GW00383890

HARRISON McCAIN

Footprints Series
JANE ERRINGTON, Editor

The life stories of individual women and men who were participants in interesting events help nuance larger historical narratives, at times reinforcing those narratives, at other times contradicting them. The Footprints series introduces extraordinary Canadians, past and present, who have led fascinating and important lives at home and throughout the world.

The series includes primarily original manuscripts but may consider the English-language translation of works that have already appeared in another language. The editor of the series welcomes inquiries from authors. If you are in the process of completing a manuscript that you think might fit into the series, please contact her, care of McGill-Queen's University Press, 1010 Sherbrooke Street West, Suite 1720, Montreal, QC H3A 2R7.

Harrison McCain

Single-Minded Purpose

DONALD J. SAVOIE

McGill-Queen's University Press
Montreal & Kingston · London · Ithaca

© McGill-Queen's University Press 2013

ISBN 978-0-7735-4321-8 (cloth)
ISBN 978-0-7735-9023-6 (ePDF)
ISBN 978-0-7735-9024-3 (ePUB)

Legal deposit fourth quarter 2013
Bibliothèque nationale du Québec

Printed in Canada on acid-free paper that is 100% ancient forest free
(100% post-consumer recycled), processed chlorine free

McGill-Queen's University Press acknowledges the support of the
Canada Council for the Arts for our publishing program. We also
acknowledge the financial support of the Government of Canada
through the Canada Book Fund for our publishing activities.

Library and Archives Canada Cataloguing in Publication

Savoie, Donald J., 1947–, author
    Harrison McCain : single-minded purpose / Donald J. Savoie.

(Footprints series ; 17)
Includes bibliographical references and index.
Issued in print and electronic formats.
ISBN 978-0-7735-4321-8 (bound). – ISBN 978-0-7735-9023-6 (ePDF). –
ISBN 978-0-7735-9024-3 (ePUB)

    1. McCain, H. Harrison, 1927–2004. 2. Businessmen – New
Brunswick – Biography. 3. Executives – New Brunswick – Biography.
4. McCain family. I. Title. II. Series: Footprints series ; 17

HD9217.C34M3387 2014   338.7'66402853092   C2013-906034-0
                                                 C2013-906035-9

Typeset by Jay Tee Graphics Ltd. in 11/14 Minion

Dedicated to All New Brunswickers

Contents

Preface

I first met Harrison McCain in the spring of 1982 when I was working in Ottawa as a senior policy advisor in the Department of Regional Economic Expansion (DREE). He – not his office – had called a day earlier, asking if he could come to see me. As I later discovered was invariably the case, he wasted no words and went straight to the point: "You're Donald Savoie. I hear you're a New Brunswicker and I want to meet with you." I had, of course, heard of Harrison McCain and, intrigued, I agreed to meet with him.

He wanted to resolve an issue with a project that involved DREE. I had no knowledge of the project, but I promised to put him in contact with the senior official responsible for the program. He stayed to chat. He wanted to know where I grew up, what I was doing in Ottawa, and when I was planning to return to New Brunswick. We became friends, and I later had many fascinating chats with him, some of which I detail in this book. I thoroughly enjoyed his company. I last saw him not long before he passed away. He walked me to my car, grabbed my arm, and said, "Bring your wife and come spend a weekend with me." One thing or another kept me from taking up his invitation – and then suddenly it was too late. I regret it to this day. I attended his funeral in the small Anglican Church in his beloved Florenceville and I wrote his obituary for the *Globe and Mail*.

Harrison McCain had a solution for every problem, he always welcomed a good argument, he had strongly held views, as well as a visceral love for and attachment to his home town and his region. He was always to the point and never had a shred of pretension. His personality was larger than life: when he walked into a room, everyone felt his presence, his energy. He had limitless ambition and energy, a vision, and inspiring leadership.

This book is the story, as I see it, of Harrison McCain the man, his roots, his business genius, his ideas, his commitment to his region, his strong interest in public policy, and his decision to go global before the word "globalization" was even in the air. It is also about entrepreneurship, public policy, and the role of government in regional economic development.

Family members decided to turn over his files to me and strongly encouraged me to write their father's story. They did not offer, nor did I ask, for any funding to support the research. The academic in me came to the fore and, as always, I wanted to be free to write as I see things.

I resisted the family's urging that I write a book about Harrison for several years. I have published widely as an academic in public policy, regional economic development, and government. I had not published a biography and I saw challenges. How could I possibly be objective writing about a friend whom I had long admired? After a good chat with Harrison's daughter Ann in September 2012, I decided that now was the time. It had been eight years since her father had died, and I concluded that I would be doing my friend a favour if I tried as best I could to paint an accurate picture of him and his accomplishments.

A few months earlier I had had a discussion with a colleague about heroes and role models in modern society. As an academic, I have quite naturally a deep respect for leading scholars and for those who broke new ground, advancing the frontiers of knowledge.

However, my heroes are entrepreneurs. I subscribe to the Schumpeter school of economics in which the entrepreneur, the agent of innovation, is the hero. It is the entrepreneur who propels economies forward. The genius of entrepreneurs, as Schumpeter argued, is their capacity to generate "creative destruction." That is, through innovation, they make possible new sectors and new industries that attract resources from old ones and grow economies. That is as it should be.

My admiration is perhaps greatest for the talented entrepreneurs from my own region, the Maritime provinces. Given the workings of national political institutions, national policies, and the national economy, an entrepreneur has to pull against gravity to succeed in my region. Yet that is precisely what K.C., Jim, Jack, and Arthur Irving, John Bragg, Harrison and Wallace McCain, among a few others, have been able to do. I thought that I owed it to one of them to write his story.

Harrison McCain was a good friend. I had deep respect for him as a man, a business person, and a community leader, and I still do. The reader should be warned that this is not a "gossipy" book, nor is it an attempt to settle old scores on behalf of Harrison McCain.

It is impossible to tell the Harrison McCain story without revisiting old wounds. I do so in the book, but it is hardly the main story. I knew Wallace McCain, though not nearly as well as I did Harrison. I also enjoyed chatting with Wallace and I have a high regard for him and for his accomplishments. However, I stress once again that this book is about Harrison McCain and not about Harrison and Wallace McCain. Frank McKenna summed it up well when he wrote that their "reconciliation is the most important part of the story."[1]

I wanted to paint as accurate a picture of Harrison McCain as I could. I know that he would not have wanted it any other way. I consider it a sign of true friendship to present the various sides of an individual. My hope is that the reader will see this as a serious book about a serious business person, about a past business era, a man, and his community, and about economic development and public policy when national economies mattered more than they do today. Still, I would like to warn readers that they may well detect a bias. Not only was Harrison a friend, but it is impossible for a Maritimer like me not to take great pride in what Harrison and McCain Foods have been able to accomplish.

This is truly a New Brunswick book. Harrison McCain, as the reader will discover, was a proud New Brunswicker. The book's cover is an original painting by well-known New Brunswick artist Bruno Bobak. The painting was discovered in Bruno's personal papers by his son shortly after he passed away in 2012. My son Julien took the photograph of the painting and I wrote the book. My New Brunswick roots go back, on both the Savoie and Collette sides, to the late 1750s when my ancestors escaped from the Acadian expulsion and made their way to what is now eastern New Brunswick.

Many helped me with the book. Allison McCain, chair of the board of directors, and his staff at Corporate Headquarters of McCain Foods in Florenceville were generous with their time. Ann McCain not only urged me to write this book, she responded to every single request I put to her to obtain information and material on her father and McCain Foods. George McClure provided valuable material, read the manuscript, and made important suggestions to improve it. James Downey and Rob Prichard did likewise. I also want to say a special thank you to all those who patiently responded to my questions as I gathered information for this book.

I owe a special debt to the reviewers of McGill-Queen's University Press. One produced a thorough, highly competent, and insightful review, which prompted me to revise several chapters. No author could be better served. I subsequently discovered that the reviewer was Professor Tony Tremblay, chair of New Brunswick Studies at Saint Thomas University.

I want once again to thank my wife Linda for putting up with my insatiable appetite for work and my long-time assistant Ginette Benoit for her continued support and good cheer in the face of my constant demands for typing and retyping the manuscript. Céline Basque also made an important contribution in incorporating the final revisions to the manuscript. Joan Harcourt and Ian MacKenzie were able to make my sentences read better. But all defects in this book are mine.

Donald J. Savoie
Université de Moncton

HARRISON McCAIN

Introduction

This is a story about a man from a small community who, together with his brothers, built a global empire. Harrison McCain was a leading entrepreneur of the last century. He had all of the strengths of a great entrepreneur and some of the weaknesses as well. He was bold and decisive, and, if needed, could hold a meeting in his own mind, without need for others to help make a decision. The meetings never lasted long, but they produced decisions and results. Though the early years at McCain Foods were particularly challenging, he seldom had time or inclination for self-doubt. His deep attachment to his business, his community, and its residents is legendary.

Driving through Florenceville, one intuitively slows down. The community sets the pace and there is simply no reason to rush anywhere. Geographically, at least, Florenceville sits in the middle of nowhere. It is a relatively isolated town in a relatively isolated region of Canada. With a population of only 1,639, Florenceville-Bristol sits in Carleton County in northwestern New Brunswick near the northeast Maine border, about 160 kilometres from Fredericton (population 56,000) and 250 kilometres from Bangor (population 33,000). If one were asked to select a community where one could grow a multi-billion-dollar firm, Florenceville would not leap to mind.

Florenceville is named in honour of Florence Nightingale, "the lady with the lamp," the good nurse who came to prominence during the Crimean war. Whoever coined the phrase "salt of the earth" must have visited the town. It is a rural community rooted in rural values. It lies at the heart of New Brunswick's Bible belt. Victoria Corner, a still smaller community a few kilometres down the road, remains home to the conservative, evangelical New Brunswick Bible Institute. Christian values and the fear of God remain an intricate part of Florenceville. Living in a Bible belt is not, of course, to everyone's taste. In fact, Alden Nowlan, the widely acclaimed poet, who did live there for a time. once claimed that the problem with Carleton County was that it did not have enough atheists.[1] I suspect that not too many Carleton County residents would agree with him.

Inspired by a vision from God and chapters 6, 7, and 8 of the book of Genesis, a local pastor set out in the late 1980s to build a replica of Noah's Ark. The replica, which sits just outside the Florenceville town limits, is two-thirds the size of the biblical Ark. Initially at least it housed a private Bible school and student dorms. Today it is a multipurpose building including rooms to rent and offices for the local church. On a recent visit to Florenceville, I counted seven active Christian churches. Harrison told me once that he had given money to all of them to build, maintain, or expand their churches. Visions from God are much more common in Carleton County than are business or economic visions.

Looking after one another, holding Christian values, being self-sufficient, working the land and working hard, extending a helping hand to their neighbours, and having a warm smile are signal characteristics of Florenceville's culture. It is a physically attractive community divided by the Saint John River. Florenceville nestles among rolling hills. It is also rich in farmland, which is where our story begins.

Harrison McCain's house sits perched on top of the hill in West Florenceville. From where he sat for breakfast, he could easily see the McCain Foods plant, the small Anglican Church, which he attended, the Bank of Nova Scotia, the school, the housing development built for McCain employees, and the community library built to honour his parents. In one brief glimpse, Harrison could survey all that mattered to him.

The community has all the strengths and weaknesses of a small town. Everyone knows everyone. It is a very tight-knit community where looking out for others is commonplace. While in Florenceville, in December 2012, a resident flagged me down at the entrance of the narrow wooden bridge, where everyone has to slow to a crawl before crossing it. He had spotted the safety inspection sticker on my windshield, which had expired several months earlier. With a friendly smile and a quick wave of the hand asking me to roll down my window, he told me, "Better get that inspection done or you will have to pay a $170 fine." I doubt if someone in Moncton, let alone Toronto, would have bothered.

There are no shopping centres in Florenceville, and when looking for a restaurant, one has to drive to Centreville, some fifteen kilometres up the road. The restaurant you will find is 1950s vintage with the benches, furniture, and menu of that era. If you like hot chicken with gravy and french fries, this is the restaurant for you. The only thing missing is the old jukebox. The easy rapport between staff and customers would be unusual in larger centres, where most would be strangers to one another.

The people of Carleton County are comfortable in this environment. It is the way of a small, rural farming community. They see no need for fancy restaurants or, for that matter, for change. They are competitive only when they have to be. Yet it is from this unlikely spot that the McCain brothers were able to build their multi-billion-dollar global firm, now employing some twenty thousand people. It houses fifty-five production facilities in twelve countries and processes 450,000 kilograms of potato products every hour. It accounts for about one-third of all frozen french fries sold in the world and sells its products in 110 countries.

The McCain business acumen can be traced back to when the first McCains left Ireland for the New World. Andrew McCain, along with his brother James, left a hamlet north of Castlefin, in Ireland's County Donegal, in the 1820s, before the Great Potato Famine, to settle in New Brunswick, one of the British North American colonies. Their sister Jane joined them a year later. Harrison McCain speculates that the brothers left Ireland so that they could own and cultivate their own land, tired of working as tenant farmers. Within a few years of their arrival, the brothers had purchased 300 hectares of land and began work on it. The McCains have continued to work the land to this day.

McCain Foods ranks thirteenth among the largest private companies in Canada. McCain also operates one of the largest trucking firms in Canada, Day and Ross. McCain's head office remains in Florenceville, though pressure to move at least portions of it to larger centres, notably Toronto, has been unremitting.

This book is Harrison McCain's story. Knowing Harrison, I am sure he would have wanted his story to be cast in a broad setting. He would not have been content with a simple chronicle of the growth of McCain Foods. He would have wanted to pass on to aspiring entrepreneurs the lessons he had learned, including his own experience in the economic development of his beloved New Brunswick and the other Maritime provinces. He would have welcomed debate on the role of government in society and the state of partisan politics, not only in his province, but in the rest of Canada. He strongly believed in partisan politics but he was never blind to its shortcomings.

I write this for several reasons but mainly to indicate that Harrison McCain had myriad interests. He was a classic example of an old saying: "If you need to get something done, ask someone who is busy." Harrison had a hand in many things and was always available to give advice. I once telephoned him to ask if he had any suggestion for me, as I was about to replace him on the advisory committee of the Order of Canada. His reply: "Yup, yup, two things, two things. One, do not give the order to a person of the cloth. Their reward is in the next life. Two, do not give it to a businessman who has only made money. That's the easy part. Give it to a businessman who has given back to his community. That's the test. How in the hell are you, anyway?" Business first, pleasure after, with Harrison McCain.

This book, then, is about McCain Foods but it is also about other things that mattered to Harrison McCain. He was the firm's public face and the go-to person when politicians, community leaders, and the media wanted to communicate with McCain Foods. I must emphasize, once again, however, that this was not a one-person show. To be sure, Harrison McCain was a driving force in the company's success. But many hands made the company the success that it has become. Wallace, Harrison's brother, was no less crucial to the growth of McCain Foods. They drew on each other's strengths. Cedric Ritchie, former chairman and chief executive officer at the Bank of Nova Scotia, summed it up well when he told me, "You have to give equal weight to both Harrison and Wallace in the development of McCain Foods. Harrison was the front-runner and Wallace was not as forward."

A third brother, Robert, actually came up with the idea of starting a frozen french fries business. A fourth brother, Andrew, like his three brothers, invested his own funds in the business in 1957, and he too deserves credit for putting money in a high-risk business start-up.

Launching a business in 1957 was not done the way it is today. This book seeks to answer a number of questions. Could there be another Harrison McCain? The answer, of course, is yes: many successful hi-tech entrepreneurs of the past thirty years provide ample evidence. The more difficult question is whether there can be another Harrison McCain from a small rural Canadian community. That answer is much less certain.

How has the role of government changed in promoting economic development over the past sixty years or so? How did Harrison McCain deal with governments and community leaders? What prompted McCain Foods to go global before globalization was on anyone's horizon? How did Harrison McCain approach business challenges and decisions? What contributions did he bring to public-policy-making? Why did he see little advantage in taking McCain Foods public? Are there lessons to be learned by aspiring entrepreneurs?

McCain Foods was born in the post-Depression years, just as governments were seeking to play a stronger role in the economy. Coincidentally, McCain Foods was founded in 1957, the very year that the government of Canada launched its equalization program, which has, over the years, poured billions into the economy of have-less regions. The program was designed to give poorer provinces a comparable level of public services with national standards, without having to impose an unsustainable level of taxation.[2]

But that is only part of the story. Since 1961, the government of Canada has been promoting economic development in slow-growth regions. That year saw the enactment of the Agricultural Rehabilitation and Development Act (ARDA). It was followed by a veritable alphabet soup of economic development departments and programs, more often than not in partnership with the private sector.[3]

Wallace McCain once told a business associate that McCain Foods built the company without government help. The associate, well aware that McCain Foods had been able to access its full share of government incentives to build its processing plants over the years, called him on his claim. Wallace replied, "Well, maybe, but Harrison looked after that, not me."[4] I once asked Harrison himself for his take on the issue. He replied, "Just look around at all the jobs we created in areas where jobs were needed. Where would people find jobs in Florenceville, Grand Falls, and Portage la Prairie? These dollars did a lot of good." Then he added, with the wry smile and sparkle in his eyes that appeared whenever he wanted to make a point half in jest, "Look, Donald. If the government is stupid enough to put money in my hands, I am stupid enough to take it."

No matter the explanation, the growth of McCain Food's coincided with more government intervention in the economy, with cash grants to help create or expand economic activities, and the firm was able, over the years, to take full advantage of it. Entrepreneurship has, in more recent years, become, in the eyes of many, the panacea for communities in search of economic development. The government of Canada unveiled a new economic development agency for Atlantic Canada in June 1987 – the Atlantic Canada Opportunities Agency (ACOA) – and directed it to focus on promoting entrepreneurship. Ottawa has since set up one such agency after another, and promoting entrepreneurship remains a central feature of its efforts. We have now reached the point where every postal code in Canada has access to a federal regional economic development agency.[5] What would Harrison McCain think of this?

What lessons do Harrison McCain and McCain Foods offer for today's entrepreneurs? Apart from government efforts to promote entrepreneurship, there has been an explosion of academic programs, academic journals, and think tanks devoted to the field. What advantages do they offer that Harrison McCain and his peers did not enjoy in 1957?

What about building a multi-billion-dollar business in a small New Brunswick town? Harrison McCain was proud of his business accomplishments and prouder still that he did it all from tiny Florenceville. Roots mattered a great deal to him, and he never wavered in his loyalty to Florenceville, to New Brunswick, the Maritime provinces, and to Canada. He drew great satisfaction from building a global business empire from a small New Brunswick town.

Harrison McCain told me a story, sitting in his study of his Florenceville home: "Two banker types from the United States asked to see me. They sat right there, right there, right where you are sitting. They said, 'Harrison, Harrison, your business has outgrown Florenceville. You need to move. You need to move. You need to move to New York, Toronto, or somewhere else. You need to move.' You know what I told them? I told them, 'Get the Christ out of here.' You know, Donald, I never saw them again."

Small-town business tycoons who stick by their community wear it as a badge of honour. Sam Walton, of Walmart fame, opens his autobiography with the observation that when *Forbes* named him the richest man in America, he could easily imagine "all those newspaper and TV folks up in New York saying 'Who?' and 'He lives where?'"[6] This brings us to yet another question: What are the advantages and drawbacks in building and maintaining a multi-billion-dollar enterprise in small-town Canada?

I seek to answer these questions through Harrison's eyes and his beliefs. So what about Harrison McCain, the man? Harrison had a number of constants in his life. He was highly intelligent, driven, a bon vivant, charismatic, energetic; he had a great sense of humour and remained throughout his life deeply committed to Florenceville and to New Brunswick. He was anything but a loner, always wanting to be around people. He was loyal to his friends. He often said that he was bilingual: he had mastered both Maritime English and profanity.

Harrison stood out among his peers. His grade 11 teacher said about him, "I thought Harrison was the type who might lead the province. He was so clever and a real gentleman, you know. Sitting in the front row, he used to be the leader in everything. Just in every avenue, he was a leader."[7]

I was fortunate to have numerous conversations with Harrison McCain. Every get-together was informative and stimulating. I was always delighted by his quick mind, he never failed to make me laugh, his love of and commitment to Florenceville was always present as an undercurrent. Former Premier Frank McKenna recalled, "Although Harrison could easily enjoy the company of presidents and kings, and world-class CEOs, and often did, he was equally home and perhaps more comfortable with the people of his own community. He loved the farmers who grew for him, and he loved the community in which he lived. Harrison McCain never forgot where he came from."[8] I do not recall ever having an extended conversation with Harrison when he did not raise the matter of economic development for his community and his province. It was always part of the discussion with me and I suspect that it was not far in his conversations with others.

There are those who will remember that, in the late 1970s and early 1980s, Toronto fundraisers were calling Canadian business leaders with an offer. They were looking for some $40 million towards the construction of a new home for the Toronto Symphony Orchestra. In exchange for a $5 million contribution, the donor would have the naming rights on the new hall designed by well-known Canadian architect Arthur Erickson. They called Harrison to see if he was interested. He answered, "Yup, yup, name it the Florenceville Dance Hall and you've got the money."[9] Harrison was dead serious. Perhaps not surprisingly, his offer was declined. The building was later named the Roy Thomson Hall after the Thomson family gave fundraisers $4.5 million.

Harrison knew only one speed – fast forward. His mind was never in neutral and never at rest. When meeting with him, even for only a friendly chat, you could tell that his mind was always engaged and you knew that he had several thoughts always at play.

He did everything fast. He spoke fast, at times with a slight stutter. He had a staccato manner of speech, often repeating himself to make a point. He drove fast, and friends did the best they could to avoid him while he was at the wheel.

I recall once sitting, chatting with him at his home in Florenceville. With no warning, he jumped up and said, "Let's go, let's go. I want to show you something." I had parked, as I always did, at the back of his house next to the garage. He took to the wheel of his Cadillac, backed out of the garage, and ran straight into my car. "Christ, Christ, what was that?" I said, "I think that you just backed into my car." "Oh, Christ," he replied, "let's go look, let's go look." We both jumped out of the car to inspect the damage. There was only a slight dent to the back fender and bumper. He took a quick look and declared, "No problem, no problem, let's go, let's go." Off we went at a greater speed than I would have preferred to visit Thomas Equipment, not far from his home. I had, however, learned my lesson well. Every time I went back to visit Harrison, I would park directly behind his garage door, blocking his exit. He had no choice but to come in my car, with me safely at the wheel. Harrison's close friends, like Donald Trafford and John Doucet, also made sure (with good reason) that they did the driving whenever they went anywhere with Harrison.

At one time Harrison took one of his managers from Europe to visit the Grand Falls plant, a distance of 80 kilometres from Florenceville. He drove fast, as usual, clicking the speedometer at 170 kilometres an hour. The manager, not wishing to upset his boss, kept quiet but was relieved to hear an RCMP siren closing in. The officer went to the driver's side, recognized Harrison, as virtually any New Brunswicker would at this point, and said: "Mr McCain, I am sorry but I have to give you a speeding ticket. You were driving much too fast." Harrison quickly responded: "Goddamn it, give me two. I'm coming back this way." Harrison was never one to waste time!

Information for this book comes from a number of sources. Harrison McCain's family gave me free access to his personal and business papers. I consulted published material on both Harrison McCain and McCain Foods, as well as several government documents dealing with McCain Foods and the economic development and business management literature.

I was given a copy of a transcript of an interview from 19 February 2001 that Harrison McCain had with his good friend James Downey, former president of the University of New Brunswick and of Waterloo University. Downey knew the right questions to ask and how to ask them so as to bring Harrison and his views to life. Reading the transcript, I could easily sense the strong bond and high level of trust between the two friends. I consulted the literature on McCain Foods, notably Daniel Stoffman's history of McCain Foods,[10] as well as the work of Paul Waldie, Gordon Pitts, and Michael Woloschuck.[11] I also interviewed a number of individuals who knew Harrison McCain well or had worked with him (see Appendix A).

THE STRUCTURE OF THE BOOK

Writing this book posed a number of challenges, given its ambitious agenda. The book is about Harrison McCain, the businessman, the family man, the public personality, and his accomplishments. That said, it is not possible to write about Harrison and McCain Foods in isolation from the work of his brother, Wallace.

Harrison was chairman of the firm and Wallace its president. Though their functions were never formally structured, both became known inside and outside the company as co–chief executive officers. They did establish separate spheres of responsibilities but had a say in all facets of the business. In brief, Harrison led McCain Foods in Britain, Continental Europe, and the transportation business. Wallace led the firm's expansion in Australia and the United States.

This book is about Harrison McCain, not McCain Foods. As a result, the reader will see that the book does not follow the growth of McCain Foods chronologically. At times, I move back and forth between decades as I focus on Harrison, his work, his family and friends, and his interests.

The story begins in Ireland when Harrison McCain's great-grandfather decided to emigrate to New Brunswick, then a British colony. He eventually settled in a farming community near the Maine border. He bought land and cleared it.

Chapter 3 reports on the business and political acumen of Harrison's grandfather and father. They were entrepreneurs to the core, grasping at opportunities in both politics and agriculture. They left Harrison and his siblings a taste for business and money to invest. Harrison showed a flare for entrepreneurship early in life, which he demonstrated as a student at Acadia University.

Chapter 4 tells how Harrison obtained his first job while fresh out of university. He put on hold his desire to start his own business and spent five years working in sales and marketing for the legendary New Brunswick entrepreneur K.C. Irving.

He quit a high-paying job to launch his own business. He had no idea what kind of business he should get into but decided to jump ship anyway and take his chances. With limited financial resources and no knowledge of the sector, he decided, with the help of his brother, to go into the frozen food business.

I was recently asked if Harrison McCain had self-doubts. If he did, he was able to camouflage them very well. I saw no evidence of self-doubt. He did tell me on occasions that the early years at McCain Foods were particularly difficult. But, as the company grew and met with more and more success at home and abroad, Harrison had, by all accounts, little time or inclination for self-doubt. I asked several close business associates to employ key words to describe Harrison McCain. I heard "energy," "determined," "strong leader," "headstrong," "inspiring," "charismatic," "innovator," "at times unreasonable," but I never heard once "self-doubt" or "unsure of his abilities."

Chapter 6 outlines a series of seemingly insurmountable challenges that Harrison and Wallace faced in building their business. The following two chapters discuss the decision to expand into foreign markets. They review the efforts, country by country, as McCain Foods grew to become the dominant force in the frozen french fry industry in the entire world.

The focus on the business left some important issues unattended. One was the governance of the family business; another was succession planning, laying the groundwork for someone to take over after Harrison and Wallace. Chapter 9 looks at this issue and the next chapter deals with the breakdown between the two brothers.

The last three chapters focus on Harrison as he led McCain Foods sans Wallace. Harrison always held a strong interest in politics and public policy, and chapter 12 examines his participation in both.

Chapter 13 turns to Harrison McCain, the husband and father. Harrison was hardly a loner, always having friends and close business associates around. He had a number of good friends and remained loyal to his family and friends through thick and thin. Most of Harrison's friends and business associates whom I consulted told me that loyalty was one of his defining characteristics.

In the concluding chapter, we ask, Could there be another Harrison McCain? The purpose is to broaden the economic development debate and see how a young Harrison attempting to build a global business would fare today in rural New Brunswick or, for that matter, anywhere in rural Canada.

1

Roots Matter

History matters in all things, and economic development is certainly no exception. To be sure, even entrepreneurship is not born in a vacuum. Institutional settings are also important to promoting business development, as Daron Acemoglu and James A. Robinson persuasively argue in their widely read *Why Nations Fail*.[1] They make the case that inclusive political and economic institutions are key to promoting social cohesion and economic prosperity. Anglo-American democracies have often led the way, down through the ages, in developing inclusive political and economic institutions. This explains in no small measure the economic successes of the United States, the United Kingdom, Australia, and Canada.

The British colonies in North America offered such opportunities to those looking for a fresh start in eighteenth- and nineteenth-century Europe. The United States and the British colonies to the north were already known as lands of opportunity by the early 1800s at a time when Europe was in political turmoil. The fallout from the French Revolution and the Napoleonic wars were being felt throughout the Continent.

Ireland had its own set of problems. Britain passed several Acts of Uniformity by the end of the nineteenth century. In Ireland, those who were not of the established church – the Anglican Church – were discriminated against. There were significant restrictions on Catholics (who formed the major part of the population) owning land, and also on Presbyterians. The McCains were Presbyterians. Poverty was also widespread. North America offered a fresh start, politically and economically.

Brian W. Hutchison writes that the earliest known paternal ancestor of the New Brunswick McCain family was John McCain, born about 1760.[2] He was from County Donegal, which sits in the border region linking present-day Northern Ireland and the Republic of Ireland. The county has suffered more than its share of economic disaster and consequent emigration down the years. Donegal had a population of 296,000 in 1841, which fell dramatically to 41,000 by 1851, and again to 18,000 by 1861. As recently as 2011, its population was 161,137, substantially less than what it was some 170 years earlier.[3]

It was not just the ambitious who decided to leave County Donegal. For many, it was simply a question of survival, and North America offered attractive prospects. The move also offered a promising new beginning, away from the prejudices of the established church and class-conscious Ireland. The transition would also be made easier by a common language (leaving aside French Canada) and an abundance of land.

Harrison McCain's great-grandfather, W. Andrew McCain, arrived in Carleton County, New Brunswick, in 1823. Though one cannot be certain, family lore suggests that Andrew and his brother James landed in Quebec City and made their way to New Brunswick. They first went to Sussex, in the southern part of the province, where they worked for a year before returning to Ireland. A year later, they re-emigrated to New Brunswick with their sister Jane and settled in the Florenceville area.[4]

The McCain clan began to accumulate land soon after they arrived. After he had been in New Brunswick for only three years, Andrew McCain was granted 100 acres – no small achievement for a newly arrived immigrant in his early twenties. But it would not stop there. He and his brother James both bought another 100 acres each within several years of their arrival. By the 1850s the McCain brothers each had 250 acres of land, and Andrew was able to fully discharge his mortgage tied to land purchase by 1860.[5] This would have been unthinkable had they stayed in Donegal.

Acquiring or even purchasing land in pre-Confederation New Brunswick was relatively easy. The greater challenge was clearing the land for agriculture. It was back-breaking work before the arrival of modern machinery.

Citizens could hardly look to government for a helping hand. New Brunswick was a British colony and the role of government was barely visible, other than in the military. The New Brunswick legislature, for example, had an extremely light agenda in 1824. It passed an act for the safekeeping of lunatics, given that "it might be dangerous to permit them to go at large." However, no provision was made to build a lunatic asylum, so the act was of no benefit.[6]

The legislature did pass an act to undertake its first census of the population, after New Brunswick had been in existence for forty years. The census was modest by today's standards. It ignored businesses and focused only on enumerating the number of residents, whether they were white or coloured, male or female, and under or above the age of sixteen. New Brunswick's population in 1825 was 74,176.[7]

Farmers were left to their own ingenuity and labour to clear the land. There was no helping hand from government, which had modest revenues. The best farmers could hope for was a word of encouragement from the Legislature and colonial officials on the importance of agriculture to the province.[8]

Life in the 1820s and 1830s in the New World centred on the church, the institution that linked citizens together in small nascent communities. The insularity of rural life and primitive means of transportation and communication made the church the central focus in the community. The church also looked after early social problems in the community, to the extent that it could, and provided many social and recreational activities. Picnics in the summer and horse racing in the winter, when ice conditions allowed, were popular activities, sponsored by the church.[9] The McCain brothers belonged to the Presbyterian Church.

This is not to suggest that Florenceville was free of politics or of related conflicts. Shortly after the McCains' arrival in New Brunswick, there were serious political and border tensions. The United States and Britain, it will be recalled, signed the Treaty of Ghent in the aftermath of the 1812–14 war, releasing all prisoners of war and restoring all captured lands.[10] The treaty did not, however, bring closure to border disputes between Maine and New Brunswick, which continued to drag on. At one point the issue was turned over to outside arbitration, but it failed to come up with a solution.

Tensions flared as New Brunswick lumbermen crossed over to the Aroostook region of Maine to cut timber in the winter of 1838–39. In February, they "seized" the American land agent who had been sent to expel them. The bloodless Aroostook war was soon underway. The United States Congress voted to raise fifty thousand men and allocated $10 million to repel any British invasion of American soil, while troops were also mobilized on the New Brunswick side as well. Tensions ran high on both sides of the border for years.

Feelings, of course, were at their peak in the actual disputed area. New Brunswick did not recognize Maine's claim to more stands of pine timber, and the people of Carleton County were in the thick of it. Armed civil posses roamed both sides of the border, and more than a few tavern brawls broke out. Carleton County's *Woodstock Times* ran a call to arms in 1839: "March, march, march in good order to meet Kennebec over the border, with the bayonet and cheer, we'll make them stand clear, and soon, very soon, run home in disorder."[11] The Aroostook war lasted for years, but full-scale military conflicts were avoided, although it led to bloody noses and broken arms among many loggers.

American and British authorities in Washington and London, however, had little appetite for another military conflict, particularly over a relatively small area, tucked away in "nowhere land." They met and finally struck a lasting deal; the Webster and Ashburton Treaty, signed in 1842, which ruled largely in favour of Maine, granting it large tracts of land that many had expected would become part of New Brunswick.

Historian W.S. MacNutt explains, "What Maine had set out to do she had accomplished. In the valuable timber county of Aroostook, British jurisdiction had effectively been denied."[12] The McCains, like everyone else in Carleton County, were not happy with the treaty, believing that New Brunswick had been short-changed.[13] Those in the forestry sector felt the disappointment most keenly, but there was little they could do about it. Political power in London had spoken and the colony had no choice but to accept its decision.

Jacques Poitras provides a thorough account of the negotiating tactics of both the Americans and the British. The American side, led by the legendary Daniel Webster, out-manoeuvred the British. In the end, however, Poitras maintains both were able to claim victory: "Six decades of contention had finally come to an end. The United Staters won more of the disputed territory ... and American lumbermen gained navigation rights to the Saint John, no small thing."[14] The British and its New Brunswick colony had reached a lasting compromise and New Brunswick residents could now get on with their business.

The agricultural sector, meanwhile, was largely spared, though losing significant tracts of land had important consequences for farmers in future years. No one on either side of the border remained indifferent, and the McCains had taken sides before the treaty ended the dispute. Aroostook County in Maine and Carleton County in New Brunswick are neighbours. Political tensions and border skirmishes are never good for business. The conflict, however, did not stop Andrew McCain from expanding both his land holdings and his farming activities. He settled his estate, land holdings, and many outstanding debts shortly before his death in 1865. He was able to deed land to each of his eight children, including forty acres to Harrison McCain's grandfather, H.H. McCain. He, in turn, quickly purchased another fifty acres with his brother William and turned them into agricultural land.[15]

H.H. MCCAIN THE ENTREPRENEUR

H.H. McCain – or Henry, as he was commonly called – was an entrepreneur at heart. He first settled on his father's farm but, within several years of his marriage to Jane Kilpatrick, he was able to purchase the farm of John L. Saunders in Florenceville. Photos of the farm (circa 1910) reveal an impressive property with a handsome house and three good-sized barns.[16]

Henry had one of the most prosperous farms in Carleton County. Many farmers in the county in the mid-nineteenth century owned farm implements in common, simply because they could not afford them on their own. Farms, for the most part, were struggling to survive, and the province itself was not self-sufficient in food production. There were also a lack of capital or credit to enable farmers to expand their farms or to buy equipment, and the means of transporting goods were still primitive.

Henry McCain's farm, however, was different. He was able to consolidate his land holdings and he owned outright his means of production and farm implements.[17] Henry also had an innovative streak: he installed a half-mile long wooden pipe from a spring to his farm, supplying both his house and barn with running water.

Though born into a Presbyterian family, he joined the Baptist church while he was still in his teens. The Baptist church in New Brunswick grew substantially throughout the 1800s, particularly in the western part of the colony. The church had just 2,000 members in 1834. Well-known Baptist preachers, from Joseph Crandall to Edward Weyman, roamed the southern and western parts of New Brunswick in search of new converts, including in Carleton County, and they were successful. By 1900 there were 156 Baptist churches and over 12,000 members in the province. One observer explains the growth: "The movement was chiefly a protest against two things – the unspiritual ministry and empty forms of the Church of England and extreme Calvinism." He adds, "The great success of the Baptists in the early history of New Brunswick must, in part, be attributed to the extreme zeal and the fact that many of their ministers and evangelists did not depend on their congregation for support, but lived on their own farms and obtained their living from other employment."[18] That was important to farmers struggling as best they could to carve out a living for their families.

The McCains, who had had difficulties with the established church in Ireland and who lived from the land, saw merit in the growing Baptist church, which provided a new spiritual beginning to them, free of old prejudices, much as New Brunswick provided new economic opportunities. Henry joined the Baptist church and became one of its most fervent members. He contributed to the building of the Florenceville Baptist Church and became a deacon at the age of thirty-one.[19]

When he was thirty-seven, Henry decided to look beyond what his own farm and his own community had to offer, taking steps that were unusual for a farmer in New Brunswick in the nineteenth century: he teamed up with his brother to start a food business to supply merchants mostly in Saint John, some 240 kilometres away. The business, however, soon ran into difficulties. Primitive means of transportation, the inability to ensure a steady stream of supplies to the merchants, and difficulties in collecting payments from them pushed the business into crippling debt. Nevertheless, shortly before his brother's death, Henry arranged to assume full responsibility for the business and all debts.[20] That business, albeit in a different form, exists to this day.

HENRY McCAIN MIXING POLITICS AND BUSINESS

Henry successfully ran as a Liberal party candidate in the 1895 and 1899 provincial elections. He only ran twice but remained a strong Liberal party supporter the rest of his life. His descendants, including Harrison, would retain a strong interest in partisan politics, and most of them would remain loyal Liberals.

Politics, government, and business opportunities flowed into one another with relative ease in nineteenth-century New Brunswick. Transparency requirements were for a different era, yet to be born, and politicians of the day saw no contradiction between doing good for their constituencies and doing well for themselves. Henry McCain was in no way different. To be sure, he sought to serve his constituency by bringing as many government activities to it as he could and had some success on this front. He also showed a keen interest in the provincial experimental farm located in the Fredericton area, taking advantage of its research facilities, for example, to grow experimental apples, which enabled him to expand his business. In time, he was able to ship some 100 barrels of apples every season.[21]

In short, Henry McCain's priorities as a member of the provincial Legislative Assembly centred on securing Carleton's share of whatever the provincial government had to offer while also keeping his eye on the main chance as far as his own business interests were concerned. He had, however, very little to say in the assembly on public policy issues, and his contribution to its debates is practically non-existent. In the 220 pages of *Legislative's Synoptic Report of the New Brunswick Legislative Assembly* for 1898, some three years after being elected, he spoke once in support of a government initiative to help farmers by providing assistance to mills for the grinding of wheat locally. He also underlined once the "great agricultural potential of Carleton county."[22] That was it for 1898.

He did, on a few other occasions, speak strongly against alcohol and giving women the vote. Arguments against universal suffrage appear to be both quaint and ludicrous to us today, but it was common at the time to believe that most women had no wish to vote and that, in any event, their interests were safe in the hands of their husbands. How could women gain the right to vote, Henry and others at the time would ask, if "they could not serve in the military."[23]

On the legislative front, he was able to claim some credit for contributing to enacting legislation that regulated the size of farm fences.[24] His main success, however, was in promoting the interests of his constituency in tandem with those of his business.

Henry showed an entrepreneur's flare by acquiring hay presses and having crews roam the county to press farmers' hay at a profit. He also took advantage of his Liberal party contacts in Fredericton and Ottawa to secure a large contract to provide hay for British cavalry horses during the Boer War (circa 1899–1902). He sent his son and Harrison's father Andrew, or A.D., to Ottawa to finalize the contract and to make certain that his own business interests were protected.[25] Henry purchased as much hay as he could from local farmers and grew as much as he could on his own to meet the demand. He also operated a new high-pressure steam-powered press to compress the hay in small bales essential for shipping by sea. At one point, he had two shifts of men working in Florenceville, solely engaged in this activity.

While still a member of the Legislative Assembly, Henry teamed up with another local Liberal party broker to convince the provincial government to build a toll bridge at Hartland, a few miles down the road from Florenceville, persuasively making the case that local farmers urgently needed another bridge to get their produce to markets.

The Liberal government awarded the contract to the Hartland Bridge Company, owned by leading Liberals from the area, including Henry McCain and Frank Carvell. The bridge company was also awarded the contract to collect the tolls and was granted an exemption from paying provincial and local taxes.[26] A few years later, the government of New Brunswick purchased the bridge and did away with tolls. The sale turned a handsome profit for the owners. The bridge, long known as the world's longest covered bridge, gained worldwide notoriety on 4 July 2012, when Google selected it as its doodle for the day to celebrate the 111th anniversary of the bridge's opening.[27]

COSTLY POLITICAL INFIGHTING

Political alliances are not forever. Local Liberal partisans pressed Carleton County party bagman and Henry McCain's supporter, Frank Carvell, to use his influence on Henry to persuade him to share the Boer War bounty flowing from the overseas sale of hay – in short, to give other local Liberals and hay producers a share of the action. Henry turned him down: he had won the contract on his own and it was his contract alone. There was no question of sharing the contract and no need to rewrite the rules after the fact. He had sent his son to Ottawa to make certain that the contract was air-tight. Carvell, however, was unwilling to accept Henry's decision to keep all the profits himself: political patronage was made to be shared.

Tension heightened further when both Henry and Frank Carvell decided to seek the Liberal nomination for the 1900 federal election,[28] and Carvell won. He was a formidable political opponent for Henry. Like Henry, he was a member of the provincial Legislative Assembly. However, he had the advantage on Henry in several respects: he had studied law in Boston, where he graduated with honours; he now had a successful law practice in Carleton County; and he was a major share-holder in the local Power Company and was a director of the New Brunswick Telephone Company. Though he won the Liberal nomina-tion against Henry McCain, the seat went, by only 255 votes, to the incumbent Conservative member of Parliament Frederick Hale. Once he lost the nomination, Henry had refused to help or provide funds to the Liberal party campaign, and his withdrawal could well have contributed to Carvell's defeat. Carvell, however, went on to win the constituency for the federal Liberal party in 1904, 1908, 1911, and 1917 (in 1917 as a Liberal-Unionist).[29]

Carvell's defeat in the 1900 election in no way diminished his stand-ing with Liberal party contacts in Ottawa, and his knowledge of the law stood him in good stead: he cancelled Henry McCain's contract to export hay to the British troops in South Africa. However difficult it may be to imagine today, Carvell was also able to see to it that the contract was re-awarded – to himself. Carvell then refused to buy hay from Henry McCain. This was a devastating blow, leaving McCain with thousands of tons of hay and no market for it. The Boer War also came to an end and Ottawa cancelled its hay contract, adding to McCain's business woes. Carleton County suddenly had a massive abundance of hay with little or no market. More to the point, McCain was essentially left trying to sell hay in a non-existent market. Still, McCain honoured all his commitments to local farmers and paid all of them for their hay he had committed to buy. He was soon in debt and, rather than declare bankruptcy or leave the county, he decided to stay the course and pay off all his debts and commitments to local farmers and the local bank.

He and his son Andrew, Harrison McCain's father, were able to secure investments of $20,000 each from two wealthy Saint John merchants and, together with Henry's assets, established a new firm – McCain Prime Co. Ltd – on 10 August 1909. The four equal partners were a Mr Knight, a Mr Prime, and the father-and-son team of Henry and A.D. McCain. The debt dating back to the purchase of hay during the Boer War was fully paid in 1914, and Henry and A.D. were able to buy both Knight's and Prime's shares. They changed the firm's name to McCain Produce with father and son becoming the new sole owners.[30] The firm exists to this day as part of McCain Foods.

Father and son did well. The First World War proved to be a boon for the potato business. Prices for potatoes rose sharply, and McCain Produce was able to capture an important share of the market and turn a handsome solid profit. They did not abandon the hay business, buying another steam press, which they were able to operate successfully. Henry also bought and sold heads of cattle and herds of sheep, again at a profit. As entrepreneurs are wont to do, Henry saw opportunities where others did not. He organized, for example, a plowing and mowing demonstration with several makes of tractors on his farm, at a time when tractors were slowly but surely replacing horses. This created a great deal of interest among local farmers and gave Henry both visibility and credibility.[31]

Henry McCain also sought to give his son Andrew wide experience in the business world from an early age. Henry gave his young son, barely in his early teens, a gentle horse and sent him out to buy and sell butter and eggs throughout Carleton County. In this way, A.D. was able to build a wide network of contacts in the county that served him well for years.

When Andrew was only fourteen years old, Henry sent him to Boston to collect a long-standing debt. One report suggests that the debtor was so taken aback by Andrew's poise at such a tender age that he gave him a cheque on the spot for the full amount. Henry later sent A.D., aged twenty, to London, to celebrate Queen Victoria's sixtieth anniversary and to explore new markets in England.[32] This early introduction to the world of new markets in a foreign country would prove invaluable to A.D. and in turn to his sons Harrison and Wallace.

However, the ups and downs of Henry McCain's business activities played havoc with his son's education ambitions. Andrew attended the prestigious Horton Academy, a residential school operated by Baptists, in Wolfville, Nova Scotia, which would later give rise to Acadia University.[33] A.D., who had the intellectual capacity to do it, set out to become a medical doctor. However, when his father ran into difficulties, he had to return to Florenceville to help his father out and would never return to pursue his medical studies. He long hoped, however, that one of his own sons would go to medical school. Paul Waldie writes that when Henry's son left Horton Academy, never to return, it was a devastating blow to the family's name in Carleton County: "It was the ultimate humiliation for the McCains. The fact that A.D. was even attending a school as well regarded as Horton was big news in the village, and his every trip home was dutifully reported in the local paper."[34] Henry McCain's business troubles, however, proved in time to be a blessing in disguise for the McCains, for Florenceville, New Brunswick, and, indeed, for Canada.

Henry McCain saw many changes come to Florenceville during his lifetime. When his father first settled in the community, the transporting of goods was often a hit-and-miss adventure, depending on the season. There were only makeshift roads, and (when weather permitted) the Saint John River was used to transport supplies and logs to markets.[35] In time, the colony would build a "great road" that ran from Fredericton to the northwest of the province via Florenceville. This proved to be invaluable to both the business community and residents in the area.

Canadian Confederation and its accompanying commitment to link the British North American colonies by railway had a profound impact on transportation throughout the Maritime provinces. The New Brunswick Land and Railway Company obtained authority in 1870 to build a railway line in the northwest region of New Brunswick between Woodstock and Edmundston. The company was renamed the New Brunswick Railway Company in 1881, after the line was completed and tied to other lines to the south and north. This provided greater flexibility and opened new opportunities for markets and enabled Henry McCain to establish still stronger ties to the Saint John business community.[36]

The railway was built on the east side of the river, with the river serving as a natural defence barrier against the Americans. Thus, East Florenceville would become the business centre of the community and West Florenceville the residential side for many. McCain Produce, and later McCain Foods, followed the Bank of New Brunswick (later to merge with the Bank of Nova Scotia in 1913), which had opened a branch on the east side in 1902. All four McCain boys would settle in Florenceville, and Harrison and Wallace would later build their homes on the west side.

LOOKING BACK / LOOKING AHEAD

Henry McCain suffered a fatal heart attack on 1 June 1920. He had built a business, then nearly lost it, only to build a few more successfully – an entrepreneur at heart. He played an active role in his community and was active in partisan politics.

He left the Presbyterian church to become a leading figure in the Baptist church. The McCains would remain loyal members of the Baptist church until Harrison's mother, Laura, a no-less loyal member of the Anglican church, would come to change the family's religious affiliation. Harrison McCain, one of Laura's six children, maintains that only one of her children stayed a Baptist, but he never told me which one.

Henry McCain was able to take full advantage of the political and economic changes in his lifetime. He seized an opportunity with the coming of the railway to expand his produce business and also saw a future for the tractor while others were still hesitant. As Henry Ford once observed, "If I had asked my customers what they wanted, they would have said a faster horse."

The arrival of tractors and automobiles had a profound impact on the hay markets. Henry saw the challenge, changed gears, and created a niche for himself in the highly competitive potato business.[37] If politics presented business opportunities, he wanted to be a part of it, and he was.

He was there at the birth of Canada when New Brunswick joined Nova Scotia, Quebec, and Ontario to create the Canadian Confederation. The province of New Brunswick was torn over its possible entry into Confederation. Indeed, the pro-Confederation party in New Brunswick was defeated soundly in New Brunswick in 1865.

The people of Carleton County, however, held a more favourable view of Confederation than did many in the province. The business community saw potential in the building of a national railway, opening up new markets for them. Carleton County residents had also become alarmed at Fenian raids along the Canada–United States border. The Fenian brotherhood, based in the United States, pressed Britain to withdraw from Ireland. This pushed Carleton County into the Confederation camp in the expectation that Confederation would provide them with greater protection.[38]

Henry McCain's most important legacy, however, was in giving his son an appreciation of the merits of entrepreneurship and self-sufficiency. A.D. McCain would pick up where his father left off in both business and politics. He had also the advantage, not given his father, of learning at a very young age how to explore new markets in a foreign land. He would, in turn, as we will see, pass on his business values and skills to his sons.

Planting the Seeds

Harrison McCain had anything but a typical New Brunswick childhood. His father, A.D. McCain, having been denied the chance to become a doctor, had picked up where his own father had left off and now had a thriving potato business. Harrison's mother, Laura, a strong-willed former school teacher, attached a great deal of importance to education. Unlike the majority of his peers, Harrison and his sisters and brothers all went to university.

Harrison grew up in a household where business was a regular topic of discussion and where doing well at school was simply expected. He entered first grade in the depths of the Great Depression. But the Depression did not impinge directly on the McCain home. For that matter, many in Carleton County were less affected than in the province generally and throughout much of Canada, partly because the government had not yet entered the social services field, and the people of the county were accustomed to being self-sufficient. It helped, of course, that this was largely a rural farming community, and small family farms could grow enough food to sustain themselves.

THE GREAT DEPRESSION

At the height of the Depression, some 30 per cent of the Canadian labour force was unemployed, at a time when the labour force participation rate was a great deal smaller than it is today.[1] Western Canadian farmers, with their reliance on export markets, felt the sting of the Great Depression to a much greater extent than their eastern counterparts.[2] The unemployment rate in the three Maritime provinces was actually lower than in many other parts of Canada, and some sectors, most notably the fishery, actually grew in New Brunswick during the 1930s.[3] Though Harrison McCain was a child of the Great Depression, his family escaped its consequences.

Even though the Maritime provinces on the whole fared relatively well, there were areas that were hard hit by the Depression. In New Brunswick's Gloucester County, for example, "no fewer than 1,100 families were homeless, penniless and unemployed during the early 1930s. In some instances, as many as four families could be found crowded together in a single-family dwelling."[4] A.D. McCain's household had no such worries; there was a live-in maid and, unlike most of their friends, Harrison and Wallace had access to a car to go to the local dances when they became teenagers.

Some residents of Carleton County also suffered reverses. Hants White, for example, wrote about his struggle as a small potato farmer in the 1930s: he was unable to make a living at it and had to move back and forth between Maine and New Brunswick to work in the forestry sector. He wrote that the problem for potato farmers at the time was the person who came between the farmer and the consumer – what he called the middle man.[5]

The decade was not entirely smooth sailing, even for A.D. McCain or for others in the potato business. The problem was hardly limited to the middleman. Some potato growers went out of business, others survived. Collapsing prices for potatoes during the Depression years buffeted the agricultural sector. The potato farmers in Aroostook, across the border in Maine, were particularly hard hit. Potato prices went from two dollars per bushel in 1925 to just twenty-one cents in 1931, a price below the cost of shipping. Mortgages and other costs, meanwhile, meant that the cost of operations remained constant and potato growers broke even only five years out of ten between 1930 and 1940.[6]

Harrison McCain saw the economic hardships of the 1930s as it affected his friends and their families, some of whom were forced to become dependent on "the parish," as was fairly common at the time. The local church was in many ways responsible for giving a helping hand to the poor and looking after their welfare. Only by 1932 did the government of Canada set up unemployment relief camps where destitute men could get three meals, work clothes, and twenty cents a day for clearing bush, building roads, planting trees, and constructing public buildings.[7] It was in this environment that Harrison came to appreciate the merits of economic self-sufficiency and to see the importance of running a tight business, such as his father was doing.

A.D. McCAIN, A MAN ABOUT TOWN

A.D. McCain's presence in Florenceville loomed large. He ran one of the largest businesses, was a prominent member of a local Baptist church, sang in the church choir, and was chair of the school board for forty-five years. He ran unsuccessfully for the Liberals in the bitterly fought 1916 federal by-election and in the next provincial general election. Though he never ran again, he remained a power broker in Liberal party circles in the county. But that is not all. A.D. was also chair of the Bath, Bristol, and Florenceville Hydro Commission and was directly involved in bringing electric power to Florenceville.

He held offices in the local Masonic lodge and was a member of the Ancient and Accepted Scottish Rite, a thirty-third degree Mason. He was a charter member of the local Rotary Club, sat on the New Brunswick Potato Marketing Board, was a member of the Union Club in Saint John, and served as president of the Liberal Association for Carleton-Victoria.[8] There is a photo of him in the family album, dated 1915, sitting at the wheel of a car gazing directly at the camera, with his head and back straight as a board, wearing a fashionable hat and a self-confident smile. This is the image of a man in charge. He would lead, others would follow. No wonder men from around the county and elsewhere came calling for advice or a favour. It was in this secure social and economic environment that Harrison McCain grew up and in which his values were planted. People I consulted report that A.D. McCain was a quiet, dignified man who was widely respected. One described him as a kind of "statesman" who was deeply committed to his community's welfare.

A.D. THE BUSINESSMAN

Unlike his father, A.D. never teetered on the verge of bankruptcy, nor did he take advantage of his political contacts to the extent his father had. In business he flew solo, unwilling to bring in as partners anyone other than his own sons. A.D. grew his business by steadily increasing the acreage devoted to potatoes, by using better-quality seeds, and working well with other Carleton County farmers.[9] He also expanded his business by selling fertilizer and equipment to other farmers. He even took over the collection of farm loans, which enabled him to expand his land holdings. Business in Carleton County in the 1930s and 1940s at times was raw capitalism. Raw or not, it enabled A.D. to expand his land holdings and business activities.

A.D.'s was not the only large potato-based business in Carleton County. Guy Porter in Grand Sault, Herbert Hatfield, and G.E. Gallagher ran sizeable potato businesses in the county and collaborated on a number of issues.[10] In 1924, after the major potato producers were accused of fixing prices to be paid to farmers, the Canadian Combines Investigation held hearings on the issue. The Carleton County farmers claimed that some 10 per cent of them had been forced off their land because they could not secure a truly competitive and fair value price for their potatoes. A.D. McCain was called to testify and admitted to making forty cents a barrel profit while paying between sixty cents and one dollar to farmers.[11]

Government officials were convinced that shippers, including A.D. McCain, though hardly the largest business in the group, controlled the potato industry to their advantage and that farmers received very little benefit. The Combines Investigation completed its review in 1925 and insisted that "the evidence establishes various agreements, arrangements and combinations at different times, fixing a common price and preventing and lessening competition in and substantially controlling the transportation, purchase, sale and storage and otherwise restraining or injuring trade or commerce in potatoes, to the detriment of or against the interest of the public."[12] No charges were ever laid because the investigation was never completed. The point was not lost on everyone, however, that shippers and processors would always hold the upper hand in the potato industry.

A.D.'s father had served him well by sending him off to learn about foreign markets and showing him how to work with American interests. A.D. was able to secure new markets abroad when the American government imposed new tariffs on potatoes imported from Canada in 1922. His reach extended to faraway Cuba and to South American countries, particularly Argentina.[13] It was no easy task in the 1920s to find new markets thousands of miles away in countries with a different language and different ways of doing business. A.D., from tiny Florenceville, had to compete against lower-cost American producers and he had to find and hire ships to transport the product. He remained an aggressive and successful businessman able to manage increasingly complex business activities throughout his career.

A.D. died suddenly of a heart attack in Florenceville on 8 February 1953, getting ready to go to South America to secure new clients and to look after existing ones.

Surprisingly for a man who spent his life running a very tight ship, A.D. died without making a will and the disposition of his assets was left to the courts. Laura received one-third of everything, including McCain Produce, and the rest was divided among his six children. Little did Laura know that A.D. had invested in the stock market and had put together a small fortune. Acting on a stock tip from a friend, he had bought shares in Algoma Steel and rode the company's growth at a handsome profit. His stock holdings amounted to $400,000, which worked out to $40,000 for each child and the rest to Laura. A.D. also left substantial land holdings that he had acquired over the years through purchases and from local farmers who could not pay their debts to him. But what about McCain Produce? Laura had never been involved in the running of the firm. Still, she decided to take over and named herself president. Her two sons, Andrew and Bob, became vice-presidents. She not only quickly mastered the business, but, like her husband, played the stock market and, like him, amassed a portfolio of attractive stocks.

LAURA McCAIN

As chair of the school board, A.D. McCain had a hand in hiring staff and in 1916 he hired Laura Perley, a twenty-five-year-old teacher from a small community outside of Fredericton. She had graduated from the province's normal school and moved to Alberta, where she taught school for two years. Two years after arriving to teach in Florenceville, A.D. and Laura were married.

The marriage almost never took place, at least according to Laura. Religion and partisan politics mattered a great deal in New Brunswick in the early 1900s, and in parts of the province, they still do. Laura's family were both Anglican and strong Conservatives. A.D. wanted Laura to be re-baptized a Baptist and to become a loyal Liberal. She refused to be re-baptized, insisting that one baptism was quite enough. She did, however, attend the Baptist church regularly but also continued to attend the Anglican church. She did in time become a Liberal.

Laura stopped teaching the year she married, and her focus from that moment on was her husband, her children, and her community. By all accounts, she had a strong personality. Harrison McCain told me that on occasions he would receive a telephone call from his mother when a lumber mill or a local business was on the point of shutting down. She would say, "Harrison, these people need jobs, now fix it." Then she would hang up. He added that he had been given his marching orders and he would do what he could to fix whatever it was that needed fixing. The mother and son bond was very strong and lasted until she died.

A.D. and Laura McCain had six children, two girls and four boys: Marie, Andrew, Robert, Eleanor, Harrison, and Wallace. Typical of the times, the boys were raised to earn a living so as to support their future families and the girls were educated to raise children and organize their future households. Middle-class parents of the 1940s and 1950s hoped their sons would become doctors and lawyers, their daughters, on the other hand were expected to be nurses, teachers, or secretaries – until they married, at which point they would leave the workforce. It is no coincidence that when Laura McCain went to Mount Allison University to upgrade her skills after a few years of teaching, she enrolled in the home economics program. As noted earlier, she also left the teaching profession when she married, never to return. This was simply expected of her in society in the 1920s and 1930s, and in some jurisdictions it was the law. After all, it was only some thirty years earlier that A.D.'s father had campaigned against giving women the right to vote.

Laura was a high-spirited woman who became widely respected in her community. She came from a long line of "driven individuals."[14] Her grandfather served for forty-four years in the New Brunswick legislature and initially, at least, was one of only a few provincial politicians who supported New Brunswick's entry into Confederation. Her cousin George Perley was a federal Cabinet minister in Ottawa, including minister responsible for Overseas Forces during the First World War. He subsequently served as Canada's high commissioner in London and was a delegate to the Paris Peace Conference in 1919.

Her great-grandfather, Israel Perley, established Maugerville in 1763, one of the first English-speaking communities in New Brunswick. He had been an American soldier in the 1776 revolution. He was also part of a ragtag liberation army that set out to take Halifax for the Americans. The group attacked Fort Cumberland (now a national historic site) that lay on the marshes that separate New Brunswick and Nova Scotia. Though they were defeated, they put up a good fight and managed to burn a number of houses that belonged to those loyal to the British Crown. One of the houses torched was owned by Christopher Harper, who had taken his family to Fort Cumberland for protection and to enable him to pick up arms in defence of the fort and the Crown. Christopher Harper was Canadian Prime Minister Stephen Harper's great-great-great-grandfather.[15]

People I consulted for this book who knew Laura McCain told me that she had a strong, vibrant personality. One observed that she liked everybody in the community and everybody in the community liked and respected her. If someone was on the old narrow bridge linking West Florenceville to the community when Laura came on, they would stop and back up to the other end of the bridge so that she could safely navigate across. No one else in the community received that special treatment. The bridge still stands. It is over 100 years old, a combination of a steel-truss and wooden covered bridge that spans the Saint John River.

Laura was a strong community activist. She started a Boy Scout troop and was active for many years in the Women's Institute, serving as provincial president for four years. She supported her husband's local Baptist Church, while remaining a practising Anglican. The Baptist Church was right across the street from the McCain house. All the children attended Baptist Sunday school every week. This, Harrison told me, was an "absolute prerequisite" in his parents' household. Actual church attendance on Sunday afternoon was not obligatory, but was "highly encouraged." Some of the children would go to the church service, but having an "excuse" was enough for others to avoid it. Interestingly, despite their having gone to the Baptist Sunday school in the morning, Laura would take one child or another with her, "complaining and screaming," to the Anglican Church for evensong late Sunday afternoon. There were very few Anglicans in Florenceville, yet Harrison reports that as the children grew up, all but one "became Anglican, all Anglican."[16]

Laura was the first woman elected to the Anglican Synod of Fredericton. She edited two widely read cookbooks and turned the profits over to the Anglican Church. She was awarded an honorary doctorate from the University of New Brunswick and was made a member of the Order of Canada in 1979. As mentioned earlier, she successfully managed McCain Produce with her two sons after her husband's death. With two such parents as he had, it's easy to conclude that Harrison's DNA was wired for ambition and success.

EDUCATION FOR EVERYONE

A.D. McCain's hope to go to university, let alone achieve a medical degree, was cut short by his father's sudden business difficulties. In his turn, he ensured that his own children would not suffer the same fate. Laura, the former teacher, also kept a close eye on her children's progress through school. If one lagged behind, she saw to it that the child was given the necessary assistance or tutorial.

Harrison did well at school from the first grade. He sat in the front row, sharing a bench with Donald Trafford, and the teacher was Trafford's mother. Harrison and Trafford would become lifelong friends. Trafford, along with McCain Foods' senior executive Mac McCarthy, became Harrison's two closest friends.

Trafford was bigger than Harrison and somewhat of a bully. He periodically beat up Harrison after class and on a number of occasions Harrison tried to avoid going to school. His mother was firm on school and his teacher held little sympathy for Harrison, given that it was her son who stood accused of being a bully. Harrison decided in grade two that he had to bring things to a head, whatever the outcome, so he stood at one end of the schoolyard and made a run at Trafford. Harrison knocked him down, jumped on him, and mercilessly flailed away, punching Trafford as fast and as hard as he could. No one stepped in to stop them, with fellow students thinking that Harrison had suffered, and the time had come to put an end to Trafford's bullying. Blood poured out of Trafford's nose and mouth. Trafford told me that it was the last fight that he and Harrison ever had: "We realized that we were now big enough that we could hurt one another if we kept it up." More is said about Trafford later, but suffice to note that Harrison and Trafford stood by one another until Harrison passed away. Harrison was Trafford's best man at his wedding and Trafford was a pallbearer at Harrison's funeral. Harrison had no more difficulty with bullies at school from that moment on and he did very well in his studies.

All six of A.D. and Laura's children attended university – no small achievement for a New Brunswick family in the 1940s. The eldest, Marie, graduated from Mount Allison and Eleanor from McGill. Andrew attended both Acadia University and the University of New Brunswick. Robert completed three years of pre-medicine at the University of New Brunswick and his first year of medicine at Dalhousie University[17] but never returned to complete his medical studies.

Robert – or Bob, as he was known – aspired to a medical degree. His studies, however, were cut short by an accident while on military training in 1942. Like other young men his age, he participated in a military training summer camp. The New Brunswick military camp in Sussex put the boys through a rigorous training regime, including firing mortars with little preparation.

In late May, Bob, together with his friend Walter Ross, took the first mortar in line. Bob placed the shell into the mortar barrel and hunched over as Walter pulled the trigger, but the shell exploded within a foot of the barrel. Walter was killed and shrapnel ripped through Bob's arm and hand. He spent lengthy periods in several hospitals and was told that his injuries would prevent him from becoming a surgeon – which was what he had wanted to be. He quit his studies and returned home to work with the McCain Produce Company.[18]

If A.D's dream was to pursue medical studies through his sons, it would now be left to Andrew, Harrison, or Wallace to step up to the plate. For his part, Harrison claims, "My father wanted me to be a doctor because I was going to be the best-off person in town, come hell or high water."[19]

Andrew was born with a serious heart condition and his parents took great care to not push him in his studies. He did, however, attend Acadia University and the University of New Brunswick, but medical studies were not in the cards for him.

Wallace had many strengths, as history would so clearly establish, but university studies were not one of them. He went to Acadia University, the University of New Brunswick, and, finally, completed a BA at Mount Allison, but it was not easy sailing. In fact, Wallace graduated mainly because his parents would accept nothing less, as he later readily admitted.[20] In truth, he wanted to be anywhere but at university and he failed most of his courses in his second year at Acadia. He wanted out, to get a "real" job in the navy. His parents would not let up, and after his dismal showing at Acadia, sent him to the University of New Brunswick. In brief, he was left with no choice but to suffer through university courses until he graduated.

It thus fell on Harrison to go to medical school, and he had the academic ability to do so. Harrison had breezed through school, was one of the popular students, and had an abundance of energy. He did not, however, want to go to university. He wanted to be a truck driver. His parents would hear nothing of this and A.D. enrolled him at Acadia University, without even telling him.[21]

Like his grandfather and father before him, Harrison showed a bias for action early. His high school yearbook says, "Confidence and initiative are a good portion of the personality that is Harrison."[22] Like Henry had done with A.D., it was now A.D.'s turn to teach his sons to appreciate the value of money at an early age, and the best way was to have them earn it themselves. In Harrison's case, A.D. suggested that he milk the family cow when his two older brothers were away. The deal was that Harrison could sell the milk and keep the proceeds, and he did.

During his high school years, Harrison enjoyed parties, a few drinks, and in Donald Trafford's words, "chasing girls." Trafford added that Harrison had a quick temper and, with a few drinks in him, he would not back down from a "good scrap," even if the other guy was much bigger. "One time," he said, "I saw this big American going after Harrison with brass knuckles. Harrison had a few drinks in him and had been after the guy's girlfriend. I grabbed Harrison by the arm and said, 'Let's get out of here.' Harrison wanted to stay and fight. I think that is why I never drank. I was kept busy keeping Harrison out of fights."

HARRISON AT ACADIA UNIVERSITY

Harrison did well at Acadia without, in his own words, "working hard." He was a bright student, so he could focus on things other than his courses, and he did.[23] Harrison arrived at Acadia in September 1945, just as the Second World War had come to an end. The government of Canada was determined not to allow the country to return to the doldrums of the 1930s, now that industries sparked by the war effort, especially in the manufacturing sector, were closing. Stimulus plans were prepared in Ottawa for a sudden economic downturn. Keynesian economics had arrived in Ottawa, as it had in many Western countries.[24]

The government of Canada also decided to be generous to returning veterans, more so than it had been after the First World War. It put together a veterans charter at a cost of $1.2 billion, which provided a range of assistance, including free tuition for university or for vocational training.[25]

Acadia's student population doubled in the immediate postwar years. This not only put a great deal of pressure on the university's infrastructure, it also brought to the campus mature men who, only a few months earlier, had been witness to war. Hard-living, hard-drinking, hard-working men of war who had been in Europe only a few months before came face-to-face with seventeen- and eighteen-years olds fresh out of the small Maritime towns.

Acadia was a deeply religious institution, with ties to the Baptist church: alcohol was not permitted on campus, boys and girls were segregated, and chaperones were still in fashion. This did not sit well with returning veterans – or, for that matter, with Harrison McCain. Groups of students got around the strict behaviour codes on campus by organizing trips to nearby Kentville to buy beer or hard liquor.

Harrison thrived in this environment. Then as later, Harrison was a social animal who enjoyed being in the thick of things. He joined others in organizing trips to Kentville to buy alcohol and was often found at the student hangout, Mom's. By his own admission, he could also be found hanging around girls residences[26] and helped organize campus events that piqued his interest, such as a torchlight parade.

Harrison's take-charge personality extended to his securing support for the construction of a student union building, which Acadia and its alumni had debated over several years, with no action taken.[27] It is worth quoting Harrison from his interview with James Downey on how he was able to deliver the project:

> There was no student union building at all, no student centre at all. Everyone met off-campus at a place called "Mom's" where you bought food and drink, not liquor, just coffee, tea, and so on. And I said we ought to have a place of our own big enough to have a restaurant and have a meeting place, so forth, and so on. So I took on the job, maybe self-appointed, I'm not sure, to raise the money for that. And we hired an architect. And I was maybe helped by two or three other people. One was an American girl, big help. But we raised the money from parents by writing a letter saying there was no place for students, and the university was too poor to put the money in a facility that produced no revenue. So could they make a donation, and if the donation was large enough, they'd have their name put on an appropriate piece of equipment like a stove or a fridge or what-have-you. And if it weren't, even a few dollars would help. And if all hands pitched in a few dollars, we'd raise the money to build the building. And we did, and we did. I think we raised something like $80,000.

Downey then asked, "Was it at Acadia that you came to realize that you were a leader – I mean that if you took action, people would get behind you?"

Harrison gave his typically cryptic response: "Yes."[28]

Harrison did well in his studies at Acadia with a minimum of effort. However, he dropped out of pre-medicine because it held little interest for him, but he still majored in organic chemistry and took economics courses in his third and fourth years. He once asked me, "Can you see me as a goddamn doctor?" I can easily imagine that his patients would have been subjected to a quick diagnosis. Notwithstanding his father's wishes, he never had any interest in studying medicine.

Harrison did not engage in many sports in high school or at Acadia. His size at five feet seven was a factor. I suspect that another was that Harrison was never prepared to lose at anything. He would later take up skiing with friends.

Harrison McCain never expressed much warmth for his alma mater. For example, he declined a special invitation to attend the opening ceremonies of the student union building, which was completed only after his graduation. He decided not to attend because he saw no point in it. The job was done. Nor was he in later years as generous a bene-factor to Acadia as he was to the University of New Brunswick and Dalhousie.[29]

In his interview with James Downey, Harrison explained why he had not maintained strong ties with Acadia:

> The place when I went there was partially dominated by the Bap-tist church and that didn't appeal to me too much. And rules were very stringent. In fact, I participated along with this American girl, whose name I can't recall, in seeing that women for the first time in the entire history of Acadia were allowed to smoke in residence. Up until that date they'd never been allowed to smoke. And they said it was because of fire, but in fact I really felt it was because the Baptists thought women shouldn't be smoking. And definitely men should not be allowed in the residence, under any circumstances. If you were, you were met in the hall, at the end of the hall by stern Kate. But people did get around her, or so they said. There was some movement in and out windows I believe. I have good reason to believe that.[30]

Harrison was never one to be confined by rules, by expected behav-iour. Still, Acadia enabled him to sharpen his interpersonal and leader-ship skills and revealed early his impatience with just talk.

Harrison McCain had an ego, and a healthy one at that. Success-ful people tend to have healthy egos. It comes with the territory. Was Harrison's ego over the top? The answer is clearly no. It was simply on a par with many successful people I have met from the world of pol-itics, economics, and academe. Indeed, I know more than a few from these worlds who have a much larger ego than Harrison, and with less reason. Anyone who knew Harrison knows that he had a profound dislike of pretentious people and there was not an ounce of pretension in him. He made it clear on more than one occasion that he had little time for "bullshitters" or, if he was in more polite company, he would say, "Him, he is full of beans."

MEETING BILLIE

Harrison had what it took with girls. To be sure, being the son of a successful businessman in his home town had its advantages. Having a driver's licence and access to his father's car on some weekends gave him a big advantage in a small community like Florenceville in the 1940s.

Harrison, however, also had more than his share of dates while at Acadia, where men far outnumbered women. He had the personality: beyond being a take-charge kind of guy, he wanted to have fun, was full of confidence, had a good sense of humour, was always well dressed, and would rarely miss an opportunity to impress.

In his eulogy for Harrison McCain, Frank McKenna recalled, "Harrison had a rare gift – command presence. An entire room would light up when he entered. He was a driven man and you could feel the energy pulsating from him." He added that Harrison "had the most wonderful smile. His whole face would light up and you would smile yourself from the sheer joy of being in the presence of such a charismatic and caring man."[31]

Harrison met the love of his life at Mount Allison University, not in Florenceville nor at Acadia University. He decided to visit his brother Wallace, who was attending Mount Allison. Wallace told him that he had picked the right moment to come because there was to be a "big dance" on campus. "Great," replied Harrison. "Get me a date. Get the best-looking woman down there. Don't get the second-best-looking one. Get the best-looking one going to that university, no fooling."[32] Wallace asked Billie McNair if she would be his brother's blind date.

Marion McNair was given the nickname Billie at a very young age and it stuck with her for the rest of her life. Her father took her for a haircut at Mr Fox's barbershop in Fredericton, where everyone in McNair's house went. Marion was three years old, wearing blue shorts.

McNair told the barber that he was going a few doors down the street to buy a newspaper. The barber assumed that Marion was a little boy and he cut her hair very short. When Marion returned home, her grandmother called her "William," later "Billie," and Marion became Billie.

That first date must have gone well because neither Harrison nor Billie ever looked back. One would not have guessed it by hearing Harrison's unromantic version of his first date with Billie: "We went to the dance together. And she thought perhaps I was unwell because Wallace and I kept running to the men's locker room. After every second dance we'd run to the locker room where we had a bottle of whisky in a trench-coat pocket and we had swills direct from that bottle, direct out of the bottle. She thought it was kidney trouble or bladder or some reason why I had to keep running back and forth to the locker room. She never caught on that I was getting more tight as the evening went on. So, anyway, I didn't forget her."[33]

Billie and Harrison were married on 4 October 1952. It was a high-profile and well-attended wedding. Billie's father was John B. McNair, Liberal premier of New Brunswick from 1940 to 1952, later named the province's chief justice and later still lieutenant-governor of the province.

McNair's influence extended well beyond New Brunswick's border. Oxford-educated, he was highly respected at the national level and in other provincial capitals for his intimate knowledge of Canada's constitution. As premier, he ran the province with a firm, austere hand. Former premier Louis J. Robichaud once told me that McNair's intellect was such that no one dared to challenge him on substantial issues, either in Cabinet or in caucus for fear of looking silly.

When McNair came to power, New Brunswick was literally on the edge of bankruptcy or very close to defaulting on its debt. A student of New Brunswick history writes, "The province's Montreal bankers were threatening to foreclose on the provincial government."[34] McNair's steady hand and his ability to make difficult decisions and make them stick, slowly brought order to the province's fiscal house. McNair demonstrated political courage in 1950 when he stared down a province-wide protest and implemented a 4 per cent sales tax. He was also able to run a succession of budgetary surpluses.[35]

Harrison quickly established a strong rapport with his father-in-law. Billie's brother, John McNair, remembers, "Dad got a kick out of Harrison. Harrison would come to our home and just be bouncing off the walls. Dad would sit, smile and just shake his head."[36] Harrison once told me that his father-in-law felt that he was a bit "breezy." Harrison's sister-in-law, Janet Scarfe, tells me that her father liked Harrison from day one. McNair was a good friend of his father, A.D. McCain, which, she said, "helped," and he particularly enjoyed Harrison's high energy level. She adds, "Like everyone else, my father found Harrison very charming."[37]

Billie's mother was Mary MacGregor Crocket, the daughter of a widely respected Fredericton surgeon. She suffered from mental illness and spent lengthy periods in hospitals, at first in Ontario and later in New Brunswick. She decided to lend a helping hand in Canada's war efforts and served as a nurse at a military hospital in Leeds during the First World War. She saw first-hand the horrors of war, and her daughter tells me that she was never the same afterward.

It fell on John McNair and daughter Billie to look after the family. Billie had one brother and two sisters, and she became the anchor in the McNair household at a young age. She carried the responsibility with poise. It also gave her a quiet inner strength and a self-sufficiency that she would carry with dignity for the rest of her life.

Harrison was proud of his father-in-law. He reminded me more than once that his father-in-law had been to Oxford, as I had been. He once told me that he wanted to take me to dinner at the Mitre Restaurant in Oxford, the finest restaurant in town, or so he claimed. I asked him if he had eaten there. "No, no, never been to Oxford but I hear that it is the best restaurant in town." It may well have been when his father-in-law was a student, but certainly not by the time I was there.

Harrison explained his affection for his father-in-law: "Well, he had a rural background. His father-in-law was a small lumberman and some kind of a farmer up in the Tobique Valley. Not well-to-do. And so they're somewhat similar backgrounds. And of course he knew my parents, who were both big gun Liberals. That didn't hurt things any. And he and I got along famously. And after Billie and I'd married and had kids, my God, he was in love with those kids. He used to take them fishing when I never would. He would take them fishing, he would take them fishing, boating, any damn thing at all."[38]

It is often said that when it comes to romance, opposites attract. This was particularly true with Billie and Harrison. Billie was quiet, strong, and unassuming, and had a deep appreciation and knowledge of fine arts. She had learned early on not to draw attention to herself and not to embarrass her premier-father. Billie also had an aura of charm and elegance, and the McNair name brought connections to the province's political and economic elites.

Harrison could not have been better served, for his relationship with Billie liberated him to pursue his goals, to focus on building a business empire, and to become a public figure. Janet Scarfe reports that, in one year, Harrison was away from home 250 days. He knew that the home front would always be in good hands. He also knew that he could have the limelight all to himself. Billie wanted none of it.

3

Getting a Job

Americans call it chutzpah, central Canadians call it guts, while Maritimers call it balls. Call it what you may, Harrison McCain was the king of it. He was never late for anything. Once, impeccably dressed, his shirt crisp, his tie expensive, Harrison was waiting for a dinner companion in upscale Scott's restaurant in London's fashionable Mayfair district when he was approached by a snobbish looking older man, who had just come in with a much younger woman. Assuming that Harrison was the head waiter, he requested a quiet table. Rising to the occasion, Harrison found one that met their wishes, pulled out their chairs and asked politely if he could do anything else for them before summoning their waiter. "Yes," said the gentleman. "We'll have a bottle of champagne." Harrison then went to the maître d' and told him what he had done. He then ordered, on behalf of the gentleman, a bottle of the most expensive champagne in Scott's (which specialized in champagne). He did not stay to see the "wincing embarrassment" of the gentleman after he received the bill.[1]

Finding a job in postwar Canada, at a time when war veterans were coming on the market was no easy task. It required chutzpah. As well, some of the women who had replaced the men who had gone overseas now wanted to stay in the workforce. In addition, the manufacturing sector, adjusting to peacetime circumstances, was shedding jobs.

Finding a job for a university graduate wishing to stay in the Maritime provinces has never been easy.[2] In the postwar period it was particularly difficult. So chutzpah came in handy for a young university graduate from Florenceville, New Brunswick.

I'M JUST EXACTLY THE MAN YOU WANT

Harrison saw an advertisement in the Halifax newspaper, the *Chronicle Herald*, for a sales job with the pharmaceutical firm Mowat and Moore. He thought that he would be a shoe-in, given that he had studied organic chemistry at Acadia. However, when he went for an interview, the firm's sales manager politely informed Harrison that three highly qualified graduate pharmacists had also applied for the job and the firm would be looking at one of them. He added, "The chances of you getting this job are zilch."[3]

Harrison did not miss a beat: "No, no, no, no – you're making a terrible mistake. Don't do that at all. I'm just exactly the man you want." He then pressed his case further with a remarkable offer. "I'll tell you what I'll do. Just because you're slow to pick up on what I think I can do in this job – you have to have a car to get the job – I'll borrow money from my old man to buy a car. Step one. Number two, I'll work for no pay. You only have to pay my expenses. No pay for a solid year. At the end of that year, you pay me my wages for the full year or shake hands, your choice, not mine." The sales manager said "No, no, we can't do that."

Harrison, of course, did not walk into the interview with that proposition in mind. After all, he'd expected to be offered the job. He came up with the idea on the spot: "I wanted a job. Jobs were very hard to find, and what was I trained for was not sales. In my mind, I should be a salesman. But I wasn't trained."[4]

Two days later the sales manager telephoned Harrison to say: "I can't even sleep at night, thinking about your offer, that you'll work for a year for nothing if I'll give you a job and then we'll settle it amicably. I'm giving you the job. You get the job. Come to work next Monday."[5] Harrison not only beat out the three pharmacists, he got the job, and he received a salary plus expenses from day one.

Harrison worked at Mowat and Moore for nearly two years. His sales territory was southern Quebec and eastern Ontario. His base was Montreal but he spent most of the time in Ottawa, living in the Lord Elgin Hotel, since Ottawa was more central to his territory.

By the end of his first year, Harrison had established himself as one of the firm's top salesmen – first or second out of fourteen. He received bonuses for his performance and outperformed everyone's expectations, except his own. He was soon looking for a more challenging job.

The hours were too short and he felt that there was not enough action to keep him fully employed. He remembered, "You couldn't see a druggist before nine-thirty in the morning because he was doing his cash from the night before. Then you started to see the doctors around one-thirty and you were all through by four-thirty."[6] The fact that the offices were also closed on Wednesday afternoons and Saturdays did not help matters. In fact, he already had his heart set on starting his own business.

LEARNING FROM THE MASTER

While at Acadia, Harrison McCain met K.C. Irving's sons J.K. and Arthur. They became good friends and remained so after they left university. K.C. Irving was nothing short of a business genius, an entrepreneur who built a business empire with a hand in virtually every sector of the economy. Starting with very little in the small New Brunswick coastal community of Bouctouche, he became one of the world's leading industrialists. By the time his career came to a close, he owned a shipyard, an oil refinery, several newspapers, pulp and paper operations, sawmills, dry goods stores, large forestry holdings, an engineering firm, and the list goes on.

K.C. Irving privately owned all his enterprises. This, he argued, enabled him to react more quickly and plan better for the longer term than if they were publicly traded companies. But there was another important benefit: he could remain tight-lipped about his business activities, and no one was able to establish his true net worth. Suffice to note that from a relatively modest beginning, he built one of the largest and best-run business empires in Canadian history and became one of the world's wealthiest individuals. K.C. Irving also had a well-earned reputation for keeping things close to his chest. In accepting a business achievement award, his grandson J.D. Irving told the gathering that, if his grandfather were there that night, he would lean over, pat him on the arm, and say, "Now, Jimmy, don't say too much."[7]

If one wanted to study one of history's great entrepreneurs, one need not look further than K.C. Irving. He saw first-hand the challenges of growing a business in a small, peripheral, and fading region. K.C. was a proud New Brunswicker who saw no need to move to a large urban centre in central Canada or the United States to build his businesses and prosper.

K.C.'s first venture into the world of business was securing a Ford dealership in the early 1920s. He was told, however, that he couldn't have his dealership in Bouctouche because it was too close to Moncton where a Ford dealership already existed. He considered Halifax, Nova Scotia, as a likely location, but preferring to stay in his home province, settled on Saint John, New Brunswick. He knew better than anyone that his region was vulnerable to large firms and government policy "from away," so he entered into partnership agreements only if he had no other alternative and, once he had the knowledge and resources to fly on his own, he did. He struck a partnership with Chevron to sell oil and gas in the Maritime provinces. He later introduced his own brand of gasoline, initially Primrose, and later Irving Oil.

I once asked his son Arthur Irving why his father got into the oil and gas business. His answer: "Because he was selling automobiles and cars need oil and gas to run. Why give that business to someone else?" The logic does not end there – if it makes sense to sell oil and gasoline, then it also makes sense to build a refinery, and, if it makes sense to build a refinery, then it also makes sense to build ships to transport oil and gasoline from the refinery.[8] That lesson would not be lost on Harrison McCain.

K.C. Irving's entrepreneurship skills were anchored in a few but unshakable beliefs. First, he was convinced of the merits of a hands-on approach: leave nothing to chance and pay attention to detail. He passed this belief on to his sons. Second, "expansion is the thing." He was a pioneer of clustering before it came into fashion in the business-management literature.

I recall being in the small northern New Brunswick town of Saint-Quentin, when Sandra Irving called about a project we were working on. I told her that by sheer coincidence, I was in front of the local Irving service station. Arthur, her husband, was soon on the phone. He said, "Thanks for the business, Donald. I know the manager, a real good guy. Please say hello to him. Could you let me know if the rest room is in good shape and clean?" Now, *that* is paying attention to detail!

K.C. Irving was a master of vertical integration. Why sell someone else's gasoline when you have an automobile dealership and service stations and when you can refine it yourself? One of his grandsons explains, "One company building and buying from or selling to one another and building a base that would allow you to export or expand into new markets and new products elsewhere. It was good then, and today it's still just as good for us."[9]

Another of K.C. Irving's firm beliefs was in work, focus, work, and work some more. His son Arthur Irving told me that his father had no sense of time and had incredible energy. He could outwork and out-last people thirty years younger. Harrison McCain once observed that K.C. Irving had "great energy, wonderful energy. Never got tired."[10] This from a man who himself had an oversupply of energy. Family lore reports that when he left Bouctouche for Saint John, K.C. asked how best he could connect with the city's business community. He was told to join the local golf club. This he did. He bought a new set of golf clubs and deposited them in his locker. The locker was never opened again and the clubs were lost when the clubhouse burned down several years later. K.C. Irving had his eyes on the business at all times.

K.C. Irving was a man of great civility, as everyone who ever met him can attest. I grew up in the same small community – Bouctouche – as did K.C. Irving. In the summer months I would often see him pull up at the local Irving gas station. One day, manning the pumps was a young Acadian from Saint-Antoine, down the road from Bouctouche. He had set his heart on becoming an entrepreneur, the goal of few young Acadians at the time. He saw an opportunity to impress the great man and maybe get some advice on how to become a businessman himself. He decided to give K.C. the complete service and then some. He poured the gas, he washed not just the windshield but all the car windows, he cleaned the headlights, and he even wiped the front and back bumpers with a cloth, all with great care. All the while K.C. stood by, arms crossed, not saying a word or showing impatience. When the work was finally done, the aspiring entrepreneur went to collect the money and said, "My goal is to be a businessman. Any advice?" K.C. calmly responded, "You will need to work a lot faster if you ever want to be successful." I am happy to report that the young man appears to have taken the advice to heart. Today he is a successful businessman producing and selling construction material.[11]

K.C. Irving was an excellent business mentor to a number of entrepreneurs, including Harrison and Wallace McCain and of course his own sons. As Henry and A.D. McCain had done with their sons, K.C. Irving made certain that his sons would understand the value of money by earning it themselves. He had them working at demanding jobs in one or another of his businesses. For instance, he sent his eldest son, Jim, Harrison's friend from Acadia, to a tough job cutting and hauling logs in the woods in northern New Brunswick. From time to time Jim would come to visit the McCains in Florenceville, which was not far from where he was working.

It so happened that when Harrison came home for a brief visit during his work with Mowat and Moore, Jim was visiting. According to Harrison,

We were having a talk. And while we were having a talk off in a quiet corner, my mother brought in a letter to my attention. It was a letter that I was to receive when I was at home. And it came from Mowat and Moore. She said, "Here's a letter, Harrison, probably from your boss or something. You'd better read it." So she handed me the envelope. I opened the letter and here was the letter saying, "Well look Harrison, you've done such a very good job for us, you've done such a very good job for us over the last year, year and a half, and so I know you're on your holidays and there's not a lot of money to go around and I thought it would help out a bit. Here is my cheque for (I think it was) four-hundred dollars, four hundred dollars, to help pay your expenses, and I hope you have a good time and look forward to seeing you in a couple weeks time." Well I was surprised to get it, but the only one person who was more surprised than me was Jim Irving. He couldn't believe that this company that I'd only worked for a year was sending me cheques unasked for.[12]

Jim went home and told his father that Harrison had to be the "king of the salesmen." From that moment on, Harrison claimed "K.C. Irving chased me to join them." Harrison initially resisted: he had his heart set on starting his own business. He turned down K.C. Irving's invitation to meet him in Saint John, but K.C., never one to give in easily, insisted on having a good talk with Harrison. They met the following week in a small community near Ottawa.

K.C. Irving made his pitch. He told Harrison that he needed "sales help and sales supervisors," adding that there was a "huge future in the oil business for me and for everybody." He asked Harrison how much money he was making. Harrison admits that he "stretched the truth," adding expenses and bonus to his salary. K.C. Irving replied that he would "add substantially" to it if he would take the job.[13] Harrison put his plan to start his own business on hold and signed on with Irving, where he would learn a great deal about running a business from the master – K.C. Irving. He also demonstrated his ability to negotiate a good deal. Harrison told K.C. Irving: "Give me 10,000 bucks and a big car and I am your man." That was a hefty salary for a young man just two years out of university in 1951 in New Brunswick. Having a big car was important to Harrison, as a sure sign of success. It also proved to be a wise investment for K.C. Irving.

Harrison McCain joined Irving Oil as one of its lead salesmen. He came to admire K.C.'s business acumen and his ability to manage his and his businesses' public image. According to Jim Coutts, one of Harrison's close friends, K.C. Irving "was the man Harrison most admired."[14]

K.C. Irving knew better than anyone how to push the envelope, how to get his senior managers to deliver that extra effort, and to how to outperform even their own high expectations. Harrison claimed that K.C. Irving was never happy if you delivered 95 per cent of your object-ives, he wanted the 100 per cent. Thus, Harrison had worked for a long time to secure a contract to supply a large power station with Irving fuel. After eighteen months he was successful. Delighted, he called K.C. to share the good news. K.C.'s response? He asked Harrison if he had been able to add lubricating grease to the deal.[15] The grease repre-sented only some 4 per cent of the deal. The message was not lost on Harrison: 100 per cent of the business is better than 96 per cent, and a successful business owner always looks into the details of any business deal or business activities.

Harrison told me that K.C. Irving was a gentleman, a demanding boss who had the ability to see how things would play out five or ten years down the road and understood that if you do not go after the busi-ness, someone else always will. Harrison said that K.C. raised plenty of eyebrows when he bought Saint John Sulfite, a small, struggling mill in bad shape financially. However, at the same time he also bought sub-stantial woodland from the province. K.C. was ahead of the pack and saw the potential in forestry when no one else did or could. Harrison once said to me, "Call it luck, strategic thinking, or taking a risk. What-ever you call it, you have to know when to pull the trigger, and Irving knew that better than anyone."

Harrison also admired how K.C. Irving managed his public image, because it, along with his reputation, was crucial to his business suc-cess. Harrison maintained that, because K.C. Irving never gave inter-views, people simply believed that he had little interest in projecting a public image. Harrison insisted that nothing could be further from the truth. K.C. Irving knew better than anyone the role a public image has in business and how to manage it. Irving cultivated the image of a tough, demanding, shrewd, austere, tireless, sober, secretive, no-nonsense businessman, never to be outgunned. "Christ," Harrison explained, "when K.C. Irving walked in to negotiate a business deal, the competition was already ready to give up and say I can't compete with this guy. The competitor would lose before the competition began because everyone knew that you could never beat K.C. Irving."

Harrison admired K.C.'s management style, which he said was based on "suggestion." It is worth quoting him at length on this point:

One, he had a style, he had a style all his own. I've never seen the like of it in all my life. I must have heard him, but I can't recall an example of him ever giving me a direct order, "Harrison, here's what I want you to do on Thursday. Go down and see Jack and do this, this, this and this." Maybe it happened, probably happened, but I can't recall it. Mr Irving ran the business with his top people by suggestion. His style. He'd make a suggestion that if we had such-and-such an account, that would fit in just exactly what our expenses and our business plans in buying this flat area, and that would be the cornerstone for a new location. And if we got that, that would convince me that we should go ahead and spend the money and get the damn thing going. If we could just find some-body that could just talk the fellows into swinging that damn deal around. And what that meant was, get your ass out there and get that account.[16]

Harrison also presented a largely unknown side of K.C. Irving. He described him as "kind and good fun. We used to have great fun." He added, "He used to sing, you know. We used to be riding in his car late at night, 10 or 11 o'clock at night, going to some goddamn place to see a service station site and, jeez, he'd start singing. He was a fine fellow."[17]

Harrison McCain worked for Irving Oil for five years, and he always maintained that he "had an excellent time there."[18] He became, at age twenty-four, sales manager for Irving Oil for New Brunswick, Prince Edward Island, and Newfoundland. He worked at 73 Dock Street at the foot of King Street in Saint John, only a few doors down from K.C. Irving – pretty heady stuff for an aspiring entrepreneur in New Brunswick in the 1950s.

Besides learning a great deal about growing and managing a large business enterprise at the feet of the master, Harrison's innate talent for business was as evident as it had been in his time with Mowat and Moore. He had a hand in growing Irving Oil, securing new clients, finding sites to build new service stations, and working with local managers to grow the business. He strongly urged K.C. to expand Irving Oil in Maine – which he did – and then on into New England. Harrison put in very long hours with Irving Oil but he welcomed it. He found it far more satisfying than having to shut down at four-thirty in the afternoon because that was when medical doctors closed their offices for the day. With Irving Oil his long hours often extended to the weekend and he could be on the road at a moment's notice, and in fact "he always kept an extra bag packed, just in case."[19]

Life in Saint John was pleasant. He and Billie had a comfortable home on beautiful tree-lined Manawagonish Road in West Saint John. Their first baby was born there and Billie's father, John McNair, became a regular visitor. Billie was quite content in Saint John, looking after Harrison and raising her newborn son Mark and daughter Ann.

But Harrison was growing restless and could not let go of his desire to start his own business. He explained, "You know, I thought I was going to walk into a place and see a place to buy some day or a place I could offer to buy, and lo and behold I'd be in business. And it dawned on me one day that I was too busy doing too many things for that to happen, and that I had to make it happen. So I quit the job. So I had no job and no money, and I had to find a business." K.C. Irving pressed him to stay, but Harrison had made up his mind. He told K.C. that he was going into business for himself and that it would never happen if he "kept working for him, waiting for it to happen."[20]

Harrison had had many discussions with his brother Wallace about going into business. Wallace was also living in Saint John, working for K.C. Irving's Thorne Hardware. He too had soon happily adapted to the Irving work ethic, putting in fourteen hours a day. Like Harrison, Wallace outperformed expectations. He helped to transform Thorne Hardware from a local building supply store to a major regional presence. When he arrived at Thorne, the firm had sixteen salespersons, but by the time he left there were twenty-five.[21]

Wallace spent a great deal of time with Harrison and Billie while in Saint John. The topic of conversation, more often than not, was how to go into business for themselves. They both wanted to follow in their father's footsteps. They looked at different possibilities – opening a hardware store, a dry cleaning business, and even buying a seat on the Toronto or Montreal Exchange. They could not, however, settle on what direction they should take. Harrison's decision to throw caution to the wind and quit Irving Oil forced the issue for him. After all, starting his own business had always been his overriding objective.

WHAT TO DO?

Harrison left a well-paid, high-profile sales manager job working with one of Canada's business giants. No job, no salary, and a wife and newborn son and daughter at home. No business to go to, just an obsessive desire to start one. The problem – he had no idea what to start. Harrison's chutzpah once again rose to meet the occasion.

Joining the family business was not an option. The potato business was not what it had been, with prices in the 1950s remaining flat in both domestic and foreign markets. The potato business in Carleton County was going through a difficult period and was also highly competitive. Mechanization was increasingly making its presence felt in the industry, and American producers were quicker than their Canadian counterparts to embrace it.[22] In addition, Carleton County producers were having little success in introducing new products. They tried "ill-tasting dehydrated potatoes, potato starch and potato feed – but none brought the profits their investors had predicted."[23] More to the point, Harrison's mother and his two brothers were already working as McCain Produce and they could not afford to pay another McCain.

Harrison had inherited $40,000 from his father that he could use to invest in a business – if he could find one that suited him. While waiting for inspiration, he did not stay idle. He got into the Christmas tree business and he spent a month in Florida selling Christmas trees. He wanted to look at business opportunities up and down the eastern seaboard and decided to finance his trip by selling Christmas trees along the way. As he explained, "I think that I had three or four hundred dollars in my pocket when I left and I had three or four hundred dollars in my pocket when I came back. It didn't cost me anything."[24] It did, however, enable him to explore business opportunities and develop further his skills as a salesman.

Still, it was hardly the business prospect that he was looking for. If he was not overly worried about coming up with an idea to launch a new business, his mother Laura was. She was satisfied that Wallace had a good job with Thorne Hardware and that Bob and Andrew were in the family business with her. She did not think that selling Christmas trees in Florida was any sort of career – nor for that matter did Harrison. Laura was worried. Harrison had little income and his inheritance would not last forever. Laura turned to Bob, whose judgment she trusted. She simply told him to come up with business ideas for Harrison.

Bob knew that Carleton County potato farmers were shipping a lot of potatoes to the Birds Eye plant in Maine that processed them into frozen french fries. He felt that there was something promising there, something worth exploring, and he was right. Fast food restaurants with french fries as a central focus were slowly making their presence felt. McDonald's, Burger King, A&W, Kentucky Fried Chicken all appeared in the mid-1950s in the United States, and the list has kept growing ever since, as did their demands for french fries. Fast food outlets had arrived to stay and they were grabbing a large share of the restaurant food market.[25]

Bob suggested to Harrison that the time was ripe for a home-grown competitor. Why should Carleton County potato farmers ship their products to be processed in Maine, only to be then shipped back to

Canada? Harrison, at least at first, did not think that it "was any earth-shaking idea. But I had nothing to do since the fall before and I was quietly desperate."[26] His life-long friend Donald Trafford told me that he saw little potential in the frozen french fries market at the time and felt that Harrison was making a bad mistake.

Harrison finally decided to go for it and to use $30,000 of his inheritance in the venture. In his interview with Downey, he said that when he left Irving Oil to start a business, he was "working full time without pay for myself." Although he had talked at length about going into business with his brother Wallace, "I wasn't representing the two of us. I paid my own bills, he wasn't paying half. I looked after myself."[27]

Still, Harrison did tell Wallace what he planned to do and asked if he wanted in the business. Wallace responded, "You go ahead and start and we'll see how it goes. I'll help you all I can, I'll put some money in and see if it's big enough for the two of us, and I'll see what I'm going to do." Harrison's response: "No, no, come right now. Come right now. Don't fool around, just make up your mind."[28]

Wallace then became the second McCain to leave an Irving business. He gave six months' notice, and during that time Harrison and Bob laid the groundwork for the new business. They visited large frozen-food producers in the United States and tried to identify potential distributors in Canada. Still Harrison later reported that everyone felt that "we were stupid. It was the wrong thing to do, but I think the more negatives we heard, the more positive we became that we wanted to go into it."[29]

Initially the thinking was that each of the four brothers should invest $25,000 in the new business venture. Wallace said no. He felt that if Harrison and he were to run and grow the business, then they should have a majority interest, and the control that comes with it. The other brothers agreed, and Harrison and Wallace invested $30,000 each and Andrew and Robert $20,000.

The sisters were not involved. Both Marie and Eleanor had also inherited $40,000 like their brothers. But women in rural New Brunswick in the mid-1950s were not in the habit of starting new businesses or investing in them. It was simply not their role – end of story.

Harrison asked his brother-in-law, John McNair, a Fredericton-based lawyer, to incorporate the new business, which was born on 24

May 1956 with the name McCain Foods Limited. Harrison was president and Wallace secretary-treasurer.[30] All four brothers became company directors. They also invited Marie's husband, Jed B. Sutherland, to join the board in the event of a tie in a vote. Five members would solve that potential problem.

Harrison had what he had long hoped for. He was in business for himself with his brothers. There would be immense challenges ahead, but the new business had a number of advantages. The fast food business, with its heavy reliance on french fries, was about to take flight and change the food-restaurant business. In addition, governments were poised to play a far greater interventionist role in the economy. Harrison with his brothers, particularly Wallace, would ride these two advantages in building their multi-billion-dollar food empire.

Both Harrison and Wallace had honed their skills at the feet of a business genius and one of the world's great entrepreneurs, fellow New Brunswicker, K.C. Irving. Both remained forever grateful to him – but now they were on their own, hoping to emulate their mentor's success.

A.D. and Laura McCain's family. *Left to right*: Wallace, Eleanor, Harrison, Laura, A.D. McCain, Marie, Robert, and Andrew.

Harrison McCain, graduation photo, Acadia
University.

Billie with her father, John B. McNair, welcomes Princess Elizabeth to New Brunswick in 1951.

Billie landed a thirty-eight pound salmon on the Restigouche.

Billie and Harrison McCain on their wedding day.

Billie and Harrison on their honeymoon in Florida.

Official opening of Thomas Equipment. *Left to right*: Louis J. Robichaud, Wallace, and Harrison. (© McCain Foods Limited, all rights reserved)

The original McCain plant in Florenceville.

Working on the conveyor belt at the original plant. (© McCain Foods Limited, all rights reserved)

Left to right: Robert, Andrew, and Harrison at the plant. (© McCain Foods Limited, all rights reserved)

Harrison at a food fair.

Harrison at his office.

Left to right: Ann, Harrison, Mark, and Peter at home, 1959.

Harrison and Billie in London, 1960s.

Left to right: Peter, Mark, Harrison, Ann, and Laura.

Gillian with parents.

Launching a Business on a Wing, a Prayer, and a Helping Hand from Government

Harrison McCain finally had what he had long wanted: a business to start, a chance to compete in the marketplace, to grow, and hopefully to turn a handsome profit. Admittedly, Harrison had a leg-up – an inheritance from his father, and brothers willing to lend a helping hand. As noted earlier, all four brothers invested part of their inheritance in the business, and two were directly involved: his younger brother Wallace, and his elder brother Bob. Bob provided both key support and advice, particularly in the early months. Harrison and Wallace, as we have seen, also had countless discussions about what business they should start while both were working in Saint John for K.C. Irving. It was never a question of if or when, only what. They now had an answer to the what, the when, and the who.

Harrison and Wallace had raw ambition, youth, energy, and an exceptionally strong work ethic. Both had gained invaluable business experience working under the ever-watchful eye of K.C. Irving. They also picked a fortuitous time to get into the frozen food business. The fast food industry was still in its infancy, but rapidly gaining momentum. Canada's population was well into a growth spurt fuelled by the baby boom of the postwar period and the arrival of many new Canadians. More important still, women were joining the workforce at an increasing rate. Two-income families meant eating out often and also easy-to-prepare meals to eat at home. Frozen french fries were a crucial ingredient of both.

But launching a frozen food firm required a great deal more than raw ambition and a strong work ethic. For one thing, both Harrison and Wallace had very limited knowledge of the industry. One had worked in oil sales, and the other had run a relatively small hardware business. The frozen food business was terra incognito to both. Little wonder that when Harrison told people what he was getting into, many told him that he was crazy.

The money the brothers had invested wouldn't, however, get them far. Nor did they have access to the expertise they so sorely needed. It certainly did not exist anywhere in Carleton County or, for that matter, in Canada. All they had was the raw material – potatoes. However, the quality of the local potatoes was in question, at least when compared to Idaho potatoes, which were considered more suited to the frozen food business. Nor was there yet a market in the three Maritime provinces for frozen food, and the large markets were thousands of miles away. Then there was transportation to consider, a daunting problem in the late 1950s, especially for moving frozen food. The transportation infrastructure and industry in New Brunswick in the late 1950s were both lacking on many fronts, particularly when it concerned frozen food. They also lacked financial resources.

THINGS TO DO

Harrison and his brother Bob had been laying the groundwork for the new business for several months before Wallace arrived on the scene, and there was a great deal to be done. The McCain brothers, to be sure, faced a very sharp learning curve. They could not learn the business at home because, leaving aside a small plant in Quebec, the frozen food business essentially did not exist in Canada. As well, few grocery stores were equipped with freezers, and those that were had only small ones for ice cream. Bob and Harrison talked their way into visiting frozen food plants in the United States to see first-hand how they could make it work at home, but a brief look inside a frozen food plant was one thing. Building one from scratch was quite another.

By the time Wallace arrived, the McCain brothers had a fair idea of the challenges ahead. Yet neither Harrison nor Wallace ever lost faith. I once asked Harrison if he ever regretted leaving a secure, well-paying job with Irving. "Christ, no," he said, "no sense looking back. We were in it and that was that. Best years of our lives, best years of our lives."

To be sure, there was no shortage of challenges. They had to find capital, build a plant, learn to operate it, secure the raw material, hire staff, identify markets, and ship the products. This all had to be done in a relatively short period, or before the cash ran out.

FINDING CAPITAL

The investment in the business by the four McCain brothers was critical. But it was hardly enough. Salaries would eventually have to be paid, including their own. A plant with sophisticated machines had to be built, a modern cold storage facility had to be constructed before sales could be made. All of this had to be done in a relatively short period, or before the cash ran out.

The first order of business was to find money to build the plant and the cold storage facility. They did what many aspiring entrepreneurs do – they sought help from a bank. In their case, they went to the local branch of the Bank of Nova Scotia, the bank that their father and grandfather had done business with, and applied for a line of credit of $150,000.

As luck would have it, the bank's president, Horace Inman, was visiting the branch while Harrison and Wallace were making their pitch. Inman spotted them, went over to introduce himself, asked who they were and why they were there. The brothers gave him a brief outline of their business plan. Inman told Harrison and Wallace to sit tight and wait for a few minutes. Very shortly he came out of the branch manager's office and told them that they had the money and were now in business. Inman knew the McCain family from his time as bank supervisor in New Brunswick. He explained, "Your grandfather did business with this bank. He owed this bank a lot of money, and when he owed it he was broke. But your father paid all the money back. We never lost a nickel from any McCain."[1]

Despite the line of credit and the $100,000 the McCain brothers had committed to the project, it was still not enough. However, luck again entered the picture when Harrison heard from friends in the Liberal party that the federal government had or was about to put in place a program to encourage the construction of cold storage facilities throughout Canada. He contacted Milton Gregg, federal Cabinet minister representing New Brunswick in Louis St Laurent's Liberal government. The Liberal McCains knew Gregg well, and Harrison met with him to see if they could qualify for the program that provided a generous subsidy of about 40 per cent towards the construction costs of a new cold storage facility. The objective was to support agricultural communities and to promote new product development. Gregg came back to say that, sadly, they did not qualify because McCain Foods was a private company. He explained that the business "would stand to make a personal gain, which the program did not allow."[2] It had to be a community-sponsored project to qualify.

Harrison had an answer. He told Gregg, "No problem. We'll make it a co-op." He went to several large farmers in Carleton County, organized a co-op and called it the Carleton Cold Storage Company. The co-op successfully applied for the grant and, in Harrison's words, "That took straight off and then on to building the plant."[3] McCain Foods continued to buy shares in the co-op and was finally able to fully absorb it in the company in 1979.

The Bank of Nova Scotia's $150,000 line of credit and the federal government's contribution were very important, but, again, still more would be needed to build a modern plant and equip it with the necessary machinery and tools. Venture capital was rare to non-existent in New Brunswick in the mid-1950s, and family and friends had little more to offer than what they had already contributed.

HUGH JOHN FLEMMING

Enter Hugh John Flemming, a good old Carleton County politician. He had defeated the provincial government led by Harrison McCain's father-in-law, John B. McNair, in 1952. Flemming, ironically, like Harrison's father, A.D. McCain, had his heart set on going to medical school. And, like A.D., Hugh John had to put his plans on ice because of his father's financial difficulties. He left school at fifteen to work in his father's lumber business in Juniper, a short distance from Florenceville.[4]

Hugh John knew the county well and was also quite aware of the problems confronting potato farmers. Potato prices had remained flat for several years and local farmers had difficulty coming up with new products. Flemming, meanwhile, sought early on to make job-creation and economic development central to his government's policy, and in time they became the most important component of his political legacy. As students of New Brunswick history know well, he pushed the federal government time and again to come up with an economic development strategy for Atlantic Canada and to make substantial investments in major hydro projects. He met with some success, particularly after his friend and political ally John Diefenbaker came to power in Ottawa.[5]

Flemming had tried, with no success, to attract some American-based food-processing firms to Carleton County. He was thus ripe for a proposal when the McCain boys came calling. He was happy to overlook the fact that the McCains were well-known Liberal party supporters. The proposed project was going to be in his constituency, would create jobs, and would modernize the agricultural sector. The fact that 1956 was an election year only fuelled his enthusiasm for finding projects that his government could support.

The mid-1950s also saw governments in many Anglo-American democracies intervening more and more in the economy to promote economic development and job creation. It was as true for right-of-centre government as it was for left-leaning governments. In Canada, for example, it was the John Diefenbaker Progressive Conservative government that introduced the first of many economic development measures for slow-growth regions.[6]

Flemming announced with considerable fanfare that he would support the McCain project for his constituency. He proudly declared, "We are convinced that this new industry will help to provide new and profitable markets for farmers over a wide area of New Brunswick."[7] The Flemming government guaranteed a $470,000 bond on behalf of McCain Foods. This, Wallace McCain explained, "was a big deal for us." It enabled McCain Foods to borrow money at a low interest rate. "Who," he asked, "was going to buy McCain Foods bonds without a guarantee?"[8]

Hugh John Flemming was not to be outdone by other provincial governments. Robert Stanfield, the Progressive Conservative premier of neighbouring Nova Scotia, was also putting in place measures to promote economic development and attract outside investors. He established Industrial Estates Limited, gave it a $23 million start-up

budget, and told its officials to build industrial parks and work with
private sector firms to create jobs.[9] Stanfield's was a right-of-centre government. The regional economic development field came of age in the
1950s, with governments of all stripes coming on board, no matter their
political philosophy. The idea was to create programs in tandem with
the private sector to achieve this aim. No government wanted to sit on
the sidelines, only to see a neighbouring jurisdiction getting into the
game and attracting private sector jobs away from their own region.[10]

It was Flemming's turn not to be outdone. He established the New
Brunswick Industrial Board in 1956, and McCain Foods was the board's
very first project. It handed out its first two loans or bond guarantees to McCain Foods – one for the construction of the plant and the
second for cold storage. The assistance was for twenty years at a 5 per
cent interest. They were the first of many loans, loan guarantees, and
grants McCain Foods would receive from the provincial and federal
governments as they grew their business.[11]

WHAT ABOUT TAXES?

Despite the brothers' $100,000 investment, the line of credit and now
the federal and provincial government assistance, money remained
tight. Harrison and Wallace never stopped looking for ways to save
money, at least in the early years. As luck would have it again, Bob
McCain was elected as Florenceville's representative on the Carleton
County council.

County councils in New Brunswick played a powerful role in the
days before Premier Louis Robichaud abolished them in the mid-
sixties. They delivered public services from education to health care
and had significant taxation powers. Harrison and Wallace asked
to meet county council in June 1956 to make a pitch for a tax break
for their new business. It was agreed that Harrison would make the
presentation, while Wallace would stand by to answer questions. This
was the start of Harrison becoming the main public spokesman for
McCain Foods.

Bob, meanwhile, sat with other council members and listened. The
pitch would not be easy. McCain Foods at the time had no employees, no product, no plant, limited financial resources, and a plan to

produce an untried product. About the only thing they had to offer was an idea to launch a business and a commitment from both senior levels of government to provide financial assistance. They came calling with only a request to secure a tax break. The McCain family, however, had a solid reputation in Carleton County, going back two generations.

As was his style, Harrison was forthright in his address. He told council, "For the past two years, we have learned, much to our sorrow, that our principal agricultural crop of potatoes is becoming a liability rather than an asset to the economy of our county."[12] He spoke about the substantial contributions the new business would make to the region and talked about the jobs to be created, the houses to be built, and the new markets farmers would now have for their potatoes. All the council had to do was to say yes to some tax concessions. He insisted that what he was asking for was not out of the ordinary, since a firm in Ontario, also in the food processing business, had recently received a tax break in that province.

Harrison made the pitch at a time when politicians enjoyed a much higher level of trust than they do today. The age of transparency was still some twenty-five years away. Bob McCain, a shareholder in the company, did not abstain from the deliberations. One councillor immediately made clear his support, well aware that council might be establishing a precedent. The council, however, was more cautious and decided to turn the matter over to a committee for consideration. Council subsequently announced that it would exempt McCain Foods and Carleton Cold Storage from all local taxes for 1957 and 1958. The tax concession was adjusted slightly when the provincial government told Carleton County Council that a total exemption of all local taxes was not legal because of existing statutes. Taxes were later adjusted to almost nothing for 1957 and 1958.[13]

GETTING GOING

In many ways securing funds and tax concessions was the easy part. The entire project would fail miserably if they didn't get some high-level expertise in the frozen food industry onside – and quickly. Harrison and Bob had paid a few brief visits to a frozen food plant in Maine, but that had mostly shown them how much they didn't know.

But growing potatoes and producing frozen french fries are two vastly different things.

The risks were high, knowledge of the sector was virtually non-existent, and Carleton County had no expertise in building, let alone managing a frozen food plant. Youth, energy, and raw ambition were about to come face-to-face with a daunting challenge in an environment that provided little help.

Reading about the early months at McCain Foods essentially speaks to an exercise in improvisation, of attempts at trying this and that to see what would work. First on the agenda was to find a site for the plant. Second was to build it. Third was to acquire the machinery and make it work. Fourth, hire staff. Fifth, make the freezing process work and ensure quality. Sixth, identify and pursue markets. All in all, a daunting agenda for two men still in their twenties, with no experience in the sector.

THE SITE

Florenceville had one distinct advantage: land was cheap. In addition, McCain Foods, at least at the time, was not looking for agricultural land. Rather, what they needed was a site with good access to water and to transportation facilities. They knew enough about the frozen food process to know that a constant supply of water was needed to fuel steam-peelers, potato cleaners, and boilers. They looked at several sites but settled on one within walking distance from McCain Produce Co., the firm started by their father and run by their mother and two brothers. They bought the land from a relative of their father's high-profile political rival – conservative politician B.F. Smith.[14]

The plant would be in their home town, Florenceville, with easy access to the Saint John River. It was also near the Trans-Canada Highway and CNR railway tracks. The land was inexpensive and the site held a number of advantages providing easy access for farmers.

BUILDING THE PLANT AND FINDING THE MACHINERY

Harrison once told me that the only thing he knew about frozen french fries when he decided to get into that business was how to eat them.

Asked to explain his business success, Harrison said, in his typically succinct way, "Good timing, good luck, right place."[15] He would repeat this mantra time and time again whenever the question was broached.

As for expertise, Harrison and Wallace once again got lucky when they learned that a pioneer in the business was living just down the road from them, working for H.C. Baxter in Houlton, Maine. Olof Pierson would earn the label "the father of the frozen French fried potato."[16] Pierson was an eccentric, MIT-trained, chain-smoking, hard-drinking, absent-minded inventor. He earned a master's degree in aeronautical engineering from MIT in 1932, and while serving in the American army during the Second World War he was given the task of working out how to dehydrate potatoes for the armed services. His success led to his joining H.C. Baxter, where he continued his work on processing potatoes, first in canned goods and later in freezing them as french fries. He invented and drove the process and indeed was directly responsible for the first package of frozen french fries sold in 1947 by the Birds Eye Company.[17] He later became an independent consultant in the frozen food business. McCain Foods was an early client, and later he advised the United Nations Food Organization.

Pierson had the run of the place on the technical side with McCain Foods because no one else knew how to build and operate a frozen food processing plant. He went to work improvising, sketching plans on the back of cigarette packages, thinking how the production process would work, and designing new machinery. Wallace explained that Pierson "had it all in his head," never one to outline elaborate plans, preferring to solve problems on the spot.[18] Harrison and Wallace were dependent on Pierson's work.

Once Pierson had put together plans for the plant, Wallace took his drawings to a local contractor, who looked at the plans and, with a puzzled look, asked Wallace, "How high do you think the walls of the plant should be?" Wallace went back to Pierson with the question. Pierson simply replied, "Well, how high do you think they should be?"[19] It was hardly the only time that he misfired in overseeing the building of the plant. Pierson later forgot, for example, to install conveyor belts on the production line in the plant.

However, Pierson had a genius for coming up with innovative solutions and inventing machinery. He single-handedly developed a steam peeler that would peel the skin off potatoes, and the basic design is still in use to this day. In its rudimentary form, however, the peeler was not without problems. It required a great deal of pressure, steam, and a controlled temperature to perform properly. Pierson's invention could not always accommodate the pressure, and at times bolts flew off in all directions. At other times, the peeler's door blew open. Carl Morris, a long-time McCain employee, recalled that in the early years he would be sitting in his office hearing "ping, ping as bolts flew off and bounced off other machines like bullets."[20]

Harrison and his brother Bob had made notes of the machines and freezers in use when they visited the plant in Maine. The problem was that money was short, so the McCains searched for machines that they could get second-hand. They were able, for example, to buy freezing equipment from a Quebec firm. They also acquired second-hand boilers from a plant in Ontario and machines to cut potatoes from California. They bought new machines only when they had no choice. Pierson went over the machines as they arrived and adapted them, when necessary, to operate a frozen french fries line.[21]

Since many of the machines had to be modified, they often had to be repaired. Long-serving McCain employees now report that in the early days they had to be "jack of all trades and if a machine needed fixing we figured out how to fix them." Lester Cox explains, "We trained ourselves, got a little manual, called the serviceman who probably didn't know more than we did. If we were lucky, we bought a piece of equipment that would work and give the results we wanted. If we bought a piece, put it on the line, didn't get results, then we had to figure out what we had to do to that piece to make it work."[22]

HIRING STAFF

Harrison and Wallace always led by example. They also improvised every step of the way. If potatoes were not available, they would process whatever vegetables or fruits that were available. A long-time employee, Betty Betts, recalled, "The first summer that I worked on peas, Harrison ran the line and Wallace worked in the field. It would be ten, eleven at night and Wallace would come dragging in, and would he ever be tired. They worked, they really worked! They knew where their first dollar came from because they worked for it. They would tell us everything that was happening, everything that they were going to do and how we were part of it. And we really believed that we were part of the McCain family, believe me."[23]

Harrison and Wallace also learned management by doing, by trying this and that, and by sharing information freely. They had no formal training, no management school training, and certainly no MBA degree. What they knew about management they had learned from K.C. Irving. Like him, they would lead by example, put in long hours, improvise when necessary, look a few years down the road, manage by suggestion, and give wide flexibility to their managers and staff to operate the way they saw fit. Harrison was never one to draft a memo when a phone call or a brief visit would do.

They hired competent staff, no small feat in Florenceville, far from major urban centres. They were fortunate, however, in having a Birds Eye frozen food plant just across the border in Maine. The McCain brothers had several contacts with the Birds Eye plant employees, including an impressive young engineer, Carl Morris, whom they set out to lure away to manage their new operation.

Morris resisted at first, though he volunteered advice, essentially acting as unpaid consultant. He became a friend of both Harrison and Wallace, meeting with them frequently, happily providing free advice on a host of issues. He enjoyed their company and became increasingly fascinated by what they set out to accomplish. After a few years, he signed on full time with the business.

Morris left a secure position with a prominent American firm. He later explained that General Foods was so well run that it would never make a bad decision, but that it took so long for senior management to take a decision that the advantages of moving quickly were often lost. There would be no such problem with McCain Foods. Decisions were quickly made and it was also acceptable to make mistakes, provided one learned from them. Morris explained, "If you were wrong, you got a heck of an education and you probably didn't make that mistake again. If you were right, you were so far ahead of everybody else and it was a major coup for the company."[24]

The McCain brothers and Morris hired staff that were of like mind. The criterion was a willingness to work long hours. Harrison and

Wallace inspired Carl Morris and the staff down to line workers to put in extremely long hours and to perform whatever tasks that needed attending to. Morris made the point that some senior managers see manual labour as somehow beneath them. This, he added, was certainly not the case with either Harrison or Wallace. They were true entrepreneurs and had everything riding on the success of their business start-up. For them, loading trucks was making good on promises to clients, it earned the respect of their staff, and it taught them all aspects of their business. Morris also reported on a brutal work agenda in the early years: "I am not kidding when I say we worked seven days a week, eighteen hours a day. But the work was enjoyable because everyone pulled together. Lots of times there would be two truckloads that had to go to Toronto or somewhere and there weren't enough bodies to load the trucks. So we'd all go over, Harrison and Wallace included, and load trucks."[25]

Harrison and Wallace were always on the lookout for strong managers. They also needed help to design and implement financial management controls. McCain Foods ran a $1,822 profit in its first year of operation and, remarkably, has turned a profit ever since. Carl Ash, manager of Dominion Bridge Company in the early 1960s in Montreal, was à Maritimer by birth who longed to go back home. He saw an advertisement for a comptroller for a growing business in New Brunswick. He guessed that it was McCain Foods, applied, and won the competition.

Ash drove home from Montreal to Amherst, Nova Scotia, every summer, always driving by the McCain Florenceville plant. He maintains that each year he drove by, the plant and company had grown. However, he joined McCain Foods only to discover that the firm had "virtually no systems at all." One manual accounting machine served the entire company. Ash told Harrison and Wallace that McCain Foods had a serious financial management problem that needed fixing. They simply told him, "Fix it." Both Harrison and Wallace were busy on other things, so Ash designed a management control reporting system that would become "the bible of the company," and its basic building blocks are still in place today.[26]

Many hands were involved in the early years and it is not possible to discuss all of them.[27] The community itself played an important part in the company's growth. The McCains were the entrepreneurs but McCain Foods was in many ways a local project. Farmers grew the potatoes, brought them to the plant for quick processing and freezing, and some of their wives worked on the production line. Everyone knew one another, and Carleton County residents had a stake in making the fledging start-up firm succeed.

If a machine broke down at the plant, the word was out in the community. Breakdowns were not uncommon, given that many were bought second-hand and some had been adjusted to fit a purpose that was different from its original one. It was also not uncommon for Harrison to visit garages throughout the county, asking mechanics if they could repair any given machine. In short, many residents of Carleton County were willing to put a shoulder to the wheel and help a couple of young local entrepreneurs turn out frozen food and french fries at the McCain plant.

The cold storage was in fact a community project designed from day one as a co-operative. Hunters frequently tramped through the cold storage to store their recent kills. The cold storage was a shared community institution and no one saw a problem with this, at least in the early years. There were no strangers around the plant, the cold storage area, or in Carleton County. Farmers knew where to bring their potatoes, McCain staff knew what needed to be done, and everyone hoped that the production line, the machines, and the power supply would hold up.

Even in the early years, it took less than a few hours for a farmer to pick a potato from his farm and then see it turned into frozen french fries. The potatoes arrived, were washed, and then immediately placed into one of eight Pierson steam peelers. They were then dumped on the trimming table, where workers looked for imperfections. From there, the potatoes were placed into a cylinder, spun around, then shot through a series of knives. The pieces then moved on a conveyor belt to a blanching drum to give them a golden-brown look. The french fries were then cooked in cottonseed oil in a fryer twenty feet long by six feet wide. Finally, the fries were moved to the cold storage area where they were blast-frozen at minus forty degrees and packed in thirty-pound cartons and stored in another room at minus ten degrees. This process, first put in place in Florenceville, has since been duplicated and introduced in the McCain Foods plants around the world.[28]

QUALITY

The McCain brothers very quickly discovered that local potatoes were not good for french fries. Wallace explained, "Our first products were greasy, black fries. If there was such a thing as Grade F, that was what we were producing. We had never heard of sugar content in potatoes."[29] New Brunswick had good potatoes but not for processing into frozen french fries. It also explains why an American in the potato business told Harrison that he was "crazier than hell" trying to start a frozen french fry business in Canada.

The American knew full well that the best potato for processing into frozen products was the Russet Burbank potato, grown mostly in the Pacific Northwest of the United States, notably Idaho. No one had grown it in Canada. There was yet another problem with New Brunswick-grown potatoes. Farmers did not make the transition from handling potatoes for immediate domestic consumption and the seed market to one designed for the frozen food market. The first are stored at low temperature to keep them firm, which is fine for the immediate retail market and domestic consumption. But in this environment the potatoes transform their starches into sugar, which produces a dark brown french fry.

Harrison and Wallace had an easy solution: get the farmers to grow the Russet Burbank. The farmers resisted at first because this was a potato that had never been grown in eastern Canada. Some, however, eventually agreed to give it a try, even though they doubted it would work because of New Brunswick's shorter growing season. They were right.

With this setback, the McCain brothers decided to diversify into other vegetables. Initially, they froze peas along with french fries. They then added cauliflower, beans, Brussels sprouts, and strawberries. Only later, when they could ensure a higher quality, would they focus the bulk of their efforts on potatoes.

To achieve a higher-quality potato, Harrison and Wallace hired Paul Dean, an American who studied food science at the University of

Georgia. He turned down eight offers to come to work with McCain Foods, but what won him over was the cool Canadian climate: he had had enough of Georgia's hot, steamy weather.

Dean talked about the satisfaction of working at McCain Foods in the early days, where he enjoyed the daily variety of challenges. "It was management by crisis. You never knew what you were going to be doing on a given day." He quite enjoyed working with Harrison, though he felt at times that he was overly ambitious. He said, "Harrison would say he was going to be the largest french fry producer in the world. I used to roll my eyes. I didn't think it was possible, because the Americans were so big. But he had great single-mindedness of purpose. He put the blinders on and he was headed right that way."[30]

A federal government bureaucrat, however, is credited for solving a big part of McCain's quality control problem. Donald Young, at the time a plant biologist and a specialist in potato variety at the federal government's Agriculture Canada Research Centre in New Brunswick, was working on producing a potato better suited for the short eastern Canadian growing season. He eventually came up with the Shepody potato, which proved to be a godsend for McCain Foods. The Shepody has since become one of the three most-grown varieties in North America and is now grown around the world. It is today the main competition to the Russet Burbank potato in the french fries industry.

I once asked Harrison about Young. His response: "Yup, yup, real good fellow, real good fella. Some of the problems solved." Somewhat more descriptive and complete, Wallace said, "Don made an enormous contribution to McCain Foods. First the Shepody ... Later guiding other global teams of agronomists for many years to greatly improving yields in Manitoba and research in areas where we planned to build."[31] Young and Harrison became close friends.

Donald Young was not the only federal bureaucrat to play a critical role in the growth of McCain Foods. Berkeley-educated George McClure had joined the federal government in the 1960s to work in the Department of Regional Economic Expansion (DREE), where he was responsible for Atlantic Canada, before he joined McCain Foods. He was a senior member of the department that led negotiations with McCain Foods in its applications for government grants, and he was with DREE when McCain Foods applied and received nearly $8 million

in subsidies for the expansion of the Florenceville plant and the construction of a new plant a few miles up the road in Grand Falls, New
Brunswick.

Harrison McCain had full confidence in McClure and gave him
wide authority to undertake a variety of tasks. Initially, he was responsible for business financial analysis of the deals that McCain Foods
were pursuing. As we will see later, he later worked in Europe and later
still became vice-president of corporate development. He was also
appointed a member of the McCain family-controlled board of directors. All to say that McClure played and continues to play a pivotal role
in the development and growth of McCain Foods.

Harrison and McClure established a very close working relationship that lasted until the end. I recall Harrison admiringly speaking of
McClure on a number of occasions. Harrison pegged him in the early
1970s to capture the European market for McCain Foods. McClure
recalls how Harrison gave him his marching orders: "He looked me in
the eyes and said 'I guess I should tell you what your mandate is. Your
mandate is to dominate the frozen french fry business in Europe.' That
was so typical of Harrison. It was the only instruction I ever got."[32]
Harrison had learned from K.C. Irving that management by suggestion was the way to go. It not only motivated senior managers, it also
delivered impressive results.

It is interesting to note that no one, including politicians, senior
public servants, and journalists of the day, believed that there was anything wrong with McClure being on one side of negotiations between
the federal government and McCain Foods one day and then going
to work for McCain Foods the next. Indeed, many saw benefits flowing to both government and the private sector when senior managers
moved back and forth between the two sectors to gain a better appreciation of each other's challenges. Sadly for both sectors, the *va et vient*
between the two has lost its currency in more recent years at a cost to
both sectors.

There was no suggestion then or since that McClure did anything
inappropriate on behalf of McCain Foods while at DREE, because
he did not. The government department had an incentive program
designed for the private sector wishing to establish or expand activities in designated regions. The criteria were clear and if a firm and

its project qualified, then it would receive the funds. It was a fairly straightforward program. Put differently, McCain Foods would have qualified for the assistance whether or not McClure worked at DREE at the time. In fact, I believe that McClure did more to promote regional economic development while working with McCain Foods than he would have, had he stayed with DREE. Today, given transparency and conflict of interest requirements, George McClure would have had to stay in government at a high cost to society, to New Brunswick, and indeed to Canada's economic development.

McClure left the safety of a senior government position in Ottawa to join a fast-growing, privately held firm because of the "energy" and "optimism" that Harrison and Wallace brought to the job every day. He explains, "It was a sense of the world is our oyster. It was ready, aim, fire. It was a remarkable feeling. The thing that appealed to me the most was a great sense of adventure."[33]

I have long argued in my writing on public administration and governance that governments have recently gone too far in promoting accountability and transparency.[34] This has resulted in governments becoming heavily bureaucratic, overly cautious, excessively concerned with process, and the consequent establishment of far too many oversight bodies looking over the shoulders of beleaguered government managers.

Governments in Anglo-American democracies have, in recent years, sought to have the public sector administration emulate private sector management practices. They have turned to performance evaluation reports and oversight bodies to fabricate a bottom line. And the efforts have largely failed. In the process, they have accomplished the exact opposite, creating one reporting level after another, imposing one reporting requirement after another, and adding substantially to the overhead cost of government.

The intent was to introduce a bias for action of the kind seen in dynamic private sector firms. However, it has accomplished the exact opposite, actually promoting a cautionary bias among senior public servants. In brief, we now have more bureaucratic and more costly government than we had thirty years ago. Governments can no longer keep up with the pace of change that the private sector must accommodate. This, as I have argued elsewhere, explains in no small measure the reason why the public sector has lost credibility with both the private sector and citizens.[35]

OPENING THE PLANT

On a cold winter day, 25 February 1957, the plant was completed and ready for a grand opening. Journalists from Fredericton, Saint John, and Moncton had come up for the event. A seventy-five-foot-long red ribbon was attached to the building and hundreds of people from Carleton County came to witness the event and applaud the McCain boys. They would later cut the ribbon in pieces for souvenirs.

New Brunswick's political and business *Who's Who* were also in attendance. Premier Hugh John Flemming was there and so was the federal minister of agriculture, James Gardiner. K.C. Irving proudly sat on the stage, happy to see his former employees take their first big step. Time alone would tell if they would succeed. Irving also bought an advertisement in the local newspapers to say, "It is people like the McCain family that keep the Maritimes growing." Laura McCain sat in the front row, dressed in her Sunday best, proud that Harrison and Wallace were now living their dream.[36]

Hugh John Flemming spoke at some length, congratulating the McCain boys and underlining the importance of the frozen food business to New Brunswick. Flemming had, by all accounts, seen the potential of the frozen food business several years earlier. As early as 1954, he had outlined a ten-point industrial development plan for the province, which highlighted the need to attract investors to set up frozen food processing plants along the Saint John River Valley. This, his government was sure, would both create direct jobs and provide new markets for farmers. He pointed to the potential of his own constituency, Carleton County, to stop, or at least slow, the flow of imported foods to New Brunswick.[37] As already noted, he had hoped to attract American investors but when that proved impossible, he was happy to provide funds to the McCains, long-time political foes to both him and his own father, who had also served as premier of New Brunswick.

The economic impact on the small community was immediate and highly visible. In the early years, Harrison and Wallace heard that some local businesses were complaining that they were not benefitted from McCain Foods. The company decided to pay its employees in pay packets with two-dollar bills. All local businesses in Florenceville, Hartland, and Woodstock suddenly saw an influx of two-dollar bills and a marked increase in revenues.[38] The McCain boys were generating economic activities in Florenceville and surrounding communities. New cars were bought, houses were built, and existing ones were modernized and painted.

Within a few years of launching McCain Foods, Harrison and Wallace served notice that they were out to generate as many new economic activities as their finances would allow. Cashing in was never part of the equation. Profits were reinvested in McCain Foods or other activities.

The McCain boys purchased Thomas Equipment ten years after they opened their first frozen food plant. Thomas Equipment was established by three brothers in nearby Centreville in 1943 to manufacture farming equipment. McCain grew Thomas Equipment and expanded its sales to Europe and Asia. Thomas Equipment could lay claim to have produced the world's first skid steer loader with hydrostatic drive in 1969. McCain also tied the work of Thomas Equipment to its own requirements and to potato harvesters.

Harrison and Wallace had learned the merits of vertical integration from K.C. Irving. They now owned a firm that made equipment to harvest potatoes, a fertilizer company, and later a major trucking firm, in addition to a frozen food plant.

Harrison took a strong personal interest in Thomas Equipment. He was fascinated by the heavy equipment it was able to design and build and often took great pride in the number of manufacturing jobs it had created in Carleton County. The company was sold in 2004 shortly after Harrison died.

LOOKING BACK

Harrison finally had what he always wanted – a business of his own. Harrison and Wallace made a very powerful combination, working to each other's strengths. All major decisions were taken jointly, with each holding a kind of mutual veto. It is now well known and well documented that Harrison was the visionary, the one who could put it all together, and that Wallace was the nuts-and-bolts man, or the guy who made it happen. A long-time employee, Ian Cameron, once compared the work of the two brothers: "Wallace is more of an operations person. Dealing with Wallace, you had to justify every penny you spent, whereas Harrison was a little bit less critical. When we had a meeting, he would have more to say about marketing and sales. They were great as a team. They had enthusiasm and foresight."[39] One thing is clear: they needed each other.

They were, however, hardly flying on their own. The other brothers, Andrew and Bob, were also involved, though both were still employed with McCain Produce. The four brothers met often, at times around a kitchen table, to review the business start-up and to chart its development. Bob, in particular, kept a watchful eye on the business and its challenges in its development years.

Harrison and Wallace were well on their way to writing a truly remarkable success story of entrepreneurship. Again, Harrison would often cite the reasons behind McCain Foods' success: "Good luck, good timing, right place." To be sure, luck and timing certainly had something to do with it. The economic environment was ripe for the frozen food industry in the late 1950s. And, as we have seen, governments were also trying to support winners with cash grants and Ottawa was prepared to make a special effort in slow-growth regions. Florenceville was an ideal candidate, a slow-growth rural community in a slow-growth province, in the Maritimes – a slow-growth region. Luck again came into play when the head of the Bank of Nova Scotia happened upon Harrison and Wallace applying for a line of credit at the local branch. And it was a federal bureaucrat who came up with a potato that would transform the frozen french fry business and give McCain Foods a leg up on the competition.

Harrison had all the attributes of an entrepreneur. He quit a high-profile, well-paying job with strong prospects for the future, not knowing what he would do next, other than wanting to start his own business. He was prepared to risk it all to pursue his dream.

Once in the saddle, he indeed gave it his all. Long hours were meat and drink to him. He performed virtually every task that needed to be carried out. He would act as the firm's president, which he was. But he would also work the production line, load a truck and package frozen food, if it were required. He took in a salary of $100 a week but paid some of his more senior people $150 a week. He and Wallace decided early on to reinvest any and all profits back into the firm. Harrison told *Canadian Business* magazine, "Some people are in business to clip dividends or make a certain amount of profit,"[40] but he was not one of them. He was in business to grow a business and businesses.

Harrison spoke like a true entrepreneur when he told the *Executive Magazine* that he was in love with the game, with the chase: "The game is action, what's going on. There's something new all the time – buying companies, building factories, hiring guys, motivating people, seeing advertising programs, taking positions on commodities, borrowing money, settling lawsuits."[41]

Throughout his career, Harrison had a relatively modest lifestyle. He stayed in his West Florenceville house until the end. He never owned a collection of fine cars and had a relatively modest collection of fine art, mainly because Billie saw to it. He never bought a winter home south but bought a lovely summer home in Saint Andrews, New Brunswick, again because Billie wanted one. In brief, Harrison was a billionaire but did not live like one.

James Downey asked Harrison about "possessions" and what they meant to him. He reminded him that Lord Beaverbrook had some six houses scattered around the world. He said, "Harrison, you don't seem to put a great deal of store in that." It is worth repeating the exchange here.

HARRISON: No, I don't have any great desire to flaunt money, spend money. I just do as I like. I have a good quality of life and I do what I want to do.

DOWNEY: You have what, just the two houses?

McCAIN: Two houses, yeah.

DOWNEY: One in Florenceville.

McCAIN: And one is in Saint Andrews.

DOWNEY: They're not houses that …

McCAIN: Not pretentious.

DOWNEY: Upper-middle-class people couldn't aspire to.

McCAIN: Absolutely. They're just good family houses.

DOWNEY: So you don't put much store by houses or cars or …

MCCAIN: Don't interest me one bit. I like fine airplanes. But they involve the company, not me.

The McCain boys would invest much of the profit in building their first frozen food plant in their home town. It laid the groundwork for solid growth year after year. They were motivated by the business and everything was working out according to plan, though there were more than a few bumps in the road. Harrison and Wallace had a fast-growing list of things to do as they sought to pursue growth for McCain Foods. The real question for them was, What now?

5

Crazier Than Hell

The Florenceville plant was up and running, though the opening had been delayed by several months. Construction problems and difficulties in finding the right machinery, often second hand, had pushed back opening day from October to late February. October would have been much better because it would have coincided with the potato harvest. But, finally, the McCain boys were open for business. They had a production line operating and staffed with forty people, mostly from Florenceville and surrounding farms and mostly women. Overnight, McCain Foods became Florenceville's largest employer. The McCain brothers had delivered on the promise to start a business and create jobs. The next immediate test was now simply to survive.

Getting the plant into full operation was no easy task. Harrison and Wallace had never worked in a factory before, let alone managed one. They had to find and work with people like O.P. Pierson, who had some knowledge of building and running a frozen food plant. O.P. was eccentric, an oddball. He was certainly different from Harrison and Wallace. He had no interest in business, and respecting a timetable was always someone else's problem, never his. His genius was with machinery, inventions, and making things work. Harrison told me that O.P. once invented a machine of some kind, neglecting to seek a patent. Someone else copied the design, got a patent, and made a fortune. To be sure, that was not Harrison's style. The McCain boys had to learn from scratch to work with the likes of O.P. Pierson. There were very few O.P. Piersons working in sales with K.C. Irving.

There were plenty of new, no less daunting challenges ahead. They had to be certain that the Florenceville plant would operate smoothly, ensure a supply of raw material, hire new staff, operate within budget, come up with ideas to find new markets, and get the product to far-away markets. Early on, as noted earlier but worth repeating here, Harrison and Wallace effected a division of labour that fit their individual strengths. Harrison was the visionary, the elder brother, the firm's public face, and the upfront person. Wallace was the operator. In some ways, Harrison was the chief executive officer while Wallace was the chief operating officer, with both having a right of veto on major decisions. Later, Harrison would become chairman and co–chief executive officer, while Wallace became president and co–chief executive officer. Purdy Crawford, the Bay Street lawyer and corporate director and a close friend of Wallace McCain, describes it as "quite a team." He explained, "They built an organization around the world from a base in Florenceville. They would take off Sunday night or Monday morning from the air strip and come back Thursday or Friday if they were lucky."[1]

There was never any question in the minds of Harrison and Wallace as to whether they would be happy operating just one plant. There were in business to grow, to compete, to capture new markets, and to dominate the french fries business. Everything else had to fall in line with those objectives. The answer to "what now?" was clear: growth. The next question was how.

FROZEN FOOD IS THE THING

Harrison and Wallace decided early on that the frozen food sector and only the frozen food sector would drive the growth they sought. They had dabbled with other activities, including establishing a snack food drive-in, with little success. Now, all activities would be anchored in the frozen food business and the focus would be on frozen french fries.

The plant was working relatively well, the early kinks were being worked out, and, there were competent staff now running it. Work on the production line was demanding and tedious, and staff turnover was higher than expected, but as time went on, machines became more efficient and production processes more automated. The plant alternated between processing potatoes, peas, and strawberries. They had little luck in freezing strawberries, however, because the technology of the day turned them into mush.

The business had grown to the point that it allowed Harrison and Wallace to hire the necessary expertise to ensure that production lines ran efficiently, with experienced engineers joining to look after the plant and machinery. This would enable both Harrison and Wallace to focus on other issues and on efforts to grow the business.

The McCain brothers had to keep an eye on their own farmland. They owned nearly a thousand hectares of productive land where they grew potatoes, peas, strawberries, and grain to feed livestock. But this alone could never supply the plant for the year and they had to work with local farmers to secure a constant supply of raw material. Today, McCain Foods harvests from its own land about 10 per cent of the raw material processed at its Florenceville plant.

They improvised on the marketing and sales front after one year in business, nearly as much as they had in building the plant. Markets for frozen food were neither stable nor predictable. They were still immature and just taking shape with sharp swings in demand. Several months after the plant opened, for example, McCain Foods had grossly overestimated the demand for frozen peas. Growing conditions in 1957 were ideal and North American growers produced a bumper crop. It made little sense to try to sell them to a non-existent market, so Harrison decided to hold them in the cold storage, and the decision was handsomely rewarded the next year when the market came back. Harrison was also able to sell frozen peas in Britain after a quick visit to London. While there, he made new contacts that would prove invaluable in future sales and in opening up the British market for frozen french fries.

McCain Foods also established a strong relationship with the Bank of Nova Scotia, that remains to this day. They had an excellent personal and working relationship with Cedric Ritchie, the local bank manager who had grown up in Bath, a short driving distance from Florenceville.[2] Ritchie and his good friend Harrison kept in contact as Ritchie climbed the corporate ladder at the bank. He was appointed chairman–chief executive officer at the bank and held that position until 1995. Harrison would later serve on the bank's board of directors.

In the early years, Harrison and Wallace did whatever they had to do and performed whatever tasks needed to be tackled. Their offices were linked by ashtrays to accommodate their two-pack-a-day habit. They shared the workload equally, with Harrison in charge of finance, sales, and other things, and Wallace, the plant, supplies, and other things. Both put long hours in the business. Looking back, Harrison McCain laughed off any suggestion that they were working from a master plan: "Those guys who think they know what they are doing when they start out are crazier than hell."[3]

SELLING FROZEN FOOD TO CANADIANS

As the plant began production, Harrison was able to secure some American clients. American packers were selling their products in Canada but had to pay a duty to bring their brands into Canada. Harrison struck a deal to package their brands, thus avoiding duty charges, which generated a profit for both the American packers and McCain Foods. This gave McCain Foods a start and it enabled them to introduce their own brand whenever they could. But Harrison knew full well that this could only be a start and that McCain Foods would soon have to promote its own brand, give it visibility, and establish its own dedicated sales network.[4] As is well known, manufacturers can generate a much higher margin and higher profits selling under their own brand than producing and packaging for others.

Harrison recognized that the real test for McCain Foods would be in marketing and sales. Aspiring entrepreneurs wishing to gain an appreciation of the work and commitment required to launch a new business successfully could do no better than read about the sales efforts of both Harrison and Wallace in the early years. Some of this is captured in *From the Ground Up: The First Fifty Years of McCain Foods*, which the firm published in 2007 to celebrate its fiftieth anniversary.

The strong working relationship that Harrison and Wallace established extended to sales and marketing. In a nutshell, they ran every major decision, every challenge by one another. James Downey recalls that he first met Harrison in 1981, to ask for what he describes as a modest gift to the University of New Brunswick. Harrison's response was, "Sounds all right, but I'll have to talk to my brother before we do anything." Harrison added, "That's the way we ran the company."[5]

It was the same in sales. Harrison and Wallace were always on the same page, pushing in the same direction. They left their homes on Sunday evenings or early Monday in different directions, knocking on doors, selling frozen french fries, at a time when most Canadians had not yet discovered the merits of frozen foods.

Some of the sales stories belong to a different era. Both Harrison and Wallace spent many nights a year away from home. Harrison was more often on the road than Wallace, with Wallace frequently staying behind to ensure that the operations were running smoothly. Marilyn Strong, Harrison's long-serving assistant, told me that he spent on average 150 days away from home every year. In 1985, not a particularly demanding travel year, he spent 130 days and fifteen weekends away from home.[6] His nephew Stephen McCain said that he once accompanied his uncle on a trip, picked up Harrison's two suitcases, and noted the high-quality leather. He told Harrison, "Quite nice luggage with very thick leather." "Yup, yup," replied Harrison, "top quality, the best, the best. They are guaranteed for a lifetime. This is my second set."

At least one of them was always on the road, and very often both, drumming sales. There were no credit cards or automatic teller machines in that era, and banking hours were very limited. It was not uncommon to see the McCain brothers going up and down the production line borrowing travel money. Florence White, a former employee, reports, "Harrison would get two dollars from one person and five dollars from another. He would always pay back the money. The faith everyone put in him was amazing."[7]

Harrison and Wallace went after every possible customer, from housewives to restaurant chefs. They had learned from K.C. Irving that no account was too small to pursue and that every single customer was valued. They started in the Maritimes, a region that they knew well and that was easily accessible by car. They attended food fairs and knocked on the doors of virtually every restaurant. They went in kitchens where fries were being cut from fresh potatoes, in the hope of showing chefs the advantages of frozen fries. They tried to tap into the catering market. There are photos of Harrison with an apron covering his tie and neatly pressed blazer, always with a big smile, promoting his frozen french fries. In Harrison's words, "We went from restaurant to restaurant, café to café, and hotel to hotel and being thrown out mostly."[8]

To save money, they stayed in cheap motels in Halifax, Moncton, Saint John, and Charlottetown. In the early years, they visited fast food restaurants that were just beginning to make their presence felt in the region, and they scored some success with Kentucky Fried Chicken and A&W outlets. They were always in and out of restaurants, so that by evening their clothes reeked of frying oil. Dry cleaning was out of the question, so they simply hung their suits out the windows of their motel rooms to air them.

They turned to brokers and distributors to promote sales in Quebec, Ontario, and Western Canada. In time, however, they decided to build their own sales team. Ralph Orr, who had worked for Kellogg's, became the first salesman at McCain Foods. Halifax-born Orr had been asked by Kellogg's to relocate to Vancouver, but he opted to stay in the Maritimes and signed on instead with McCain Foods as head of sales for the Maritime provinces.

Orr's arrival enabled Harrison and Wallace to focus on the rest of Canada. They continued to work with brokers and distributors, but they also hired two salesmen to look after central Canada – Dick McWhirter, also from Kellogg's, and Peter Laurie. Laurie worked out of Ottawa and McWhirter was appointed sales manager for Ontario, later to become national sales manager.

McWhirter remarks that Western Canada was a particularly tough market to crack: "Who wanted to buy a truckload of frozen potatoes from New Brunswick? The first question from the distributor was, 'Where the hell is Florenceville?' Also many said, 'You're crazy, McWhirter. We've got enough potatoes in Manitoba and Alberta to satisfy us all.'"[9]

The competition at the time, however, had more to do with fresh potatoes than with another frozen food firm. which, essentially, did not exist in Canada. In any case, the necessary infrastructure was simply not there: crucially, large freezers were few and far between in both supermarkets and in fast food restaurants.

As well, the fresh potato held a lot of appeal. Restaurant owners were proud of serving only fresh potatoes and were sure that their customers would not accept a frozen product. They also argued that fresh potatoes helped their bottom line because they were cheaper. Fresh potatoes, at the time, sold for one and a half cents a kilogram, compared with about nine cents for McCain frozen french fries.

McCain Foods, however, came up with a convincing sales pitch: in short, they compared apples with apples. Harrison, Wallace, and the three salesmen would ask chefs to peel, cut, and cook fresh potatoes. They would then have them weigh the raw material and take into account the cost of the cooking oil. Harrison and the others would then prepare easy-to-cook frozen french fries, inviting the chefs to savour their taste and texture. They would then also calculate the cost per serving, showing that frozen french fries were in fact less expensive than making them from fresh potatoes. They also explained that frozen french fries hold a consistent quality twelve months of the year, while those cut from fresh potatoes vary by season because after being in storage for months, they lose quality, freshness, and appeal. In addition, french fries from fresh potatoes required more staff hours to prepare, adding to the cost.

In brief, the McCain brothers and their three salesmen were essentially creating in Canada a new market, not competing in an existing one. The sales pitch was more difficult, but when it worked there was a very good chance that they had found themselves loyal and permanent customers.

Harrison and Wallace never cut back their sales efforts as their firm began to grow. In fact, if anything, they were more and more on the road. They had a large territory to cover and Florenceville was hardly the hub for the Canadian market. Harrison travelled more often than Wallace. As he explained, "Somebody had to deal with farmers, whoever was producing and supervising the plant activity, and so forth. So there'd be one fellow on the road all the time and one fellow in the office most of the time." As already noted, the McCain brothers decided from day one to "plow back" into the firm whatever profit they made. Harrison, looking back, said they reinvested "every nickel we made, and every nickel we could borrow."[10]

Harrison and Wallace decided in 1965 to buy a second-hand Piper, which they flew in and out of whatever landing strip was available between Fredericton and Edmundston. McCain Foods paid $25,000 for the plane. "Probably [we] didn't have the $25,000, we probably borrowed it," said Harrison, "but it was the price of getting going," and they hired a pilot part-time to fly the plane. Later, they would build their own strip behind their houses.

THE FAMILY

While Harrison and Wallace were regularly putting in fourteen-hour days, often seven days a week, both their families were settling in Florenceville. The families moved from Saint John, a relatively large urban centre at the time, to small-town Florenceville. Billie had grown up in Fredericton in relative luxury and lived in Saint John for several years. Living in Florenceville and married to a husband who was on the road more often than he was at home required a major adjustment. Harrison said that Billie was always fully supportive and well aware of the risks.[11] He once told me that Billie had incredible inner strength, which came in handy on many occasions as he and Wallace set out to build the firm.

Billie and Harrison had two children born in Saint John: Mark, in 1954, three years before the family moved to Florenceville, and Ann, born in 1956. Peter, Laura, and Gillian followed in 1957, 1959, and 1966 respectively, all born in Florenceville. So Billie had a house to manage and five children in their early years to raise virtually single-handed, in a community that she did not know well and at a time when Harrison's focus was on the business.

Billie learned at an early age to be stoic and independent, and the inner strength that Harrison referred to served her well. She never complained about Florenceville or Harrison's frequent absences. She had to learn to cope with his bruising work schedule and she did. She focused on her home and family and took part in few community activities. She did not then, or later, seek the limelight. The one strong interest outside of her family that she retained throughout was a heart-felt appreciation of and support for the arts and artists.

Billie and Harrison initially moved into a small two-bedroom house in East Florenceville, not far from where the plant was being built. Later, once McCain Foods was up and running, both he and Wallace built lovely homes in West Florenceville. Harrison's was a two-story Cape Cod–style house with a spectacular view of the valley and the plant. Harrison joked that his friend Reuben Cohen, the Moncton financier and owner of Central Trust, turned him down for a mortgage. Cohen's take was, "Who in his right mind would give a mortgage to someone wanting to build a big house in Florenceville?"[12] This may well explain why Harrison added to his home over the years, building a guest house and a swimming pool. Wallace chose a site next to his elder brother's, and both brothers were only a few doors from their parents' house, where they had grown up.

Harrison had only loving words for Billie in all conversations I had with him about her. He was very fond of her and appreciated her support in the way that husbands did in the 1950s, 1960s, and 1970s. It was a different era, when women were mostly expected to stay at home and limit their horizons to the family hearth. Frank McKenna summed it up well: "Harrison adored his wife, Billie. He was devoted and talked incessantly about Mark and Peter and Ann and Laura and Gillian."[13]

I had many conversations with many people who knew Billie. Universally, she was regarded as a loving, kind woman who was liked by everyone who came in contact with her. When I was beginning work on this book, I spoke with Christine Morris, a widely respected New Brunswick journalist. It was to Chris that Harrison had famously responded, when she asked him about the reasons for his success, "Right place, right time. Next question." She told me that she had had twelve questions for him but the interview "lasted all of about 50 seconds."[14] Unprompted, Chris told me that Billie had to be one of the nicest persons she ever met. Many New Brunswickers would agree.

FARMERS

Local farmers now had a reliable stable local market for their potatoes. Before McCain Foods built its plant, farmers had to ship their crops to large urban centres, such as Toronto and Montreal. They had only a six-week window, between September and October, to do so. Prices fluctuated and local farmers were at the mercy of the seasons and outside forces – not to mention a less than reliable transportation system to ship their potatoes thousands of kilometres away.

Cedric Ritchie argued that McCain brought stability to potato prices for Carleton farmers, not only because it created a new local demand, but also because the plant operated twelve months of the year. He explained that the McCain plant "brought value-added processing to the area and that created steady employment. Before, it was all seasonal employment."[15] McCain Foods offered to sign pre-season contracts with potato farmers to buy all or some of their crop at an established price. Farmers still had to cope with the weather and crop risks, but McCain assumed full market risk.[16]

Many farmers were proud of the local boys doing well. Some of them had family members working full-time for McCain Foods. New economic activities and an influx of outsiders moving to Florenceville to work with McCain Foods and to buy or build new homes was all to the good. However, a number of other farmers and some local residents had concerns.

Farmers watched as the McCain brothers accumulated wealth while they themselves saw only marginal improvements to their income. Some also felt that the McCain boys were gaining far too much influence over the county's farming community. They wanted more competition between processors so that they could gain a greater share of the economic benefits. But they were never forthcoming, however, about where the entrepreneurs, the financial resources, and competition should come from. The competition came from the open market where farmers could sell their potatoes to supermarket chains or wholesalers.

Like their mentor K.C. Irving, and as already noted, the McCain brothers pursued vertical integration. They sold fertilizer, farm equipment, and seed potatoes. Their dealings with local farmers gave the McCains an unfair advantage in the eyes of some. As well, Harrison and Wallace preferred to deal with individual farmers and had little time for a collective approach.

The two brothers attached considerable importance to legal contracts. As Wallace explained, "The contract is written for dishonest people. It's a tough contract. There isn't any question about it. And the contract, I agree, is one-sided."[17] But a contract was a contract and it had to be respected. Two farmers decided in 1964 to ignore their contracts with McCain Foods and sell their potatoes to another buyer. McCain Foods took them to court and won, and the two farmers had to struggle with a crippling debt for several years. To be sure, the McCain victory was not lost on other local farmers.

Harrison and Wallace were surprised in the mid-1960s to hear that 248 county residents had signed a petition asking county council not to grant new tax concessions to McCain Foods. Since the McCain brothers were quickly getting rich, the petitioners thought it was only fair that the firm pay its fair share of taxes. The point here is that not everyone in Carleton County was in the McCains' corner. The petition did not work.

I asked a long-time potato farmer from the Florenceville area if Harrison McCain was fair with local potato farmers. His answer: "Harrison McCain was a tough businessman. He was all business. He always drove a hard bargain and never gave an inch. But I will tell you this. Harrison was honest as the day is long. If he gave you his word, you could take it to the bank. If he owed you a penny, he would pay you. If you owed him a penny, it was best to pay him."

For his part, Harrison McCain said that McCain Foods played by the rules of the marketplace. He would ask, "If you know any farmer who will sell potatoes to me any cheaper than he would sell to anybody else, I'd like to meet him. I don't know one. They sell to make the best buck that day. The guy that pays the best buck gets the potatoes."[18] The head of the Western New Brunswick Potato Agency said in 1979, "On average over the years, McCain contract prices have proved a little higher than market prices after counting the cost of preparing and shipping table potatoes."[19]

Harrison insisted in 1982 that "New Brunswick statistics will show ... that over the last twenty years the McCain pre-season contract price for potatoes in over half of these years has been higher than the average spot price."[20] A few years later, Harrison told the *Atlantic Advocate*, "With perishable agricultural products, the market doesn't recognize cost. It only recognizes supply and demand ... Two years ago farmers were selling at a profit – no complaints were still heard then, and the company had no choice but to pay higher prices."[21]

THE GROWTH: THE ONLY GAME IN TOWN

From the outset, Harrison McCain's goal was to grow the business. He did not want to sell it, to collect dividends, or cash in his chips. Every year the McCain brothers reinvested all the profits, and every year they added new equipment to the Florenceville plant or expanded its capacity. Harrison explained, "You bet the bundle every year, year after year. If you're wrong once, you're out. We kept pushing the business as hard as we could, borrowing all we could, building, and borrowing, and building. We were risking it all on deal after deal."[22] That, as well as anything, defines entrepreneurship.

In 1976 McCain Foods decided to build another plant in Grand Falls, eighty kilometres up the road. Harrison later explained that his thinking was to discourage someone else from building a frozen food plant there. For Harrison, growth not only meant expansion, it meant beating down the competition.[23]

But there was another reason. New Brunswick politicians were pushing Harrison to invest in the northern part of the province. Politicians from that era tell me that they met with Harrison to encourage him to build a plant in the Acadian Peninsula in northeastern New Brunswick. They argued that the Acadian Peninsula had been at one point a strong potato-growing area. The region was in urgent need of jobs and the government offered Harrison a helping hand. Harrison and Wallace agreed to build a plant in a francophone region in need of jobs, but they would build the plant closer to home in the northwestern part of the province.

As already noted, McCain Foods arrived on the scene precisely at the moment when governments everywhere were looking to intervene in the economy and to support economic development, particularly in slow-growth regions. In more recent years, because of the difficult fiscal position confronting many governments and because many observers became critical of governments providing cash grants to private firms, the level of government assistance to McCain Foods during its rapid growth period is no longer available to anyone, even to those in slow-growth regions.

Harrison always defended his decision to turn to federal and provincial grants, loans, and loan guarantees to grow the business. He argued that critics "forget that you don't get a government grant because you're a good fellow; you get it because you promise to perform by supplying a certain number of jobs." He added that government assistance does not fully compensate for locating a manufacturing facility away from large markets. He asked, "Did General Motors decide to move to the

Maritimes to collect a grant? Why doesn't Stelco come down and collect these 'huge government grants'? Who else do you want to name?
The Ford Motor Company? General Electric? Why don't they all come
down and get these great grants? A grant only goes toward compensat-
ing. It doesn't pay the bills. Even in Ottawa they don't understand that.
It's a long story."[24]

Harrison summed up the importance of government grants for
regional economic development in this fashion: "The best investment
the federal government can make is a well-placed DREE grant. The
best thing since tea."[25] He added, "Without the loan guarantee from the
provincial government in 1956, the land where the McCain plant sits
would still be pasture land."[26]

Jim Casey, owner of the highly successful manufacturing firm
Paderno in Prince Edward Island, worked at one time as a development
officer for DREE in its New Brunswick office. He was asked to review a
McCain Foods proposal to build a plant in Grand Falls, New Brunswick,
to produce frozen pizza. He carefully studied the proposal and drove up
to Florenceville to meet with Harrison. He told him, "I had a careful
look at your proposal. You will be importing most of your raw material
from away and exporting your products to large markets a thousand or
so miles away. So, why do you want to build the plant in Grand Falls,
New Brunswick?" And Harrison's answer was to the point: "Because I
am from Florenceville." Nothing more was said about location.

Harrison would also look to local government for a helping hand.
He decided to revisit Carleton County council and ask for a review
of the tax break it had put together when the Florenceville plant was
being built, which he now believed was not sufficient. He and Wallace
went before county council again in January 1959. Harrison told them
that in just two years McCain Foods had generated over half of a million dollars in wages and purchases from local farmers. He then went
on to say that McCain Foods was operating at a disadvantage with
competitors in other regions, who were being given tax concessions.
He persuasively made the case that a higher tax break from local council would enable McCain Foods to compete, expand, and create more
jobs at home.

Bob McCain was still a member of council and he could be counted
on to put in a good word for his brothers behind closed doors. Within

a few days, the county council agreed to tax McCain Foods only $1,500 a year for ten years, increasing it to $2,000 a year for the following five years, and to $2,500 for the last five years of a twenty-year tax deal. The Hugh John Flemming provincial government quickly gave its seal of approval, as required by law.[27]

A HELPING HAND FROM OTTAWA AND FREDERICTON

McCain Foods was also able to secure a number of federal grants to expand its Florenceville plant and to build its Grand Falls operation. The very first grant awarded under Ottawa's Regional Development Incentives Act (RDIA) went to McCain Foods in the amount of $2,925,000 to expand its Florenceville operation.

McCain Foods also received numerous federal regional development grants to expand existing facilities and to build new ones, including the Portage la Prairie plant in Manitoba, in the heart of the province's potato-growing region. DREE provided a $2.4 million subsidy, and the Manitoba Development Corporation gave a $7 million loan guarantee towards the $9.4 million total cost.

McCain Foods unwillingly became embroiled in a heated political debate about financial assistance to private firms in the early to mid-1970s in Canada. David Lewis, leader of the left-of-centre New Democratic Party (NDP), launched a high-profile debate on "corporate welfare bums," arguing that many private firms were benefitting from overly generous federal government grants for economic development.[28] DREE and McCain Foods became a target.

The media soon revealed that McCain Foods had already secured some $22 million in federal government "handouts" by the mid-1970s. Harrison agreed to give a CBC interview with Adrienne Clarkson and hard-hitting journalist Gerry McAuliffe, insisting that he had nothing to hide. Clarkson agreed in the immediate post-Watergate period to co-host a new CBC investigative documentary program – *The Fifth Estate*. The no-holds-barred interview pushed Harrison on issues from plant security to dealing with farmers and government subsidies. The interview, "Citizen McCain," was aired nationally on 8 December 1976. Harrison did not perform well and the interview gave McCain Foods a black eye, at least in its public image. Many politicians and observers leapt to McCain's defence, including a senator who questioned Clarkson's Canadian citizenship.[29] But the damage was done.[30] Harrison had learned an important lesson in public relations: do not always presuppose the best scenario, never take anything for granted, especially with the media, and never go unprepared.

Media reaction, however, did not diminish the appetite of McCain Foods for government assistance. Indeed, the firm did not miss a beat when the Flemming government lost to Louis J. Robichaud's Liberal party in 1960. Harrison developed a very close relationship with Robichaud and more is said about this later. Suffice to note here that the Robichaud government gave McCain Foods well over $3 million in loan guarantees.

Given my strong interest in the regional economic development literature, I had several discussions with Harrison about his capacity to secure funding from government. He told me that he always played by the rules and that McCain Foods only applied for programs that were available to everyone. As we will see later, for his part, Louis J. Robichaud always had a particularly high opinion of Harrison McCain and his business acumen.

Ottawa's RDIA was designed to subsidize firms that invested in designated slow-growth areas, and its focus was exclusively on manufacturing and processing firms. This squared nicely with the operations of McCain Foods in Florenceville and, for that matter, in any potato-growing rural region in the country. In brief, DREE and its RDIA program squared quite nicely with McCain Foods, its location, and its growth strategy. The subsidy was non-repayable and was calculated on the basis of number of jobs created and construction costs.[31]

The RDIA program delineated which applicants were eligible. First, a firm could not qualify if it was probable that the facility could or would be established without receiving the incentive, although this was not easy for government officials to determine. Second, a firm could not start construction of the facility until the government had given the green light. This was easy for government officials to determine but, in many instances, it meant a frustrating delay in getting a project off the ground. Indeed, many firms complained to the government that they were forced to deal with too much red tape, delays, and bureaucratic processes, and that while they waited, construction costs went up. Third, a firm could not qualify under the act if there was already capacity in the sector: the government did not want to push an existing firm out of business.

Again, McCain Foods was an ideal candidate for the program. The frozen food industry was new to Canada, so there was little worry about creating an overcapacity in a particular region or putting an firm out of business by helping a start-up. The RDIA program favoured regions where McCain Foods wanted to locate: slow-growth rural areas in slow-growth regions. Rural potato-farming communities in northern New Brunswick and rural Manitoba were precisely the kind of slow-growth areas in slow-growth regions that DREE's RDIA program was established to help.

Though not in the early years, the one criterion that could have disqualified McCain Foods from receiving a subsidy was whether the firm would have proceeded with the project if it had not received a grant. Dan Usher summed up the problem well: "It is like trying to determine the number of babies that would have been born in the absence of the family allowance program."[32]

The one criterion that Harrison found annoying, if not difficult to accommodate, was the firm's inability to start construction until the government gave construction the green light, but government officials were unflinching on this criterion. If a firm proceeded with the project without approval, it meant, at least to auditors, that it did not need the subsidy. What this required of Harrison McCain was patience – of which he never had an over-abundance.

The wait, however, was well worth it for Harrison and McCain Foods. RDIA subsidies fuelled a good part of the growth of McCain Foods. In some instances, as in Portage la Prairie project, they accounted for 60 per cent of the total cost. It meant that McCain Foods did not need to go to venture capitalists, sell equity, or launch an initial public offering (IPO) in order to get things moving. It thus enabled the McCain brothers to keep it all in the family.

Harrison was always committed to McCain Foods remaining in private hands. I once asked him why. It is easier, he told me, to plan for the long term when a firm is privately held. Shareholders, he added, are invariably interested in the short term only. Like K.C. Irving, he also attached great importance to keeping information away from public scrutiny. He saw no advantage in sharing information about McCain Foods and plenty of disadvantages, including giving the competition a window on the business. He also told me once that he did not want shareholders asking why he decided to buy a Falcon jet. Harrison was much more direct when a journalist asked him why he wanted to keep McCain Foods in private hands: "My business is none of your business."

We may also recall Harrison's comment when he was asked to explain his success: "Right place, right time." No doubt that was true. To launch a frozen food business just when fast food restaurants and eating out were beginning to grasp the public imagination was for-tuitous timing. But so was the decision to expand the business in designated regions precisely at the time when the federal government offered attractive grants to the private sector to invest in these very regions, largely thanks to RDIA. The idea was to attract outside invest-ors and businesses to locate some of their activities in slow-growth regions, and the government would make up the cost of locating in them. The McCain brothers stayed where they were in the middle of potato-farming regions and were able to draw substantial benefits from the program. The RDIA program was done away with at the same time as the government scrapped DREE on 12 January 1982.[33]

Some might have seen the end of these programs as a serious blow; however, all was not lost for McCain Foods. The Ontario caucus in Ottawa and ministers from Ontario in the Trudeau Cabinet sounded the alarm in the early 1980s when a recession hit central Canada and its manufacturing sector particularly hard. The federal minister of finance tabled a document in Parliament titled *Economic Development for Canada in the 1980s*, which argued that regional balance in Canada was changing as a result of economic buoyancy in the west, optimism in the east (because of energy projects on the horizon like Hibernia and Sable Island), and unprecedented softness in key economic sectors in central Canada.[34]

As is now well known, the economic recession in central Canada in the early 1980s was sharp but also short-lived. As for the optimism in the east, this turned out to be essentially a creation of finance officials in Ottawa. No matter, the department's document led to an overhaul of Ottawa's regional economic development.

Trudeau appointed Ed Lumley from Ontario as the new minister responsible for economic and regional development, and he rose in the House of Commons on 27 June 1983 to unveil a new approach. He explained that "combatting regional disparities is difficult even in good economic times … It is much more difficult in a period when Canada's traditional industries are suffering from soft markets, strong international competition, rapid technological change and rising protectionism.[35] Lumley's solution was a new program that would no longer apply only to certain designated regions. The new program would be accessible even in downtown Toronto and could accommodate a variety of activities including industrial diversification, the establishment of a new plant, and the launching of a new product line.[36]

This was no problem for McCain Foods. By the mid-1980s, the firm had expanded as much as it wanted to in slow-growth regions in New Brunswick and Manitoba. The new program allowed funding to introduce a new product line to expand in central Canada and Alberta, and that suited Harrison McCain just fine.

Harrison did not need lobbyists to do his bidding with governments. In fact, he told me on more than one occasion that he had little use for lobbyists. He said that he always played by the rules, went through the application process, and fully answered all questions. He had an excellent relationship with politicians, particularly those from the Liberal party. But he also worked well with other political parties. He was close to Richard Hatfield, another Carleton County politician, the Progressive Conservative premier of New Brunswick between 1970 and 1987 and a member of the Legislative Assembly from Carleton County. I have never heard of a politician or a public servant, from either the federal or provincial, suggest that Harrison McCain had ever attempted to influence them or do anything inappropriate in his dealings with them.

As mentioned earlier, Harrison McCain and Premier Robichaud had a particularly strong friendship. Robichaud set out to change the face of New Brunswick with an ambitious socio-economic agenda several years after he came to power. He began by seeking out the best and the brightest to join the provincial public service to shape and implement his Program of Equal Opportunity. When Ross Thatcher defeated the left-of-centre New Democratic Party in Saskatchewan in 1964, he tossed out a number of competent senior public servants.[37] Robichaud saw his opportunity and came calling, and he attracted more than a few to New Brunswick.

Donald Tansley was one of them. Robichaud appointed him deputy minister of finance and industry in 1964, and he later served as deputy minister of fisheries and oceans in Ottawa. Shortly after arriving in New Brunswick, Tansley went through the province's books and financial commitments. He looked at loans and loan guarantees for McCain Foods and was taken aback by the lack of proper documentation. With Robichaud's blessing, he approached Harrison McCain, outlined the government's concerns, and stipulated the accountability requirements that had to be met. Harrison listened attentively and said, "Goddamn it, you're right. Let's fix it. You do what you have to do and you tell us what we have to do and we'll do it, no questions asked."[38] End of issue.

Harrison and Tansley subsequently became good friends. In retirement, Tansley became an activist for the Canadian Committee for Five Days of Peace in the late 1980s, which sought to promote the idea of a five-day moratorium in both Palestine and El Salvador and then immunize children on both sides of the conflict against diseases. The thinking was that if you could establish peace for five days, why not ten or thirty days and then why not six months. Harrison wrote Tansley to congratulate him on the initiative, enclosing two cheques for $4,500, one from himself and another from McCain Foods.

These were just two of many cheques that Harrison would write over the years in support of social and community causes, from 1957 until his death in 2004. Harrison would often ask that his identity not be revealed to the recipients. He also told me that many came asking for a sizeable financial contribution and in return would adorn the building with the Harrison McCain name. He consistently turned them down, insisting that donors to a good cause should not expect anything in return.

TRANSPORTATION

Sales was the lifeblood of McCain Foods. Harrison and Wallace were, to be sure, excellent salesmen. Indeed, sales played to their strengths. But this was only a part of the puzzle, a good part to be sure, but it was not enough.

The Florenceville plant was located far from large markets. Transportation of frozen food was a particular headache, especially in the late 1950s and 1960s. In an attempt to solve this problem, Harrison and Wallace turned their attention to a local trucking firm, Day and Ross, which Elbert Day and Walter Ross had founded in 1950 in nearby Hartland.[39] They had one truck hauling Carleton County potatoes to Montreal. Shortly after opening its Florenceville plant, McCain Foods became Day and Ross's biggest client. Day and Ross grew in tandem with McCain Foods so that by the late 1960s the firm operated 400 trucks. To accommodate the requirements of McCain Foods, Day and Ross had to invest substantial resources in modern up-to-date refrigerated trailers.

McCain Foods pushed Day and Ross hard to grow, to cut rates, and to provide prompt service. At one point, McCain Foods actually bought three trucks to help Day and Ross deliver their frozen products. Harrison and Wallace pushed the firm to take on larger and larger shipments and to modernize by incorporating new technology. This pushed one local carrier into bankruptcy and another close to it. Maine Maritime was in desperate financial shape by the early 1960s but it held at least one valuable asset – a licence to haul in Ontario. This was enough to convince the McCains to buy Maine Maritime.

Day and Ross was also having problems. Early on Walter Ross decided to leave the trucking business and sold his interest to Elbert Day. Day was having a hard time turning a profit, living from "invoice to invoice." Day explained, "I was the last one who got paid. I took what was left and it wasn't very much. We used to work all day and then load a load of potatoes."[40]

Day asked Joe Palmer, a tough-talking Carleton County farmer to join him in the business. Palmer eventually bought out Day in 1963, but he too continually struggled to keep the business afloat, so Harrison met Palmer with an offer to buy Day and Ross. Palmer explained, "The McCains had money and no management in the trucking business and I had management but no money. So we merged the two companies."[41] The McCains suddenly owned one of the region's biggest trucking firms.

McCain Foods' decision to buy Day and Ross and Maine Maritime did not flow from a comprehensive business plan. It was a pragmatic decision to get products to market in Quebec and Ontario. This it did. But Day and Ross continued to struggle even after the purchase and was only kept afloat because McCain Foods had deep pockets and they needed a dependable carrier to move their products to market.

Day and Ross had a number of underlying problems. It had weak senior and middle management and operated in a highly competitive environment against firms like Armour Transport who were solely devoted to the trucking business. Day and Ross lost $20 million in 1991 alone, which McCain Foods had to absorb.

Harrison told me on several occasions that hiring John Doucet in 1992 as chief operating officer, later chief executive officer, turned Day and Ross around. Doucet, an Acadian, had already established a strong track record with a trucking firm in Montreal. Doucet remains CEO to this day. Harrison and Doucet also maintained a strong friendship until the end. I never understood why Harrison mentioned John Doucet as often as he did until I undertook research for this book.

I made it a point of sitting down with Doucet for a lengthy interview. Doucet is a straight-talking, unpretentious, tough, hard-working, hard-nosed business executive who is not averse to swearing to make a point. He speaks of Day and Ross and McCain Foods from two distinct periods: one during Harrison's time and the other after Harrison stepped away from the business shortly before he passed away.

Doucet enjoys telling Harrison stories. He reports that Harrison would "suggest" a to-do list often in all-too-brief hard-to-read handwritten notes. One time, he got a note suggesting that he should buy the "derelict" place next door. Doucet's next-door neighbour was an elderly woman living by herself and unwilling or unable to take care of her modest old unkempt home. Doucet described her as a "wonderful older lady who meant no harm, but her house was a complete mess, an eyesore." He went up to her house twice with the intention of making an offer to buy her house. He reports that he "simply could not do it, I just could not do it." He added, "She was a good decent person who did not know or did not have the financial resources to keep her house neat and tidy."

A few weeks later, he told Harrison, "Look, I can't do it. She is a lovely old lady and that's that. I just can't do it."

Harrison responded, "What the f— are you talking about, John?"

He added, "I am talking about the derelict shed next to your office."

John said, "Well, Jesus Christ, Harrison, why didn't you tell me? I have worried about that goddamn house for two weeks. Had I gone ahead and bought the place, what the f— would I do with the old god-damn house? And, by the way, Harrison, that shed belongs to us."

Harrison replied, "Well, then, John, get rid of that goddamn shed."

On another occasion, Harrison called John about buying the Bank of Montreal branch next door to the Day and Ross office in Hartland. The conversation went like this:

"Well, Jesus Christ, Harrison, I don't know how to buy a f— bank."

Harrison: "No problem, no problem, John. I'll get you the name of the guy in Montreal or Toronto who looks after the bank's real estate and you will call him and tell him you want to buy the bank."

Doucet did just that.

The Bank of Montreal employee told him, "No, we are not interested in selling the Hartland branch. We just put $100,000 into a new roof."

Doucet said, "Jesus Christ, have you ever seen the old building?"

"No," said the bank employee.

"Have you ever visited the branch?" John asked.

Once again, the answer was, "No."

Doucet strongly urged him to come down and take a good look at the "old building." The bank employee never did visit the branch but called a few weeks later to say that the bank would be interested in selling. Doucet negotiated a $60,000 selling price, and in addition the bank agreed to pay a monthly rental fee to keep a machine in the branch for several years. Doucet called Harrison with news.

"Christ," said Harrison, "how in the hell did you do that? Hell of a price, John, a hell of a price." Then he added, "Now, don't you worry about the bank, John. That bank has plenty of money." The purchase suited Harrison well, given that he was also a member of the board of directors of Scotia Bank.

Doucet simplified the business, insisting that "transport is not that complicated. We're only moving boxes around when you get right down to it." The challenge was to get the box to its destination on time and on budget. Doucet told me, "Christ, when I arrived at Day and Ross, I had to tell the fellas there, 'The freight doesn't belong to us. You guys can't just keep the stuff here. We have to deliver this stuff.

Delivering is our business.'" Doucet introduced proactive tracking to Day and Ross. The process required the driver to deliver the shipment on time. Failing that, the local terminal manager had to call the customer between 8 and 10 a.m. to explain the delay. Doucet explains, "The terminal manager soon got the message that if they didn't want to spend the morning on the telephone, they had better get the freight delivered on time." Doucet also dropped customers who failed to pay invoices on time.[42]

When Doucet arrived, Day and Ross had $180 million in revenue and was losing money. Today, it generates $850 million a year in revenues and is highly profitable, shipping to all ten Canadian provinces and throughout the United States. It has a fleet of 2,500 owner-operated and company-owned trailers, working out of forty terminals in Canada, one of the largest trucking firms in the country, employing about 4,200 people. When Doucet arrived, McCain Foods accounted for about 50 per cent of Day and Ross's business. Today, it accounts for only about 8 per cent. Doucet tells me that he signed on with Day and Ross because of Harrison McCain, his charisma, his can-do attitude, and his willingness to "let me run the show the way I wanted to." He adds, "Harrison's strength is that he could read people, identify their strengths, and inspire them."

The McCain brothers had a challenge growing a frozen food business in a peripheral region of Canada thousands of kilometres away from major markets, so they did what they needed to do. If local trucking firms were not up to the challenge, they bought them, hired competent senior managers to run them, and invested the resources to turn them into successful firms. Harrison took great pride in the fact that, like himself, John Doucet was a New Brunswicker. And John stood by Harrison until the very end, visiting him often in his last days at his Florenceville home.

LOOKING BACK

By the mid-1960s, the McCain brothers had built a successful firm in the high-growth frozen food industry. Their presence was being felt throughout the region and in the food industry in central Canada. John Bragg, the blueberry magnate from Nova Scotia, told me that he

went to see Wallace and Harrison McCain, asking if there was a segment of the frozen food business that he could get into that would
not be in competition with McCain Foods. They told him to try frozen onion rings. To this day, Bragg still makes frozen onion rings for
McCain Foods. According to Bragg, "Only in the Maritimes do you
get a forty-year contract on a handshake."[43] Bragg told me that, when
he met Harrison with ideas to sort out the arrangement, Harrison told
him, "Now, now, John, John, you are not going to tell me how to negotiate this deal. Here is how it's going to work."

After ten years, McCain Foods had grown to the point that the competition took notice. And Harrison McCain would remain deeply loyal
to his community, the Maritime provinces, and to Maritimers.

McCain Foods was in the business to grow, end of story. Large firms
were taking note, and some came calling to see if the McCain brothers would be willing to sell at a handsome profit. Heinz, Imasco, and
General Foods, among others, offered to buy McCain Foods, enabling
Harrison and Wallace to quit their punishing long days and to enjoy
the fruits of their labour. No deal. Harrison and Wallace wanted no
part of it. It is worth quoting Harrison at some length on this point:

> And as the company grew and attracted attention, why we had
> lots of opportunities to sell it. Major food companies and cigarette
> companies and so forth wanted to buy it. I remember one
> memorable conversation with one of the tobacco companies. And
> they pressed their case quite vigorously, and we went next door to
> pick up a hot dog for lunch and their guy again pressed the case
> very vigorously.
>
> And I said, "Well look, this tobacco business you've got. Is that a
> good business?"
>
> "Oh," he says, "It's just a wonderful business. It's huge, it's a
> smashing business," and so forth.
>
> "Well," I said, "how much do you make?"
>
> He said, "What do you mean?"
>
> I said, "What percentage of your sales do you make as a net
> profit?"
>
> He said, "Two-point-seven-eight per cent last year."
>
> I said, "That's all smoke and no fire."

And they left angry. They didn't want to hear that kind of talk from a young brat.[44]

Harrison and Wallace put everything aside to grow McCain Foods. They also had no interest in cashing in or going public. They were in for the long haul. They were also on a roll and decided to expand outside of Canada. They first turned to England and only later decided to tackle the American market. The frozen food industry had already taken root in the United States, where substantial firms were already in the business. Harrison and Wallace felt they were not sufficiently well-heeled to take them on in the mid- to late 1960s. The American market could wait.

6

Florenceville Conquers Europe

Frank McKenna observed, "Harrison McCain was a globalist before the word was invented."[1] Harrison simply concluded that if he was in the frozen french fries business, then his job was to buy potatoes where people grew them, process them, and sell them where people eat them.[2] He was always one to simplify things, and he had seen his father explore new markets in England and Latin America some fifty years before.

Much as there never had been a question of whether Harrison and Wallace would launch their own business, there had also been no question of their pursuing distant markets. The only question was where. In the long run, the answer was virtually the world, but they had to start somewhere.

It will be recalled that Harrison's father, A.D. McCain, had gone to Britain at a very young age in search of new markets for potatoes. Britain also held a number of advantages for his sons. It was, relatively speaking, close to home. The distance from Florenceville to London is about four thousand kilometres, actually closer than from Florenceville to Vancouver by about four hundred kilometres. There would be no language barrier, and potatoes had been a staple of the British diet since Sir Walter Raleigh introduced them to the English in the sixteenth century.

The large United States market could wait. Allison McCain, son of their brother Andrew and the first of his generation to join the firm, summed up the situation well: "Our major competitors grew up in the United States and stayed in the United States. Because their own domestic market is so large, they didn't have as much need as we did to expand internationally."[3]

OFF TO BRITAIN

As we have seen, Harrison went to Britain a few years after the Florenceville plant opened to sell surplus frozen peas. Here he met Mac McCarthy, a Yorkshireman with whom he formed a very close friendship that lasted a lifetime. Mac, as he was commonly known, was at the time production director of a local frozen food company. It was he who bought the frozen peas from Harrison, the first of many business deals Mac had with, and later for, McCain Foods.

McCain Foods began selling french fries in Britain in the early 1960s produced at its Florenceville plant. At first, it did not sell them under its own brand. By 1965, however, McCain Foods had sold over $1 million of frozen food products in Britain through wholesalers: the McCain brand was fast becoming known, at least to distributors and the competition. Through his own efforts and those of his friend Mac, Harrison was able to establish a beachhead in Britain in only a few years. He soon decided that the time had come for a full-blown McCain presence in Britain.

Harrison enjoyed competition in all things, not just in business. Stanley Wagner, part-owner and managing director of the British company Caterpac, came to visit him in Florenceville to work on a proposed business deal. Caterpac consisted of twelve frozen-food distributors in Britain, and Harrison wanted to purchase the business. Wagner was a loud, heavy-set man with a reputation for outdoing anyone with practical jokes or, as Harrison put it, "cute tricks on everyone that came within sight." But when put to the test, Harrison could give as much as he got.

Harrison enjoyed the tale of this visit:

Stanley Wagner came to visit me one time in Florenceville and see if we could do a little business. And so after we talked in the office for awhile, it was getting late in the afternoon, so I said, "Stanley, come on. We'll go over to my place and have dinner." So he drove over in the car with me. Now if you know Florenceville, you know

that there's one section of the town that's made up of very decent
people but unfortunately poor for a long, long while. And the
housing looks it. Quite a lot of it is decrepit looking and unkempt
looking and so forth. So you have to pass through that to get up
to where I live. So as Stanley and I passed one of these houses, the
worst-looking house, I pulled in to the driveway and said, "Well,
here we are." And I said, "There's Billie hanging out my draw-
ers." And Stanley's mouth just dropped open. He couldn't believe
it. He was speechless. He didn't know what to say. "Let's go in the
house, let's go." I had him. I had him right dead to rights. So after I
watched him writhe and suffer for a minute or two, I backed the car
back onto the road and we went on to my place.[4]

McCain Foods bought Caterpac in 1965; it became the building
block for McCain Foods (GB) in 1966 which is responsible for England, Wales, Scotland, Northern Ireland, and the Republic of Ireland.[5]
The McCain clan had come full circle from leaving Ireland as farmers
in the early 1820s, now returning in style.

Harrison hired Mac to run McCain Foods in Great Britain. At first,
Mac worked from his home. His wife answered the phone and took
care of the paperwork while he travelled, hustling frozen french fries
to a market that had deep roots in fresh-cut potatoes. Mac adopted
the same method as Wallace and Harrison had used earlier, what Mac
called the approach of the door-to-door vacuum cleaner salesman:
"With our french fries we would go in and try to persuade the caterer
to ... to fry our french fries and compare the quality and cost with
the product they were using, usually chips from fresh potatoes." It was
a tough uphill battle, breaking the local food industry away from its
traditional approach. As the McCains had found in Canada, most restaurants did not have freezers, and on occasion Mac would supply one
in order to get frozen french fries into their kitchens.[6]

McCain Foods was at this time importing its fries from Florenceville. However, it was not long before Mac, Harrison, and Wallace were
asking themselves if there were not a better way to supply the British
market. Building a plant in England was an obvious option but the risk
was high. The company was anything but firmly established, and its
finances were stretched. If building a plant in Britain turned out to be a

bad call, it could well bring down McCain Foods. Harrison recalls how he arrived at a decision:

> One night I was dining in a well-known restaurant with McCarthy and a couple more guys in Grimsby, England. And there was a flash report over the radio that was replayed at the restaurant. The British pound had just been devalued by a huge amount, something like 40 per cent. And I said, "To hell with that, I'm not putting up with that. We'll build a plant here." Otherwise you'd have to give up the business because you'd be non-competitive, you see. Our prices would be moved up enormously. And we'd just be stuck. To hell with that, we're building a plant. So McCarthy was given the job of finding the site. And he found the Scarborough site where we built a plant.[7]

Harrison, by the mid-1960s, concentrated his efforts on recruiting top talent and striking deals to expand McCain Foods. He explained that "the game is action, what's going on. There's something new all the time: buying companies, building factories, hiring guys, motivating people, overseeing advertising programs, taking position on commodities, borrowing money, settling lawsuits." He added, "Unfortunately, I have to go to damn meetings, read reports, a lot of things I don't like doing."[8]

McCain Foods officially opened its first British plant in Scarborough in 1969, and the McCain luck held; it was the right moment. American-styled fast food restaurants were increasingly moving into the British market and large supermarkets were beginning to invest in commercial freezers. The Scarborough plant was well-equipped with the most modern machinery and, at the time, was the largest frozen french fries plant outside of North America. The four McCain brothers and Laura McCain, together with local civic leaders, attended the official opening, a major civic event in the community.

But the start-up was not without problems and Mac had to deal with issues similar to those the McCain brothers faced when they first opened their Florenceville plant. Employees did not know how to work the machinery and equipment often broke down. The plant's effluent capacity often malfunctioned and, too often, flooded the plant. Harrison turned to Milford Kinney, one of McCain Foods' key supervisors in Florenceville, and asked him to pick three of the best workers at the plant and go show the people in Scarborough how to fix things.

This they did, and within several months the plant was running smoothly. The turnaround also identified competent managers at the plant who would later help others set up plants in Continental Europe. McCain Foods was soon fast gaining recognition in the British market, and only a few years later, the company decided to build a second plant in Britain, one that was capable of processing some 225,000 tonnes of potatoes a year.[9]

Getting the plant up and running was not the only challenge as McCain Foods moved into Britain. As had been discovered in Canada, not all potatoes are well-suited for frozen french fries. Under European plant regulations, importing potatoes from North America to Britain required a great deal of paperwork, which only added to the start-up headaches. After considerable effort, McCain Foods was allowed to import eight Russet Burbank seed tubers. It took five years to grow a sufficient quantity of Russet Burbank potatoes, which, as we have seen, are particularly well suited for producing frozen french fries, but the effort and patience paid off.

That was not the end of McCain Foods' troubles. British potato farmers were set in their ways, having grown table potatoes for the retail market for generations. In addition, they very often owned large estates that were supervised by professional managers. It was not easy for some "smartass guy from the colonies telling them what to grow and that what they were growing was the wrong kind of potato."[10]

But every challenge was met and decisions were handled quickly. There was no bureaucracy, no working board of directors, and no quarterly reports to attend to that slowed decision making. A phone call to Harrison or Wallace, a quick consultation between the two who regularly put in fourteen-hour days, was all that was required. They made a point of being always readily available and they were always quick to move a major initiative forward.

Harrison took the lead interest in Britain, much as Wallace would do later in Australia. There was always an easy flow of information and a very high level of trust between Harrison, Wallace, and Mac McCarthy. McCain employees began to refer to Mac as the third McCain because many of them saw in him the same drive, determination, bluntness, and commitment to McCain Foods as they saw in both Harrison and Wallace. Mac also put in extremely long hours and he too made himself readily available. Employees knew that Mac had Harrison's full confidence.

Mac soon moved out of his home office into proper commercial space. He drove growth for McCain Foods in Britain and attached a great deal of importance to motivating staff. Howard Mann, former CEO at McCain Foods, summed Mac: "One of his great strengths is his willingness to give a clear, concise opinion. He is a very difficult man to be misunderstood."[11]

Mac was able to secure a contract to supply McDonald's with french fries in their British restaurants – a definite coup. He then added to this success by signing on Burger King and Kentucky Fried Chicken. These contracts convinced the fast food restaurant business in Britain that McCain Foods could be counted on to provide a high and consistent level of quality control. The McDonald's British contract also paved the way for contracts with McDonald's in other countries. Harrison often said that McDonald's was a loyal customer and that "if you have them as a customer, it is yours to lose."

The British experience was a useful model as McCain Foods turned its attention to Continental Europe. First it would test the market and export its frozen fries from Britain. It would then hire distributors and sales staff to promote the McCain brand with restaurants and other potentially large clients. The final step was to build, buy, or modernize an existing plant and produce frozen food products locally.[12]

Harrison explained back in 1988 McCain Foods' strategy to expand in other countries: "We always establish a beachhead in a foreign country by shipping product in from an existing operation. Even if it doesn't make any money, we are going to establish that beachhead and build volume until we have sufficient load to justify a factory. We built the base volume in England by supplying from Canada, then we built a factory. Now we have six factories there. We used England as a base to establish a beachhead in Holland and Belgium, and then we bought factories there. Then we used Holland as a base to invade France. And now France is a base from which we dominate the french fry business in Italy."[13]

MARKETING

In his interview with James Downey, Harrison mentioned marketing as an area in which he had substantial interest. He was at home with the subject and happy to spend time and effort on its development. He could even put up with long meetings on the topic.

Harrison went with private labels only when he had to or when McCain Foods first set foot in a foreign market, but the moment he could, he introduced the McCain Foods brand. To project the right image was important to him – he willingly spent time personally shaping McCain Foods booths and displays at food fairs. He could easily become bored when having to immerse himself in the details of an issue – except marketing or the firm's public image.

He insisted on being consulted when television advertisements were being prepared. I once told Harrison that years ago I had quite enjoyed the TV ad in which a boy, no more than four or five years old and wearing thick glasses, was happily and silently chomping on McCain french fries. The ad can still be seen on YouTube and has been described as a Canadian classic. Harrison said that they had received a deluge of positive comments in response to the ad and that, with some effort, were able to track down the young boy, by this time in his mid-twenties, and ran another advertisement with him. Not surprisingly, perhaps, it failed to have the impact of the earlier ad.

As already noted, projecting the right image was important to Harrison, whether for McCain Foods or himself personally. He was always well dressed, no matter the occasion, as on the day I was at his home, simply looking forward to a chat with a friend who always had interesting stories. Like most academics, I never pay much attention to how I look or how I am dressed. That day was no exception. Harrison, however, was impeccably attired. In fact, I do not recall ever seeing him casually dressed: his pants were never wrinkled, his shirt was always pristine, or, if he wore a sweater, it looked as if he had put it on for the first time.

On at least one occasion, however, Harrison decided to dress down. He was meeting the head of a large food company in Toronto whom he had known for some time and decided to wear an old, worn-out suit with loose threads around the arms and wrists. It was completely out of character for Harrison. The individual accompanying Harrison was puzzled, knowing that it was highly unusual for him to wear worn-out clothes. Harrison explained, "Look, I know this guy. He is very, very rich. I want to strike a good deal. I want to squeeze every penny I can out of this deal and I want him to know that he is richer than me." It did not, however, work out as planned. The leading businessman knew Harrison, found it quite unusual for Harrison to wear a thread-bare suit, and he would not be easily fooled. He welcomed both in his office and, after a good long look at Harrison's worn-out suit, asked, "Harrison, how was your trip coming up in your private jet?"

Harrison, when in London in the early years, always stayed at the luxurious Savoy Hotel, on The Strand, one of the city's best addresses. As long-time McCain Foods employee Ralph Orr explained, "If you called someone and left a message that you are staying at the Savoy, it looked good. It was a smart business tactic."[14] This choice of hotel was of course in keeping with Harrison's desire to present a strong public image.

Harrison's aim was to have the McCain brand, with the eight-point star sitting neatly on the "i", highly visible on all its products and in company advertisements. McCain Foods had to be adroit in designing its marketing plans if only because the firm was more often than not creating a new market, not competing in a mature one. The objective was to create a new market for frozen food products, not simply for McCain french fries, rather than follow an established market. This goal permeated McCain's marketing strategy, particularly in the early years.

McCain Foods has always had to strike a proper balance between a production-driven culture and a marketing culture. Paul van der Wel, a McCain Foods executive, explained the difference. The emphasis in a production-driven culture is selling what is being produced, while in a marketing culture it is to sell what the market wants: "A marketing attitude says that you must adjust your agriculture and quality control to what the market wants. If you don't have the best potatoes, you have to make compromises but, in general, quality goes above production efficiency. You have to satisfy the needs of the consumer. Otherwise, your reputation goes down the road. Anyone who worked at McCain Foods, while Harrison was there, knew full well that he would not allow the firm's reputation to be hurt, but when it was, he would invariably become directly involved in efforts to remedy the situation."[15]

NEXT STEP: THE NETHERLANDS

George McClure joined McCain Foods in June 1970 to work directly for Harrison on a variety of projects. McClure reports that he was also closely involved with Wallace, Bob, and Andrew McCain, Carl Ash in finance, Carl Morris in manufacturing, Tim Bliss in engineering, Arch McLean in marketing, Dick McWhirter in sales, and Joe Palmer in transportation. He wrote to me to say that Harrison had enrolled him at McCain University, where he learned from the best.

After he had been little more than a year with the company, McClure was pegged to develop the European market, and Harrison gave him his marching orders: "Mac is doing a great job in Great Britain. We have no business in Europe. Here's what I want you to do. Go to Europe. Put your hands in your pockets. Walk around. See what you can learn." McClure added, "There was no more discussion. I spent six weeks in Holland, Belgium, France, Germany, Denmark and Sweden. I came home, wrote a report. I recommended that we start in Holland. The rest is history." That summed up Harrison's management style. He knew how to delegate, to trust his senior executives, and to give them space to get the job done. Harrison also knew how to measure performance and to hold someone accountable.

The Netherlands held a distinct advantage. It was in the heart of Europe's best potato-growing country and actually was the home of the first french fry, which was invented there in the early 1800s when someone dropped a strip of potato in boiling fat. It is also well located in northern Europe between potentially large markets: Germany to the east, and France to the west. Politically, the Netherlands had and still has few enemies. It joined the European Economic Community – later the European Union – in 1958. It was and remains a relatively business-friendly jurisdiction.[16] Thus, while McClure recommended to Harrison and Wallace that they should locate their first European operation in the Netherlands, he also urged them to look on Europe as a single market, a fairly innovative thought in the early 1970s. The brothers gave him a thumbs-up on both counts.

McClure opened a one-man operation, much as "Mac" had done in Britain several years earlier, but he held one significant advantage – he knew the ways of government. McClure knocked on the door of the Canadian embassy in The Hague, asking for help but found that the commercial attaché was about to go on a two-month leave. He did what would be inconceivable today, though it likely proved one of the best investments ever made by Ottawa's Department of Foreign Affairs and Trade, at least in the Maritime provinces. The attaché, given that he would be away for two months, offered to lend McClure his office during his absence. Current government policy, with its emphasis on transparency and the avoidance of conflict of interest, not to mention the array of oversight bodies looming over the operations of government departments, would simply not countenance such an arrangement.

Not only was McClure able to make full use of the office, the attaché's administrative assistant helped to secure appointments for him. McClure started from scratch, calling on restaurants and other potential clients. And just as Mac had done, McClure first imported frozen fries from existing McCain plants. But that was not without problems, given import duties and shipping difficulties and costs. The bigger challenge, however, was convincing chefs that frozen french fries were better than chilled or freshly cut french fries.

McClure built McCain's presence in Europe step-by-step. He first imported the product, then hired a few salesmen to help him. He identified potential clients and then went about selling frozen french fries to them, much as Mac had done – the vacuum cleaner salesman approach. As in England, McCain Foods was soon pondering how best to produce frozen products in Europe. To be sure, McClure would need to pick an area rich in agricultural land where farmers had grown potatoes for generations, and he did not have to look further than the Netherlands. The key question was whether to build a plant or purchase one. He recommended buying, to speed up the McCain presence in Continental Europe. He had in mind buying one of two plants and, in the end, McCain Foods bought both. Both required upgrading but they gave McCain an immediate presence in Continental Europe and a capacity to produce frozen french fries close to potentially large markets. There were now three plants operating in Britain and Continental Europe, and more were to come.

Mac McCarthy's Scarborough plant would look after clients in Britain and France, while McClure's two plants would look after those in Continental Europe. The sales effort bore fruit, and, as operations in Britain and in the Netherlands continued to grow, it was not long before both were looking to expand their horizons.

Mac was increasingly comfortable with and confident in McCain's ability to provide frozen french fries to the British market. It became easier as more and more customers accepted them for their restaurants and grocery stores, and he met with one success after another. Fast food restaurants were expanding and corner variety stores were slowly losing their market share to supermarkets well-equipped with freezers. Mac was also a tough, demanding executive who kept a close eye on the plant and the sales people. He oversaw an expansion of the Scarborough plant in 1972 and added more storage space, then opened a new plant in Whittlesay in Cambridgeshire, which, at the time, was the largest frozen french fries plant in the world. Harrison's loyalty to his New Brunswick roots was evident when he asked Carleton County–born Cedric Ritchie, his long-time friend and now chairman of the Bank of Nova Scotia, to officially open the new plant.

Mac ran a tight ship, but he inspired loyalty from his staff. He was known to everyone, from senior managers to line workers, as "Mac." Mac explained that it was part of the McCain Foods culture: "There's nobody in my company in Britain who called me anything but 'Mac,' whether they swept the floor of the factory or they were the marketing director. I was Mac to every single person. And Harrison was Harrison and Wallace was Wallace throughout the whole company."[17]

Mac, like Harrison, had a temper, and both had highly vocal disagreements laced with more than a few choice words. Allison McCain, who worked with Mac and was close to his uncle Harrison, reports, "You never knew how Mac would react when you walked in with a problem or a solution." He adds that Mac and Harrison had a very close and, at times, tumultuous relationship. Harrison would, from time to time, attend management committee meetings in Britain, but you always knew that he and Mac had worked out all disagreements before they walked into the meeting.

Mac made the McCain presence loom large not only in the frozen food business but also in British society. In fact, many people believed that McCain Foods was a British firm. Prince Charles was one such: when he was on a royal visit to New Brunswick, Premier Frank McKenna informed him that the province was home to McCain Foods. Not so, the prince replied. He knew McCain Foods and it was a British firm. Mac had a similar experience. No less than the British minister of agriculture told him about the "great example of that British company McCain which started from small beginnings in Scarborough."[18] Mac was made a Commander of the British Empire in 1993. After his death on New Year's Eve, 2012, the *Grocer* referred to him as the founder of McCain Foods, and in two newspapers he was called the founder of McCain Foods U.K. The *Scarborough News*, however, got it right.[19]

CORPORATE CULTURE

Harrison and Wallace both wanted an informal corporate culture, in which senior managers had easy access to them and to one another. They were pragmatic managers to the core. They believed in keeping things simple, in having no elaborate processes, and in solving problems as they arose. The fact that McCain Foods remained in family hands made their aim achievable.

The corporate culture the brothers established also showed a tolerance for errors, as Nick Vermont (CEO of McCain Foods in Britain, Ireland, and South Africa since 2005) recalls: "I had run a consumer promotion that had come in something like five times over budget in terms of redemption and therefore cost. And I had spent about two weeks of sleepless nights wondering how I was going to tell Harrison this. And I gingerly got up and did my presentation and in the end I said, 'Well, I do have to confess that I got it horribly wrong and it's cost five times what it was budgeted for.' Harrison replied, 'Nick, Nick, I don't mind if you were five times over budget, don't mind that at all, if it meant that it costs five times as much, and I don't mind anybody making a mistake once. But just never make the same mistake again.'"[20]

That said, Harrison had an incredible fine eye for details. I read a memo that he wrote on 10 April 1985 on the possible purchase of a plant in Spain. He took into account the smallest of details from where the sunlight came in, to the level of insulation, the height of the walls, and the shape of the roof. I also read a monthly report that he sent on

29 November 1968 to Wallace McCain, Carl Ash, Carl Morris, and several other senior managers. He congratulated the group for the strong growth in sales (up 25 per cent for the month and up 10.8 per cent in the year after ten months). He also reported that for the first time in several years, downtime due to mechanical failures had been reduced to almost zero, but that maintenance cost was still too high. He wrote that during the month of October, the Florenceville office spent $7,559 on telephone and telexes, which was $2,400 over budget. He then added, "Please, gentlemen, use telexes more and use telephone less and please use the telephone to discuss business problems succinctly. Self-discipline in organizing a bit better what you want to say as compared to windy chats could likely save us $4,000 per month."

In going through his personal files, I came across about a hundred small black books full of observations and detailed assessments of business opportunities. A long-time McCain Food employee told me that Harrison would work on his little black books in private, often when returning from a business trip. He added, "We never knew what he did with them, but we knew that they mattered."

The small black books contained information about anything and everything about McCain Foods. Parts of one detailed the cost of buying potatoes one year, parts of another were, in many ways, a human resources management tool. In one case, for example, Harrison detailed the commitments he made to a senior executive – a trip for him and his wife to Italy. Another black book listed what he liked about a processing plant and what he found lacking in another.

EXPANDING THE EUROPEAN MARKET

George McClure was certainly not one to be content with the status quo. Indeed, his mandate was to grow the European market and he had the full confidence of Harrison McCain as he set out to do so. He knew that Harrison's tendency was to push the envelope at all times. Harrison, on the other hand, knew that in McClure he had a safe pair of hands, capable of accomplishing an objective.[21]

It did not take long for McClure to look beyond the Netherlands and the two plants that he had negotiated to purchase. Since both plants were working smoothly and servicing existing clients, McClure could now turn his attention further afield. Within a few years, his expanded sales team had secured new clients in Germany, France, Italy, Austria, and Denmark.

The question was often raised as to whether McCain should sell under its own brand, create new ones for specific countries, or sell to others for rebranding. The McCain publication to celebrate its fiftieth anniversary reports on a debate that lasted into the night. The question was Germany. Should McCain operate under its own name or rebrand, using a German name, as the best way to move into the German market? The debate was heated, with the majority of those present convinced that a Germanic name was required. By 8 p.m. Harrison had said little, sitting back while the others had their say. Finally, he brought the debate to an end: "Boys, that was a great conversation. Great. Lots of input. Now here's what we're going to do. We're going to call it McCain. We're going to call it McCain. Now let's go and eat."[22] It was the right call: "Today, McCain products, bearing the McCain brand, have a strong position in Germany's retail market for frozen foods."[23]

OFF TO FRANCE

I once asked Harrison which country and which government he most liked to do business with and which the least. His answer: "France," for the most and "Colombia, Colombia," for the least – adding, "Never been there and don't want to go there."

"France," I replied. "That surprises me. Big government and lots of bureaucrats there."

"Yes, yes, tons of them, tons of them. It takes them a great deal of time for them to get their act together. But, you know, when they start pushing, they push hard and they all push in the same direction. They know better than anyone how to square the interests of France with your firm's interest ... They can be tough, they can be demanding, and they can be slow. But in the end, they get it done, the right way."

Harrison was posthumously made a chevalier de l'Ordre de la Légion d'Honneur, one of France's highest honours. He also took an active interest in and made a substantial financial contribution to La Francophonie when it met in Moncton, New Brunswick, in 1999. In

addition, he took a strong interest in and was also a charter member
of the comité Canada-France to promote business and trade between
the two countries. Prime Minister Pierre Trudeau and his French
counterpart, Pierre Mauroy, had decided in November 1982 to establish the committee. Harrison McCain was joined by the likes of Paul
Desmarais of Power Corporation, Jean de Grandpré of Bell Canada,
and Red Wilson of Redpath Industry on the sixteen-member committee. Harrison's files reveal that he not only took its work seriously but
that he also spent considerable time pursuing the committee's agenda.

McClure was aware that France was a potentially lucrative market,
even as he flew over to open McCain operations in the Netherlands.
France had a large population, a thriving potato-growing region, and,
not least, a potato-loving public. As anyone who has visited France
knows, *steak-frites* is a very popular dish in brasseries throughout the
country.

But *frites* from freshly cut potatoes are one thing and selling frozen french fries with a foreign brand name attached to them are
quite another. But, as he had in Germany, Harrison was firm that the
McCain brand be used in France with its distinctive logo and its eight-
pointed star remaining intact. This strategy worked well, in France as
elsewhere, and McCain Foods was soon successfully penetrating the
French market with the fries coming initially from the plants in the
Netherlands and Britain.

The french fries and frozen food market was growing very fast,
going through the same social changes through which North America had gone several years earlier. The fast food restaurant business
was starting to make its mark and more and more women were joining the labour force. The male breadwinner model, in which only the
man worked, began to break down in France and throughout Europe
in the 1960s.[24] Today, over half the labour force in France is made up
of women.[25]

To tackle the European market when it did proved to be a very
savvy decision by McCain Foods. The American frozen fries industry
was fully engaged at home and had yet to discover the potential that
lay in Europe. Further to the advantage of McCain, European firms
were not as aggressive in their marketing as McCain, and some were
actually selling their frozen food plants to McCain.[26] Europe, notably

Great Britain, soon accounted for more and more of McCain Foods revenues. As early as 1970, nearly half of McCain's revenues came from Great Britain.

In France, Harrison followed the established pattern: first, introduce products, then import them from plants in other countries, and, once a presence has been secured, make plans to build or buy a plant to secure the market, all the while making certain to promote the McCain brand to potential clients.

In the 1980s, the newly elected French socialist government of François Mitterand sent out strong signals to McCain Foods that it should build a local plant. Failing that, it would impose tariffs on their imported products. McCain Foods had no experience in dealing with a socialist government anywhere, and in the late 1970s McCain had been watching nervously as Mitterand was fast gaining political momentum. He had even struck a political alliance with France's Communist party. The folks at corporate head office in Florenceville were not quite sure what to make of a "socialist" government and, to be sure, there was unease about dealing with one that included communists. Mitterand won the 1981 presidential election and his election platform had promised that he would lead a highly interventionist government.[27] On economic issues, Mitterand's socialist agenda stood in stark contrast to the approach taken by two powerhouse neo-conservatives: Margaret Thatcher, elected British prime minister in 1979 and Ronald Reagan, who became the American president in 1981.[28]

McCain Foods was soon on the lookout for a French site to build a plant – even though their senior officials, including Harrison, were apprehensive about the economic measures Mitterrand would be introducing. Still, McClure scoured the potato-growing regions, looking for a site. Months and months went by with little progress. McClure returned to Canada to work out of the Florenceville office, while continuing to commute to France in search of a site. In an inspired decision, he finally turned for help to Alain Thiers, the former secretary of the French Potato Growers Association.

The search for a site ended when the two men came upon an abandoned copper-wire factory in Harnes, in the potato-growing region of northwest France, near the Belgian border. It was ideally suited to the purpose, and McClure took an option to buy it. He then led the discussions with the French government, fully expecting that they would be difficult. He approached France's regional development agency, outlining McCain's plans and exploring the prospect for government financial assistance. There he was pressed to work with a majority of French partners. McClure did not even have to check with Harrison – the answer was a definite no. McCain Foods was a family business, no partners welcome. Later, he was told that the project could go ahead, this time with minority French partners. McClure's answer was still an uncompromising no.

McClure decided to turn to the local farming community for help, inviting a number of them to visit the Scarborough plant. Here they met with Mac and, crucially, with local farmers who told their French visitors that McCain Foods was an excellent customer and an important new market for their potatoes. That did it. When the French farmers returned home, they applied pressure on government officials to approve the Harnes project. The government finally relented and permitted McCain Foods to proceed with the project with 100 per cent foreign investment.[29]

The Harnes plant finally opened in 1981 to wide acclaim. It had the best machinery and equipment available and it broke new ground in environmental protection. Its state-of-the-art technology became a showpiece of how to build a modern, environmentally friendly processing plant. Gratifyingly, French government officials brought a large number of visitors to tour the plant.

The problem of the suitability of locally established potatoes for frozen fries arose here, as it had in both Canada and Britain. Harrison McCain would often say, "You cannot make a good french fry from a bad potato." By the early 1980s, however, McCain Foods had the financial resources required to fix quality problems. It hired agronomists to look into the issue and within a few years local growers were able to deliver top-quality potatoes to the Harnes plant.

GO TO HELL AND SELL IT

The McCain french fry label was now widely available throughout Western Europe. It had momentum, name recognition, and resources, both financial and human, to fuel growth. Harrison's unyielding insistence on promoting the McCain brand rather than using private labels was now paying off.

Harrison always kept a close watch on Europe and on all marketing efforts. Despite his stance on promoting the McCain brand, he saw the wisdom in tailoring marketing strategies to different national markets. A message could sell well in Germany but not in France, in Italy, but not in Spain, and so on. He had no problem with tailoring the McCain message to accommodate local circumstances.

Harrison would listen to market advice but he could just as easily dismiss it as embrace it. McCain Foods in Canada came up with a new product in the mid-1970s: super fries were different from the original McCain french fries in that they were cooked in more oil. This gave them a different taste, a more deep-fried taste. British marketing staff were adamant that the super fries would not sell well in Britain and resisted their introduction for five years. Finally, an exasperated Harrison McCain told them, "Go to hell and sell it." They were renamed oven chips and became an instant bestseller, and within a year the new fries had twice as many sales as all frozen potatoes combined.[30]

It is important to stress again that, from day one, Harrison had strong instincts for marketing and sales strategies. He often took his own advice and he was often right. As already noted on several occasions, he attached a great deal of importance to his own public image and that of McCain Foods. It was he and George McClure who handled the media and dealt with senior government officials. He had all the self-assurance, the energy, and, increasingly, the track record to inspire the firm's marketing and sales staff, and, when he felt necessary, to chart a new course.

LOOKING WEST AND SOUTH

When Harrison and Wallace took stock in the early 1980s of their European operations, they could take full satisfaction in having managed bumps in the road and in laying the groundwork for future growth. Their business model worked – move into a new national market with products from their plants in Canada, Britain, or the Netherlands, define a marketing strategy, then build or buy a plant. In England they had modernized and expanded the Scarborough plant and built new ones, first in Whittlesay and then in Grantham. There were also the two plants in the Netherlands, and the showpiece at Harnes in France.

Again, they were poised to search for new markets and grow existing ones in neighbouring countries, and now turned their attention to Belgium, Germany, Italy, and Spain. McCain's was amongst the first to move into these countries; its proven marketing strategy and the fact that they had the processing capacity to respond quickly to new demands served them well.

Harrison McCain relented on one point as they moved into new national markets, only because he had little choice. The demand for low-cost products forced McCain Foods to go with no-brand products in some countries. Large supermarket chains wanted low-cost products with their own brand name. The issue was straightforward: if McCain Foods would not accommodate them, then someone else would, and that was enough of an argument for Harrison to designate two plants, one in England and another in France, to look after private labels.

The emphasis, however, remained on marketing the McCain brand so that when one thought of frozen french fries, one would think of McCain. McCain met with success in various settings, including Italy, the land of pasta. Even the Vatican, according to the head of McCain in Italy, became an important customer.[31]

McCain Foods conquered European countries one by one, building a large presence in supermarkets in Germany, Belgium, and Spain. And in Italy it sold ten times more frozen french fries than its nearest competitor. It now accounts for about one-third of the frozen french fries in Europe.

Harrison and his key advisors in Europe defined a model to introduce frozen french fries to new markets. Harrison, as his little black books revealed, was becoming more cautious and began to weigh the options very carefully. In the early years, Harrison and Wallace would bet the farm from year to year on a new plant. No more. They had an approach that they would implement country after country.

THE BERLIN WALL COMES DOWN

The minute the Berlin Wall came down, McCain Foods was quick off the mark. The firm quickly bought land for future expansion plans but it did more than that. It immediately pitched tents, brought in freezers, and started selling McCain products under the McCain brand shortly after East European countries opened their doors to the West.

McCain followed the established pattern, initially bringing in products to former communist countries from their plants in Western Europe. It waited, however, until the transition to a market economy was well on its way before it started to build processing plants. The delay enabled McCain to test what sold better in the new markets and how best to adjust both products and marketing to capture a bigger share. Indeed, the success of McCain Foods throughout Europe is based on its ability to adjust to local conditions and to its early presence in emerging markets.

As McCain Foods successfully penetrated new markets, it also began to add to its processing capacity as it became clear that national governments in former communist countries would not impose undue regulations and requirements. At the same time, it continued to expand capacity in Western Europe. McCain Foods bought a major Belgian frozen food company in 1986 and acquired a plant in Béthune, France. In 1990 it acquired yet another plant in the Netherlands, in Lelystad, and in 1998 it announced plans to construct a $84-million french fry processing plant in Matougues, France. Selling McCain french fries to McDonald's in Moscow would also open doors to sell to other McDonald's restaurants in other countries.

As McCain Foods grew and expanded in Europe, Harrison McCain had to adjust his management style. To be sure, he no longer had to stay in cheap motels and he could now afford to have his suits dry cleaned. He explained, "When you start a small business, you do everything yourself. After a while, it becomes apparent that it isn't going to work forever."[32]

The challenge was to learn to delegate, to focus on the more important issues, to motivate managers, and to assess performance. Harrison read widely from the management literature, economics, and politics. He told the *Financial Post*, "I don't know how anyone can get by without reading. I remember what Truman said about Eisenhower – 'when he said he's been too busy to read a book for seven years, I knew the country was in trouble.'"[33] Harrison's personal library had about seven hundred books dealing with three broad themes: management, economics, and politics. One can find books on Trudeau, Nixon, Richard Hatfield, the Bronfman family, E.P. Taylor, the Duponts, Lord Beaverbrook, and "The Valuation and Pricing of Privately Held Business." I also recall well Harrison telling me about the work of Tom Peters and Robert Waterman.

Harrison once told me that he wanted to write a book about lessons learned in growing a business.[34] He never did but he thought about the themes that he wanted to address. MBA students may want to take note that Harrison believed that Henry Mintzberg had it right "most of the time." He also told me that one of Peter Drucker's articles – "Getting Things Done: How to Make People Decisions" – had a great deal of merit and that he wanted to explore further the points Drucker made from a practitioner's perspective.[35]

To be sure, Peters and Waterman prescriptions resonated with Harrison McCain: the importance of being close to the customer, promoting a bias for action, hands-on management, and simple form and lean staff.[36] Harrison had little tolerance for sending issues through cycle after cycle of analyses, and committee reports to many management and administrative layers. Harrison told a Toronto audience in 1988, "At McCain Foods, Florenceville Office, the corporate staff isn't too heavy, it is my brother and me along with a financial man and a chief engineer. That is the entire world corporate staff. Being lean may be a way to save money. But that is not the best reason. The best reason is to get things done faster."[37]

Harrison did learn to delegate as McCain Foods expanded operations. He said, "There aren't many occasions where our top twenty fellows feel they can't make the decision except for certain areas."[38] Harrison saw his role in simple terms: he was there to think about deals and acquisitions, identify talent to run things, motivate managers to keep an eye on the purse strings, review the annual business plan, and measure results. He insisted that acquisitions was a strong way to grow at the international level and he delivered. Between 1983 and 1988, close to 50 per cent of the growth at McCain Foods was fuelled by acquisitions.[39] Harrison always paid close attention to striking the right deal at the right price in acquiring existing firms. As already noted, he had a dislike for attending long, drawn out meetings and reading reports, except ones on planning marketing and sales initiatives.

By the end of the 1990s, McCain Foods decided that the time had come to build new processing capacity in Eastern Europe. Its products were selling well there and in Russia.[40] With the enthusiastic support of the local Polish government, McCain announced that it would construct a $80-million plant in Strzelin.

Again, there was strong pressure to change the McCain brand to a more user-friendly name, better suited to Eastern Europe. One advertising agency insisted that otherwise McCain Foods would fail to capture the significant share of the market it sought. Harrison told the agency that he would agree to change the name to "McCainski" if it could "guarantee" success. The agency declined and Harrison turned to another agency to promote McCain products, using the McCain brand. Once again, he made the right decision.

McDonald's opened its first outlet in Russia, in Moscow's Pushkin Square in 1990. Muscovites lined up for hours on a cold January day to get their first taste of McDonald's fast food. Russia did not at the time have a single frozen french fry plant, and McDonald's imported all its fries from McCain's European plants.

LOOKING BACK

McCain Foods conquered the frozen french fries market from England to Russia. Harrison's explanation "Right time, right place" is valid, but it is only part of the story.

A prime factor in the firm's success lay in the character of Harrison and Wallace themselves. They were formidable and indefatigable entrepreneurs. They put in excruciatingly long hours, led by example, and enjoyed every minute of it. Critically, they had a flair for hiring talented managers, whom they then encouraged to make things happen, even if they should stumble. They kept decision-making levels to a strict minimum and were always available when decisions were required. Problems were there to be solved, not to be contemplated and debated from position papers.

Michael Campbell, a long-time senior McCain Foods executive, reports that when he walked in to see Harrison with what appeared to be an impossible problem, he always walked out of his office convinced

that the problem could be solved. He adds that Harrison's can-do attitude was nothing short of remarkable and contagious.

A senior European manager recalls calling Harrison on a Saturday
morning with very bad news. The Netherlands plant in Lewedorp had
caught fire and burned to the ground. Harrison's response was quick
and to the point: "Make a proposal, we are going to rebuild." The manager got onto it immediately with engineering expertise and sent a telex
to Harrison the very next Monday with a proposal. Within twenty-four
hours, Harrison responded, "Please proceed." No committee and no
lengthy decision-making. Harrison simply checked with Wallace and
off went the two-word reply.

David O'Brien, another long-time McCain Foods employee, maintains that Harrison had two sides to his personality. He wanted people
to think that he could shoot from the hip, a stereotypical swashbuck-
ling entrepreneur. But, O'Brien insists, "make no mistake, Harrison
knew how to assess a deal, and he was very cautious and deliberate."
O'Brien also made reference to Harrison's little black books, containing
information about McCain Foods, the frozen food business, the competition, and senior staff.

That is a typical example of the management style of Harrison and
Wallace McCain, a style that captured for them a large share of the
European frozen food market. This style took hold throughout the
organization and it instilled a strong can-do attitude. That style and
attitude would now be put to test in other markets.

Fighting Down Under, in the United States, and on the Home Front

There was still the large market in the United States beckoning. And Florenceville would remain the anchor from which a game plan would be developed.

Florenceville and New Brunswick were constants in Harrison's life. As time went on, McCain Foods experimented with many new products, some of which failed to get out of the gate, such as salmon pies and chicken and chips. Harrison had a strict business approach to all new products: if they failed to turn a profit or gain market share within a certain period of time, they were gone, end of story, and on to something else.

There was one product that Harrison wouldn't drop – fiddleheads – even if the economics did not add up. This is not surprizing since fiddleheads have been eaten in New Brunswick for centuries, first by the Maliseets,[1] the Algonquin-speaking indigenous people of the St John River valley. Indeed, fiddleheads were so central to the provincial image that in the 1970s they became a New Brunswick symbol. Premier Richard Hatfield used to take a brown paper bag filled with fiddleheads to federal-provincial conferences as a treat to share with the Canadian prime minister and his fellow premiers. So why did Harrison veto fiddleheads? He explained, "If they said tomorrow 'We're losing our shirt packing fiddleheads,' I'd say, 'We're not quitting,' just because it's New Brunswick. The other products are all based on hard numbers: What's the market share? What's the margin?"[2] It was affection for his province that led to Harrison's decision. He would not give up on a New Brunswick icon like fiddleheads. That said, McCain

Foods no longer produces frozen fiddleheads with the cost of procuring the raw material becoming prohibitive.

As we have seen, Harrison and Wallace decided early on to split responsibilities. Apart from separating functional responsibilities, Harrison took the lead in Europe and in the transport business, Wallace in the United States and Australia. In the early years, they shared responsibility for Canada. Turf as an issue did not surface until the late 1980s, and even then it was a side issue. For both, it had always been simply a matter of getting the job done. They each could and did easily walk into the other's area of responsibility, no questions asked. The level of trust between the brothers was very high, with each holding a kind of right of veto over major decisions.

Harrison's appreciation of Wallace comes through in his 2001 interview with his good friend James Downey, long after the breakdown with his brother had occurred. Harrison had this to say: "Wallace is a very effective executive. He knows what he's doing and he's a smart guy. He's an excellent executive, he's an excellent executive."[3] Indeed, Wallace was as successful in Australia as Harrison had been in Europe.

THE BASE WAS SOLID

By the time Harrison and Wallace turned their attention to the United States, McCain Foods was on solid ground. Harrison and Wallace had bet the farm as they entered the British market in 1965, as they had done in the early hungry days in Florenceville. They no longer needed to worry that the whole edifice might come tumbling down.

Their reach was now extensive. McCain Foods established a sales organization in Australia in 1968, then purchased and expanded a french fry plant there in 1970. It opened a new plant in Grand Falls, New Brunswick, in 1971 and a pizza plant in 1976, built a new plant in Australia in 1975 and in Portage la Prairie, Manitoba, in 1979. It purchased a second plant in the Netherlands in 1973 and a first one in Spain in 1976. It acquired a plant in Easton, Maine, in 1976 and opened a second plant in England in the same year. In 1978, it bought a third plant in the Netherlands and in 1979 opened new pizza plants in Australia and England. It purchased the Sunny Orange plant in Toronto in 1980 and opened yet another french fry plant in France in 1981.

McCain Foods continued to expand at this rate throughout the 1980s (see Appendix B for a detailed chronology of major developments at McCain Foods between 1956 and 1993).

It will be recalled that McCain Foods actually turned a profit in its first year of operation, if only of $1,822. It was the start of successive profitable years that have lasted to this day. Harrison's friendship with Bank of Nova Scotia's Cedric Ritchie served McCain Foods well. When Harrison was on the road, he always had with him a signed letter from Ritchie saying that the bank would honour a cheque for any amount signed by Harrison McCain, and the letter came in handy on many occasions. Harrison once flew to Australia to buy a business with a $15 million cheque in his pocket. The local bank refused to accept a cheque for such a large amount. Harrison produced Ritchie's letter and after a call to the Bank of Nova Scotia, the cheque was accepted. It was claimed at McCain Foods that Harrison and Wallace's financial strategy boiled down to 1-800-call-Ritchie.[4]

DOWN UNDER

On a scouting trip to Australia in 1971, when visiting the Daylesford plant with an eye to buying it, Wallace was taken aback by what he saw in the heart of the country's potato-growing region. He called Harrison: "I was in a field today; they were planting potatoes and right across the road, in another field, they were harvesting potatoes."[5] That was something inconceivable in the northern climate of Canada, Britain, and Continental Europe.

The start-up in Australia had many obstacles to overcome. McCain bought the Daylesford plant, Wallace having decided that they would have to produce frozen french fries in Australia if the firm was to compete successfully. When it had first set up its sales team in 1968, McCain had shipped its french fries from its Florenceville plant. More often than not, however, the boxes arrived in Australia badly damaged. Refrigerated ships in the 1960s lacked the capacity and sophistication to ensure that the product would always arrive thousands of miles away in an acceptable state to sell.

As had happened in other countries, growing and processing potatoes in Australia specifically for frozen french fries proved to be more difficult than Wallace had anticipated. Australia has no frost but it has few dry days in summer. Moreover, potatoes harvested at certain points in the year contain too much sugar to produce frozen french fries. The Daylesford plant had no storage facility and its production capacity was not up to McCain standards. There were still other problems: the plant had a leaky roof, which meant that it flooded whenever it rained, its effluent system did not work properly, and it could produce only 1,000 kilograms of french fries per hour, compared with 15,000 at the other modern McCain plants. One problem simply led to another.

In one of his occasional visits to Australia, Harrison met with farmers unhappy with McCain Foods' payment for their potatoes. The farmers believed that a highly profitable company like McCain should pay more than it was to the people who actually grew the potatoes, because they were struggling just to make a living. Harrison asked them, "Do you know how many french fry processors there have been in the business around the globe?" Some of the farmers responded, "Something like ten or twenty." "No," replied Harrison, "there have been ninety-five, and all but a handful are still in business."[6] Harrison's point was that the frozen french fry business was highly competitive and unless a firm was able to keep a constant eye on the input cost, the chances of surviving were very slim. Harrison had done his homework and had jotted down the information in one of his little black books.

Wallace decided that, given the drawbacks of the Daylesford plant, it was best to start afresh by building a new plant in nearby Ballarat. But here too the task was not easy. Relations with government officials were difficult and the firm building the plant went out of business in the middle of its construction. Then there were the labour unions and unhappy farmers. At least in the early years, there were also problems with meeting quality standards for its products. McCain Foods was not a local firm and it took time to gain an appreciation of how government and labour unions operated.

Wallace McCain was not one to give up. He knew that the timing was right, and he was determined to stay the course. Though later than in North America, fast food restaurants were starting to make their presence felt, always good news for the frozen food industry, as was the fact that women were joining the workforce in growing numbers, which, as elsewhere, meant families would be eating out more often.

Wallace persevered throughout the 1960s and 1970s, and he was right to do so. Australia was and remains a wealthy nation, as well as being a strong potato-growing and potato-eating country. McCain Foods now also out-produces and outsells the competition by a wide margin. It currently has several manufacturing facilities in Australia and New Zealand. In addition, Australians buy more McCain products per capita of any market in which the company operates.[7]

Anyone looking for evidence of Wallace's tenacity and substantial contribution to the growth of McCain Foods need look no further than Australia. Ian Cameron, sent from Canada to work on the Australian project, later commented, "If it had been a public company, you'd have closed here ... It would have been easier to walk away ... You had to wonder whether there was any future in it."[8] Labour problems, crippling production problems with the Daylesford plant, construction delays, and unhappy potato farmers were not easy challenges for Wallace to overcome. In addition, the final construction cost of the new plant was twice what was first envisaged. Wallace's success in Australia proved his mettle as the "excellent executive" Harrison declared him to be in his interview with James Downey.

Wallace also demonstrated his talent as a strong manager in Australia. He knew when to get involved, what issues required his attention, and what and how to delegate. He had a no-nonsense, straight-up management style. John Clements, who ran the operations in Australia, explains, "In most large companies there is a lot of politics going on. I know because I worked in two such companies before I went to McCain. People jockeyed for positions. In McCain, it was virtually non-existent."[9]

Wallace also led McCain's entry into the New Zealand market, where he too adopted the "drink the local wine" strategy. Harrison first coined the term to describe the firm's strategy when entering a new foreign market. As we will see later, the strategy was designed to pay close attention to a country's socio-economic and business circumstances. Initially, he imported frozen french fries from the firm's Ballarat plant in Australia and later introduced other products, from frozen pizzas to frozen desserts. He subsequently bought a company and built a plant in New Zealand. Within a few years, McCain Foods was able to turn a profit in both Australia and New Zealand.

Harrison consistently argued that a family-owned, privately held company was far superior to a public company, that it was, for example, invariably in a better position to look to the long term. Harrison also often argued that, unlike a public company, McCain Foods did not have to wash its dirty clothes in public.[10] To be sure, McCain Foods had plenty of dirty clothes to wash in its early years in Australia and plenty more in the early 1990s, as we will see.

EAT OR BE EATEN

Harrison and Wallace were in business to stay in business. Everywhere they went, they set out to eat the competition rather than be eaten by it. They were constantly on the lookout for businesses to acquire. They roamed the world seeking – and finding – deals. They were now also in the business of frozen pizza, frozen vegetables, and desserts. As they bought up plants from Britain, to the Netherlands, Spain, Australia, and the United States, their products were appearing on the grocery shelves in many countries.

Again, a John Clements observation: "They were always more keen on expansion than on milking the company for profits in the short term. There was tremendous willingness on the part of the two McCain brothers to spend capital and allocate resources to any new project that looked promising."[11] By the early 1980s McCain Foods was no longer the young Canadian upstart. It was now going head-to-head with large multinationals like Heinz and well-funded national firms like Edgell in Australia and Simplot Foods in the United States.

TAKING STOCK IN 1981

Harrison McCain took stock of McCain Foods' strategy in January 1981 in a memo to senior staff. The company's growth had been on an impressive trajectory from the day it was born. The decision to reinvest profits and focus on England, Continental Europe, and Australia to fuel growth was being handsomely rewarded.

Harrison reminded senior managers that the strategy had centred on three themes:

1   Expand the food business in Canada.
2   Expand the frozen french fry business internationally and add other lines soon after McCain Foods had been nationally established.
3   Expand the trucking business in Canada.

He then took stock of the company's progress, country by country. In Canada the firm's products were mostly mature, the orange juice business was new, but had strong growth potential. In Britain, Harrison saw still future growth by aggressively pushing the McCain Foods label in french fries and pizzas. He also saw potential in the orange juice business there. He argued that Continental Europe still offered "lots of growth opportunity." Germany offered "wonderful opportunities" in the retail business, and he suggested that the company should take "a giant step forward" in France by lowering prices. The goal was to quickly grab a large share of the market as soon as the Harnes plant opened. He added that reducing prices would be very effective in the short term, but "stupid over the long term." Spain's economy was in "bad shape," but the fast-food business and McCain Foods were making progress. He saw strong growth ahead for the industry in general and expected McCain Foods to ride that growth. He added that Australia was coming along quite nicely and "is developed second only to Canada."[12]

The future? Harrison called for a shift in the Canadian strategy because the current business model could not generate sufficient growth. He identified several possibilities that will come as a surprise not only to the reader, but also probably to many current McCain Foods employees and even to some of the McCain family members. He identified the oil business as holding potential and considered actually setting up shop in Calgary. He also looked at buying the Ponderosa chain of restaurants. He contemplated investing in the emerging IT sector and had this to say: "I don't think by background we can build a large data processing business, but it is a good possibility to make some big bucks in quite a short period of time, and I favour pushing it forward and possibly merging it with someone else and becoming an investor in that area."[13]

Harrison and Wallace made a run at buying Canada Packers in the late 1970s. The brothers had quietly accumulated 10.3 per cent of

Canada Packers, fuelling takeover rumours. The McLean family and associates controlled 34 per cent of the company's shares and, in a move to stop a takeover, Canada Packers quickly bought 3.5 per cent of the McLean shares.

The McLean family was strongly opposed to McCain Foods buying Canada Packers and refused to give Harrison or Wallace a seat on its board of directors. In a memo to senior staff in January 1981, Harrison wrote, "Although I believe it would be dangerous to try to finance the purchase of Canada Packers at this moment, I have no doubt but that we will do it in due course. I would be inclined to think when the investment opportunities in Europe diminish somewhat, and the cash flow in that area goes up, we could easily handle this acquisition because our earnings growth is much faster than theirs. Three to five years from now, we will be able to handle it safely."[14]

The McLean family stood firm and Harrison and Wallace decided, with no forewarning to Canada Packers, to sell their shares, which they did, for $53.6 million or 3.5 times what they had paid.

Harrison's memo, particularly his interest in investing in oil and the IT sector, suggests that he was not altogether willing to see McCain Foods stick to its knitting. Again, Harrison and Wallace were at heart entrepreneurs and risk-takers. But they also did their homework and had every possible acquisition carefully reviewed. McCain turned down and continues to turn down more deals than it accepts. In one of his memos, Harrison said that as a good rule of thumb, McCain Foods should turn down nine deals for every one it decides to pursue.

In the end, however, McCain Foods maintained a conservative approach by staying "focussed on the business it understands."[15] It continued to buy frozen vegetable plants and a frozen dinner business in Australia, orange juice plants, frozen pizza operations, and dozens of frozen french fries plants around the world (see Appendix B). They were able to turn a profit within a year or two everywhere they went.

Harrison and Wallace knew that the task of building what looked to become a worldwide empire would never be completed until they tackled the big market south of the border. Competition in the United States, however, would be unlike anywhere else. Here, McCain would not be creating a new market, but going head-to-head in a relatively mature one. For the first time they would be taking on large, well-resourced, and well-staffed firms that had been in the business for some forty years.

Harrison concluded his January 1981 review by suggesting that he and Wallace should spend still more time on the road. The goal was less to look at how the various plants and McCain organizations were operating and more to scout out possible acquisitions. He wrote, "We will have to spend more time looking, asking questions, probing, in Toronto, Alberta and British Columbia. We should spend more time in Toronto, buying more lunches, make more contacts in the financial and industrial communities." He also wrote that the time had come to move aggressively into the United States market.

GOING DOWN THE ROAD TO THE UNITED STATES

Harrison concluded his strategy memo by writing that the company should pursue "same strategy as present" in both Britain and Europe, with only some tweaking in Australia and Canada to expand activities. The United States? He wrote, "I think we should try to find another food company in the US that is profitable, pay the top price, and move it into our business. I think First Boston Corporation could probably find us the company."

The McCain brothers knew better than anyone that they could not be the biggest frozen french-fries producers in the world without getting a good foothold in the American market. The United States was home to the original fast-food restaurants, from McDonald's and Kentucky Fried Chicken, to Burger King and Wendy's. Tempting – but it was also home to large and well-established frozen food firms like Simplot, Lamb Weston, and Ore-Ida. McCain Foods, meanwhile, had been in the American market on a modest scale since 1969, exporting from its Florenceville plant.

McCain bought a small frozen french fry plant in Washburn, Maine, in 1975 and another the following year in Easton, Maine – both within easy driving distance of Florenceville. This squared nicely with the company's strategy: move into the United States market cautiously. More to the point, the objective was to move into the market first as a regional player. Starting in Maine had two advantages: it was close to home and the big American producers were all located in the western states. McCain could pursue the large northeast market and take advantage of lower shipping costs. Initially at least, it focused on private-label business from the region's supermarket chains rather than promoting its own McCain label.[16]

McCain later bought another plant in Presque Isle, Maine, this time from the large American company J.R. Simplot. McCain had, three years earlier, acquired yet another plant in Maine. In all cases, it modernized and upgraded the plants, and later closed the Washburn plant. McCain Foods was now an important player in the frozen food industry in the northeast region.

Harrison and Wallace's appetites, however, would not be so easily satisfied. The northeast market was only a slice of the highly competitive frozen french fry American market. Still, United States operations were turning a profit, year after year. In 1981 McCain Foods almost doubled its sales from the previous year, going from $14.5 million to $27 million. However, the ratio represented less than 4 per cent of global sales and less than 2 per cent of total sales and profit. Eight years later, in 1989, the United States still accounted for only 17 per cent of McCain sales (compared with 35 per cent in Canada, 41 per cent in Europe, and 7 per cent in the Australian market), while profits were even more modest as a percentage of total profit (4.5 per cent in the United States, 41 per cent in Canada, 46.5 per cent in Europe, and 8 per cent in Australia).[17]

It is important to stress once again that Harrison and Wallace remained hesitant about engaging in open competition with large American firms on their home turf. McCain's tried-and-true formula would not be so easily applied in the United States. To be sure, having established a beachhead in Maine was the easy part. The strategy to "drink the local wine," which had been critical to the success of McCain Foods in foreign countries, would not be so easily pursued in the United States. Harrison McCain would later recommend this strategy to those wishing to expand abroad, as he explained to business students in a speech to the Richard Ivey School of Business:

· Study and grasp local market conditions for our products and our raw materials, especially potatoes.
· Engage energetic local managers.

- Develop local sales and marketing channels for McCain products.
- Understand the local practice of potato culture by observing and listening before prescribing and acting.[18]

To "drink the local wine" worked better in an immature market than in a mature one like the United States, which is in reality a collection of several regional markets. A marketing strategy for the southeastern states, for example, needs to be different in tone, message, and in some instances products from the California or the Midwest market. Put differently, creating and keeping customers in the United States requires tailoring marketing strategies to different regions. While the strategy was well suited to Europe and Australia, it was less so for a series of American regional markets.[19] It also explains in part why McCain first concentrated on acquiring existing businesses in the United States.

The McCain brothers felt that there was more than one way to jump feet first into the American market. It could, for instance, diversify its stock of products, rather than focusing exclusively on frozen french fries, thus creating a stronger presence in the regional markets. McCain Foods had already successfully moved into the orange juice market in Canada. Why not try the same route in the United States?

The break came when Wallace received a telephone call in October 1985 from an acquaintance telling him that Bodine, a Chicago-based orange juice company, was about to be sold to ConAgra, the large Nebraska-based multi-brand, multinational food company. George McClure, the trusted senior advisor and manager at McCain Foods, took a quick look at Bodine and liked what he saw.

However, time was tight and if McCain Foods was interested, it had to move fast. The sale to ConAgra was to close on 31 October, 1985. Wallace called Bodine, urging its senior executives not to sign off on the sale until he could meet with them. Wallace, however, was already committed to a business trip to Australia and he asked Harrison if he could go to Chicago to negotiate a deal with Bodine.

Harrison was soon off to Chicago with McClure and his senior legal advisor, determined to acquire Bodine for McCain Foods. There were some unsettling developments, however, including a recent and sudden sharp drop in both revenues and profits. There was no time to undertake due diligence, given that Bodine was about to be sold in a few days to a competitor. Harrison bargained hard, as he was wont to do, and he struck a deal to buy Bodine for $7,225,000 at the last hour on the last day, 31 October 1985. He celebrated by opening a bottle of Canadian Club and calling Wallace to tell him, "You own a juice factory."[20]

Within a few weeks, it became clear that something was fundamentally flawed with Bodine. The company was losing money to a greater extent than had been projected, suggesting that McCain Foods had paid an inflated price for Bodine. But the news would soon get much worse. The United States Food and Drug administration was putting together evidence to charge senior Bodine officials with fraud. The FDA brought nineteen charges against them for adulterating food and mislabelling products. Specifically, their "pure" orange juice contained distilled water, beet sugar, and grapefruit juice.

Three senior Bodine officials pleaded guilty; one was sentenced to thirty months in prison and all three had to pay hefty fines.[21] Both Harrison and Wallace reacted strongly to the news. Both were hardnosed businessmen but both were, as Donald Trafford said of Harrison, "honest as the day is long." They were rooted in Florenceville values, and honesty and integrity stood high on the list of moral attributes. Bob Crossman, who worked closely in sales with Harrison in the late 1960s, told me that one of Harrison's defining characteristics was his integrity. He said that Harrison once told him, "Do not worry about signing a piece of paper. There is a lawyer somewhere in the world who will successfully defend you in any court. Don't worry about that. However, if you cannot look another man square in the eyes, shake his hand, and give him your word and then stick to it, then you are no good, just no good and no good to anyone." Crossman added, "Harrison believed every word of what he said and I believed him."

The McCain brothers would never adulterate a product, as Bodine had done, under any circumstances. Given the dire developments, they looked for ways not to pay what they still owed to Bodine, some $3.6 million. They hired an accountancy firm and retained lawyers to mount a case. They were certain that they were on solid ground and took the former Bodine owners to litigation. Surprisingly, the Chicago jury ruled in favour of the former owners, no matter the prison sentence and the fines. Wallace shot back when told of the verdict, "I can't believe that the criminal won."[22]

Back at the plant, Wallace made sure that henceforth only pure orange juice was produced. With Harrison's blessing, he appointed his son Michael to turn things around at Bodine, and slowly it was able to regain the confidence of retailers. McCain Citrus also invested in five new plants in California, New Jersey, New York, and Massachusetts. Harold Doucet, a long-time McCain Foods manager, explained, "By buying other companies and combining them, we got certain synergies. We kept working it and working it. In the end, we were good operators because we employed the high-volume, low-cost discipline that had made the French fry business successful."[23] In 2000, McCain Foods sold its United States juice business to a group of venture capitalists and turned a handsome profit.[24]

FRENCH FRIES STILL THE THING

When Harrison and Wallace decided the time had arrived to crack the American market beyond the northeast states, they first bought a plant in Othello, smack in the middle of the rich potato-growing area of eastern Washington State. Within months, they invested $35 million to modernize and expand it. Good chunks of its sales were from the lower-profit private label segments of the market. The McCain brand was still not well known outside of the northeast and it scarcely posed a threat to the big American frozen food firms. This was, of course, consistent with Harrison and Wallace's intention that McCain Foods should move cautiously into the United States market.[25]

In the meantime, elsewhere, McCain Foods was growing at an impressive rate. It reported sales of over $1 billion in 1985, and by 1988 sales topped $1.5 billion. There were some forty production facilities in eight countries producing not only frozen french fries, but also frozen green vegetables, desserts, pizzas, juices and beverages, oven meals, entrees, and cheese.[26] It now had the financial muscle to move into any new markets, including the United States, and it did not have to bet the farm to do so.

Harrison and Wallace continued to aggressively pursue large institutional customers throughout North America, targeting fast-food restaurants. McDonald's, given its pre-eminence, was an important potential client. Its high profile was such that both Harrison and

Wallace paid a visit to a senior McDonald's buyer, but by all accounts, the meeting did not go well: McDonald's was interested enough that its officials asked to tour the McCain Florenceville plant where the french fries were being produced, and Harrison's response, as always, was to the point: "Tell us what you want and we will produce it. We know how to make French fries and we don't need you guys to tour our plant."[27]

Harrison was already well briefed on McDonald's purchasing strategy. As he explained in a memo to senior staff, McDonald's purchasing agents were known for "always complaining and threatening about quality" and for "pitting one plant against another on quality and on the buying price." McDonald's also attached substantial importance to "process" and to the "natural look" of their french fries. They asked producers to incorporate special equipment in their production process because they insisted that it was not possible to do "an ordinary steam blanch and make the product they require." On pricing, Harrison discovered that the deal McDonald's had with large American frozen food firms was cost plus 12 per cent and by cost they meant "factory door cost plus general and administrative expenses."[28] He also discovered that once MacDonald's became a client, it tended to remain a loyal client.

Initially, Harrison and senior McDonald's purchasing agents stuck to their guns. McDonald's insisting on touring the plant and Harrison insisting that they would not. In time, thanks to the diplomatic intervention of Mac McCarthy in Britain and others in North America, including several senior McCain Foods executives, McCain and McDonald's eventually developed a strong partnership, McCain now supplies frozen french fries in McDonald's restaurants in some sixty-five countries, including the United States, and is the largest producer of MacFries.

BATTLING THE IRVINGS

Prince Edward Island is known for *Anne of Green Gables*, its red earth, and its large potato crop. Local food processors began experimenting with freezing fruits and vegetables as early as 1950. C.M. McLean began freezing blueberries there in the early 1950s and expanded to

Nova Scotia in 1961, building a frozen blueberry plant in Springhill and later another in Prince Edward Island.

However, C.M. McLean had serious health problems and in the mid-1960s his son Mitch, also called C.M. McLean, left Irving Oil to work in the family business. The plants expanded into the frozen french fry business, but they struggled for years.

K.C. Irving lent C.M. McLean money to keep the business afloat, but by the mid-to-late 1970s it became clear that the firm would have to be sold or go bankrupt. Mitch McLean offered to sell the plant to McCain Foods, but Harrison and Wallace turned the offer down. As Wallace explained, "We thought no one would buy the plant because it had almost gone broke three times."[29] The Irvings, however, took over the plant, if only because C.M. McLean could not repay the loan they had made as well as meet its bank obligations. K.C. Irving was not about to let the business go bankrupt and lose his investment. K.C.'s eldest son, J.K. Irving, later said that the family had been involved with the business in some capacity since 1973.[30]

The Irvings' decision to enter the frozen french fries business sent shockwaves through McCain Foods head office in Florenceville. Harrison and Wallace knew, better than anyone, how K.C. Irving ran businesses and what a tough competitor he could be. McCain would never go into the oil, shipbuilding, and forestry business, so why, they wondered, should Irving want to stray onto their turf? Indeed, McCain Foods had bought its oil from Irving from the day it opened its first plant in Florenceville, at times negotiating with Irving Oil after it had received more generous offers from others in the gas and oil sector. Day and Ross similarly bought its gas and diesel fuel from Irving Oil. The McCain–Irving relationship quickly soured, however, when Harrison retaliated to the threat to McCain's hold on the french fry business by switching both firms to Petro Canada.

The media had a field day with the story, referring to the feuding giants as the "Hatfields and McCoys."[31] One of the first marketing decisions that the Irvings had to take was how to brand their frozen french fries. Harrison maintains that both K.C. and his son J.K. Irving were at the meeting when "McLean" was chosen. Later, the Irvings marketing people told them to drop "McLean" because it was doing "McCain more good than McLean."[32] Very shortly, the rebranded "Cavendish" appeared on the market.

It soon became clear that the Irvings would not be satisfied with a single frozen french fry plant in Prince Edward Island, when they announced plans to build a "super" $85-million plant on the island. Irving also hoped for generous subsidies from both senior levels of government, including $40 million from the federal government alone. As it happened, the Summerside air base, which had been a major employer in Prince Edward Island, was about to close and both the federal and provincial governments were at the time aggressively searching for a major, private sector project that would help to replace the jobs that would be lost on the island. Irving, through Cavendish, responded to the call with a proposal that would create hundreds of jobs and new demands for Prince Edward Island potatoes.

Irving also bought land next to the McCain Grand Falls plant with the intention of building another frozen french fries plant there. It made plans to clear land in northern New Brunswick in the Edmundston–Saint-Quentin area, to grow potatoes to supply the proposed plant. Irving also made it clear that it would be applying for government assistance from both the federal and provincial governments to build the Grand Falls plant.

Harrison and Wallace would not sit idle and let their old mentor take over their business on their own turf. Harrison hired Simon Reisman, the former federal deputy minister of finance and Canada's lead negotiator in the Canada-US Free Trade Agreement negotiations, to make a public policy case against the large government subsidies Irving was hoping to receive. Reisman was quick off the mark, declaring that such a subsidy "is insane" and added that it would be "seen in the US as the most blatant kind of bad trade practice."[33] Reisman warned the Canadian government that the United States would react badly and introduce countervailing measures.

Responding to an inspired suggestion from a senior federal official, Harrison and Wallace announced in late January 1990 that they would build a new frozen french fry plant in the town of Borden, Prince Edward Island, without government assistance if the provincial and the federal governments dropped negotiations with Cavendish to build its super frozen french fry plant. The strategy worked and, with great fanfare, McCain Foods let it be known that their project would involve no government assistance. It did, however, accept government assistance to build a water-treatment facility.

The McCain brothers won the battle. Cavendish cancelled its plans to build the super plant in Prince Edward Island and a new plant in Grand Falls. Today, a big-stop Irving service station sits not far from the land where Irving had planned to build its Grand Falls plant.

The McCains and Irvings, however, never stopped respecting one another, both sides have told me. They regarded the spat as "strictly" business and both families continued to socialize with one another. After hiatus of three or four years, the two families started to sell and buy from one another once again. As Wallace explained, "It wasn't a personal feud, it was business. It could have been anybody,"[34] and Harrison said, "It was tough, real tough for a while. But everybody got over it. No problem, no problem." New Brunswick is a small province and the "Hatfields and McCoys" knew how to separate business from friendship.

LOOKING BACK

Harrison and Wallace had a distinct management style. They showed the way by out-working everyone, by carefully hiring competent managers, and by motivating them. Harrison, for one, attached much importance to measuring performance. He often said that you could not manage what you could not measure. And measure, he did. It is worth repeating his views on measurement:

> The major component of that logical, purposeful pursuit of profit is appropriate measurement. Nearly every McCain office has a slogan posted saying, "If you can't measure it, you can't manage it." We believe that, and we follow it. All of us talk about our problems in general terms. In fact, the exact measurement of those factors generally point to an improved situation. We measure and we compare the measurements: factory-with-factory, company-with-company, McCain vs. the competition, the cost of raw products, money, labour and packaging – and on and on. In a complex operation, with comparison, it is much easier to find the upper limit of the

potential that can be achieved. Bluntly, we improve the profitability of nearly every company we buy in the first year by installing an effective management information system that lets the executives decide what to do about the problems that the system points up. Most companies that we acquire think they have a good information system. We know they do not.[35]

Harrison's little black books measured everything that could be measured, from the performance of senior executives to plant productivity.

By 1990, McCain Foods had become a juggernaut in the frozen french fry world. I toured the Florenceville plant in 2012 and asked, "Is anyone working here?" The plant is now highly automated. Farmers still deliver their loads of potatoes. From there they are moved by conveyor belts to an inspection booth staffed by two people. They are then washed, cut, sorted, frozen, and packed in bags and boxes with a minimum of workers. It's all a far cry from the first Florenceville plant in the 1950s, designed by the eccentric genius Olof Pierson. When Pierson died in 1993, his passing was noted around the world. Apart from his many subsequent accomplishments, he was universally hailed as the inventor of the frozen french fry. Harrison reminisced: "It's all true. I remember O.P. Pierson as a very kindly man, very bright, not quick to decide things. Wallace and I were in a great hurry to get things done, but he had the right ideas in the end. He had a very inventive mind. The frozen french fry was O.P. Pierson's idea. Much of the equipment to make them couldn't be bought commercially, so he built the individual machines to get the work done."[36]

CRACKS ARE APPEARING

By the late 1980s, despite the success of the business, cracks were starting to show in the relationship between Harrison and Wallace. They both tended to put governance on the back burner because business always took precedence. Harrison summed up the brothers' approach to governance: "There aren't many occasions where our top 20 fellows feel they can't make the decision except for certain areas. For example, only my brother and I borrow money. We can't have 20 fellows borrowing money. Number two: in our group you can't hire or fire a director – and there's a director for every one of our companies – unless my brother and I agree. That's important. Loyalty is a two-way street. You've got to give it if you're going to get it."[37]

For Harrison and Wallace, boards of directors were for public companies, not for family-run enterprises. Harrison once said that he could only recall the board of McCain Foods "meeting two times in twenty-six years, maybe three. I don't think I was at any of them."[38] He and Wallace looked after all decisions and consulted the other brothers only when the need arose. Harrison and Wallace ran McCain Foods, end of story.

Time and the next generation of McCains would catch up with Harrison and Wallace. Who would take over as chief executive officer? Who would run McCain Foods after they were gone? Who would manage the interests of the four families when Harrison and Wallace were no longer at the helm? These questions go to the core of corporate governance in any family business, and by the mid- to late 1980s, they were crying out for attention from the McCains.

Succession problems are too often the Achilles heel of family-owned businesses, and Harrison was concerned about looming conflict, as is evident from his personal papers, which, starting in 1987, contain many newspaper and magazine articles on souring relationships in family-owned businesses. Indeed, as early as 1985, he knew that trouble was brewing in his own family business.[39]

Harrison watched as a number of high-profile family businesses in Canada started to unravel. It became clear that the third generation of the Billes family would not be running Canadian Tire. The family-run Steinberg food empire started to run into problems when Sam Steinberg appointed his son-in-law to take over. Harold Ballard's family business, the Toronto Maple Leaf hockey team, did not survive deep family divisions. Charles Bronfman transferred assets to his private holding company simply to avoid family conflicts. He explained, "Most wealthy families by the second or third generation start quarrelling. Unfortunately, it would seem that the more wealth people have, the more there is to argue about, and instead of being content to be in that very fortunate position, they start squabbling."[40]

Harrison and Wallace had a truly remarkable ability to manage complex business issues and operations: they were the leading entrepreneurs of their generation in Canada. It was another matter and altogether more difficult to manage the overlap between family and business than to grow a global empire.

The statistics are grim. Although data vary somewhat by country, one keen observer of family business and leadership, reports that "only three out of ten family firms make it through the second generation and only one in ten through the third."[41] The most difficult moment in managing a family business is when there is a transition or a planned transition from one leader or, in the case of McCain Foods, from two leaders, to the next generation.

8

Governance: Someone Else's Problem

As we have seen, for twenty-five years governance was not on the radar screen for Harrison and Wallace, nor did there seem to be any reason why it should be. This attitude, as we have also seen, is not uncommon in family-owned businesses, especially in the first generation. The story has recently become quite different, however, for publicly traded firms.

The Sarbanes-Oxley Act of 2002 forced publicly traded firms in the United States to comply with new corporate governance and transparency requirements.[1] Canada and many other countries were soon to follow.[2]

The act came in response to a series of scandals on both sides of the border, involving Bre-X, Cinar Corporation, Livent, Enron, and WorldCom, among others. Outright fraud, cases of flagrant conflict of interest at senior levels, abuse of perks by senior management, and gross mismanagement led to a crisis of confidence among shareholders. The purpose of the act was to strengthen the role of shareholders in their dealings with management.

The reforms set in motion by the Sarbanes-Oxley Act led to an overhaul of corporate governance throughout the Western world. Gone are the days when the president-CEO of a public company could, at the stroke of a pen, add chairman of the board to his title and run the firm with an iron fist, no questions asked. James Gillies, quoting the chair of the Central Steel Corporation, compared the value of directors of companies until the 1990s to "parsley on fish – decorative but useless."[3] Family business and private firms, meanwhile, were largely untouched by the reform movement. They were and are private firms of no concern to anyone but the family members as shareholders. Harrison put it in a nutshell when he told a journalist, "My business is none of your business." Yet family-owned businesses are encumbered with a unique challenge: how to ensure the long-term success of the firm while also keeping family peace. Indeed, the question could easily be reworded: how to manage the family? Yet, as the Organisation for Economic Cooperation and Development (OECD) maintains, "Family run firms tend to believe that principles of good governance do not really concern them."[4]

A growing number of family firms, however, have established advisory boards, which are quite different from boards of directors in that, as their name implies, they provide advice, not governance. They are selected by owners rather than elected. Advisory boards hold a number of advantages for owner-entrepreneurs: they can assist them in looking to the long term and outside the inner circle of family members and managers, and they can also warn of trouble ahead and bring a fresh perspective to succession planning and to emotionally charged family-related issues.[5] Harrison and Wallace did not establish an advisory board.

LOYALTY TO THE BUSINESS

Founder-entrepreneurs are a special breed and Harrison and Wallace were archetypical founder-entrepreneurs: studies have found that the kind of people attracted to this high-risk, high-adrenaline life "do not like to be subjected to control" and "have great difficulty taking direction from others." More to the point, "they dislike structures, they like to be independent."[6] That is, of course, why they strike out on their own. Governance and management were, at McCain Foods, dominated by Harrison and Wallace. The system worked well because the brothers worked well together. There was remarkably little tension between them as they concentrated on building the business.

John Ward outlines three stages that a family business undergoes: (1) the founders as controlling owners, (2) the sibling partnership, and (3) the cousin confederation.[7] In the first stage, corporate governance is far from the minds of the founders-entrepreneurs simply because they control all the decision-making levers. Their energy is devoted to growing the business, succession issues are still years down the road, and the founders-entrepreneurs are firmly in the saddle. If there is any tension, it is with the business competition, not among family members.

The dynamics change as family-owned businesses move into stages two and three. Founders-entrepreneurs never find it easy to let go. For one thing, they must come to terms with their own mortality or when to take their leave. For another, they have to face the question of who will take over, which is never an easy question to answer when more than one family member aspires to the job.

NOT IN MY LIFETIME

Fred D. Tannenbaum tells the story of a founder-entrepreneur who dies and asks God when was there a family-owned business that was governed in compliance with the rules of good corporate governance? God ponders the question and answers, "Not in my lifetime."[8]

No doubt succession planning is one of the most insidious problems in family-owned businesses. Manfred Kets de Vries writes, "Choosing a successor shatters the fiction that all children (or cousins) are equal. Singling someone out may lead to discord." He adds that in many instances, "family logic often overrules business reason,"[9] and when that happens, something fundamental comes undone. Business reason built the business and if it is cast aside, then trust will not be far behind.

As discussed previously, family-controlled firms offer a number of advantages over publicly traded companies. It is easier for them to take the long view, they enjoy greater independence of action, and they have a greater tendency to plow profits back into the company, as has been the case with McCain Foods. They are also less bureaucratic and impersonal and they do not have to attend to as many transparency and reporting requirements as publicly traded firms do.[10]

But there are also disadvantages, with nepotism and interfamily squabbling being perhaps paramount, both of which have the potential of creating a full-blown succession drama.[11] With publicly traded firms, a chief function of the board of directors is to manage succession planning, but there is no such body to keep the temperature down with private firms.

In the spring of 1997 Raymond Garneau, the long-serving chair of the board and president-CEO of Industrial-Alliance, Canada's fifth largest insurance company, invited me to sit on the company's board of directors. I asked, "What do you expect from me? What would be my role, given that I know precious little about the life insurance business?" His response: "I wish some of the other members of the board would ask me the same question. There may come a point when you and other members of the board will have to decide to fire me. Essentially, your role boils down to this: you and the other board members will have to decide whether I stay or go or, if I go, who takes over."

What Garneau was seeking were directors who would be dispassionate, even disinterested in him as an individual. Their task was to assess his performance as objectively as possible on behalf of shareholders. Should we decide that he was no longer up to the job, the board would strike a committee of its members to select a successor. The committee would then seek out the most qualified individual and make a recommendation to the full board. In some instances, the committee would present a short list of highly qualified individuals. This is a straightforward process and it works well most of the time.

Things are never this simple for family-owned firms. It is difficult, even impossible, for family members to be dispassionate, disinterested about other family members. When governance and succession first appeared on the horizon, Harrison and Wallace simply put the issue aside because neither ranked it very high on their to-do list.

As late as 1981 the brothers were too busy to think about succession planning, and besides, neither one had any intention of leaving any time soon. The children were still young and none of them would be in the picture for years. It was taken for granted between the brothers that if one of them were to die, the other would take over. There was just one hypothetical disaster that concerned them at this time: what if both were to die in the same accident?

Harrison and Wallace easily reached an agreement on this remote possibility and, without informing anyone in their families or at McCain Foods, they prepared a document and put it in a sealed

envelope that was to be opened only if they both died at the same
moment.

March 31, 1981
TO WHOM IT MAY CONCERN

In the unlikely event that Wallace McCain and Harrison McCain
are killed simultaneously, we desire and recommend the following
action be taken by our legal successors and supported by our
Management Group.

A Member of the Wallace McCain family and the Harrison
McCain family and the Robert McCain family are to be promptly
elected to the Board of Directors. We would hope that each of those
families can individually agree on a Board Member to represent the
particular family. Presumably, Andrew McCain will be a serving
Director, but if for any reason he is not, a member of his family is
to be made a Director.

C.M.A. McCarthy is to be made Chairman, President and CEO
of McCain Foods Limited. He will commute from the UK to
Canada.

Within 12 months, a President is to be appointed, at which
time Mac McCarthy would remain as Chairman and CEO, but
the President would take over whatever share of responsibilities
McCarthy and the Board want handed to him.

After an additional 12 months, a decision is to be made by the
Directors as to whether or not Charles McCarthy is to remain
as Chairman and CEO, or only as Chairman, with the President
becoming the CEO. If the Directors decide that neither of these
moves is in the best interest of the company, they are free to make
any change they see fit.

H. Harrison McCain
G.W.F. McCain

It is interesting that Mac McCarthy, a close friend and early business associate of Harrison – but an outsider – was to assume control
of the company if the two brothers did in fact die together. Wallace at

the time was quite content with this solution. Things, however, would begin to unravel a few years down the road.

THE FAMILY

Andrew and Laura McCain had six children: two daughters and four sons. As we saw earlier, only the four sons became shareholders in McCain Foods. Robert McCain passed away in June 1977, Andrew in October 1984, Harrison in March 2004, and Wallace in May 2011. Andrew had six children: two boys, Allison and Stephen, and four daughters, Kathryn, Linda, Margie, and Nancy. Robert had two boys, Andrew and Kirk, and two daughters, Beth and Mary. Wallace had two sons, Michael and Scott, and two daughters, Martha and Eleanor. Harrison had two sons, Mark and Peter, and three daughters, Ann, Laura, and Gillian.

The second generation, as children, would naturally have taken for granted that Harrison and Wallace were in charge of McCain Foods, if they paid any attention to the firm at all. As they got older and attended school and university, some worked at summer jobs at McCain Foods. Indeed, later on, not all of them were interested in joining the company.

When the children arrived on the scene, they would learn that the four brothers held common shares roughly in the percentage proportions of 33/33/17/17. It will be recalled that when Harrison's brother-in-law John C. McNair incorporated McCain Foods, he included a provision establishing a board of directors as required by statute: the four brothers and their brother-in-law, Jed Sutherland, were named directors. It was agreed that the board – operating company (OPCO) – would have an odd number to break a tie, if necessary. There was no need for a tie-breaker, however, because the board rarely met. To be sure, Bob and Andrew were often consulted, but informally. All four lived in Florenceville and all were in the potato business. McCain Produce supplied McCain Foods with potato seeds and harvesting equipment. It was an amicable family arrangement.

Harrison resolved any issue that would normally require a board decision. For example, when Robert died in 1977, there were tax implications for his family, and his death created new shareholders for McCain Foods. Harrison led negotiations on behalf of the company with lawyers and accountants to declare a special dividend to enable Robert's family to meet capital gains tax. Once the matter was resolved, lawyers recommended to Harrison that a directors' and shareholders' meeting of McCain Foods be held "to authorize" the action. The board and shareholders simply did as they were told. Harrison was always consistent on one point: if someone in the family needed or had to sell shares, then the company's treasury would buy them. McCain Foods was a family business and shares stayed within it.

New Brunswick Justice Ronald Stevenson, in his April 1994 arbitration report concerning the dispute between the brothers, writes that the OPCO "board seldom met," confirming Harrison's claim. He adds, "Harrison McCain and Wallace McCain made all operational and strategic decisions and communicated those decisions to the other directors. OPCO's minute book shows that few matters of substance were discussed at formal meetings. Most of the minutes are standard formal minutes of annual meetings ... many of those meetings were not in fact held, the necessary minutes were prepared and circulated for signing by the directors or shareholders. The copies in evidence suggest that the signatures were not always obtained."[12] When Robert died in 1977, he was replaced by Roger Wilson, the firm's corporate counsel, and when, in 1984, Andrew also died, he was replaced by Mac McCarthy. This replacement role, however, was limited to rubber-stamping whatever Harrison and Wallace agreed needed to be done.

A new board – the holding company (HOLDCO) – was established in 1984, just months before Andrew's death. Harrison explained that it was just "for tax reasons. I don't really know what the tax reasons were but there was some kind of tax advantage for us."[13] The same OPCO directors were appointed to the new HOLDCO board – Harrison and Wallace McCain, Andrew McCain, brother-in-law Jed Sutherland, and Roger Wilson. When Andrew died later that year, Mac McCarthy was also named a director of this board.

At first, HOLDCO had no more say in the operations of McCain Foods than had OPCO. But things would change. Robert and Andrew's children had come of age and they wanted a window on the business so as to keep an eye on their investments. McCain Foods was now into the second and third stages of John Ward's three stages of family business.

First, Robert's children, and then Andrew's, began asking for a seat on the board of directors. Robert's son Andrew, with his mother and sisters, wrote to Harrison that many things had changed since Robert's death in 1977: "We feel that our ability to contribute to the board has developed. This is the time when we … should have direct input to the crucial issues facing the company. Perhaps our viewpoint will assist in devising the most appropriate structure. In any event, our family should have a choice, as it is our investment which will be affected."[14]

Harrison agreed. He wrote in a memo to Wallace as early as 17 September 1984, "Slowly but positively, the next generation of shareholders must be made aware of what the company is doing and what its prospects and problems are. In that regard, a couple of years ago I started a monthly briefing session for my nephews resident of Florenceville so they could get an explanation of those factors of the company's operations that are important. I presume that is some value to them. I now think we should take another step. I suggest that you, Andrew and I each propose one of our children as a Director of McCain Foods."[15]

A year later, Harrison wrote in a note, "Our family shareholders will have their entire fortune involved in the company and they have a right to participate in an effective functioning Board of Directors in the *major* decisions affecting the company's future. I note that some members of the Robert McCain family began attending the annual meetings of OPCO in 1981 and the annual HOLDCO shareholders meetings from the time of its incorporation in 1984. Some members of the Andrew H. McCain family, meanwhile, began attending in 1986."[16] The cousins were now forcing the issue – they wanted a seat at the table.

A two-tier board at McCain Foods was born, which would in time become highly controversial. It shifted some of the power away from Harrison and Wallace towards all shareholders. HOLDCO, the shareholders' board, would be composed of representatives of the four families and only one outsider, George McClure, the firm's vice-president. The board would consist of two representatives from Harrison's family, two from Wallace's, and one each from Andrew's and Robert's families. A new, more formal decision-making process was set in motion, which would give the shareholders a say in some decisions that in the past belonged only to Harrison and Wallace, notably when deciding on acquisitions and dividends.

As we will see in the next chapter, Wallace consistently favoured a single board made up of himself and Harrison, four other McCains representing the families, and four outsiders. Wallace was concerned about placing too much power in the hands of the second generation of McCains. Harrison, however, preferred a two-tier board, with the shareholders – or the family board – holding effective power.

THE NEXT GENERATION

Sons, daughters, nephews, and nieces were coming of age by the mid-1980s. The boys, in line with family tradition, would find opportunities with McCain Foods, the girls less so. By the 1980s, six members of the second generation of the McCain family, all males, were employed at McCain Foods. Allison McCain, Andrew's son, had worked in Australia but was now manufacturing director in England. Harrison, as early as 1982, in a memo to Wallace, identified Allison as a potential president of the firm. Allison's brother Stephen became vice-president of operations at McCain Produce Inc., which became part of McCain Foods after his father died.

Harrison's two sons were also employed with McCain Foods. Mark was a sales representative early in his career, then left the firm, only to return in 1990 as a business and investment analyst. Peter also began as a sales representative but left to work towards an MBA, which he obtained in 1987. He then returned to work in financing and marketing and also as executive assistant to his father. He was appointed in 1990 vice-president of export sales.

Scott McCain, Wallace's son, worked first as a production trainee in Canada and England and then began climbing the management ladder. He worked as foreman, supervisor, and production manager in Florenceville. He later was appointed vice-president of cheese operations in Ontario and then manager of the Grand Falls operations. Later still, he became vice-president of operations responsible for some factories as well as human resources and distribution.

Michael McCain, Wallace's second son, went to work with the firm fresh out of university. He worked in retail in Ontario and in marketing and management information in Florenceville. With Harrison's blessing, he was later appointed president of McCain Citrus in Chicago.[17]

He reported to his father who had overall responsibility for the firm's US operations.

Family considerations were fast catching up to business ones. Harrison and Wallace, starting in the mid-1980s, began to exchange a series of memos on board composition and succession planning. The quick telephone chat or a late afternoon discussion over a drink of Scotch were being replaced by the written memo, a sure sign that trouble was brewing.

Harrison saw first-hand the problems that can arise in a family-run business on a visit to Florida in March 1986. He had gone to meet with Lykes, a family firm with large landholdings and involved in businesses from frozen orange juice to banking. Harrison was interested in purchasing the frozen orange juice segment. He wrote to Wallace to say that, though the family had not been pricing shares in the company realistically in the past, they were planning to start pricing it properly and also to sell some shares. Harrison told Wallace, "All the troubles came from either the in-laws – either husband or wife – and the divorcees, which they have to buy out." There was no governance structure at Lykes to address the problem and so selling shares appeared to be the only viable solution.

As for the McCains, Wallace continued to prefer a single board while Harrison supported the two-tier board. Wallace wanted a McCain to take over one day while Harrison felt it important to get the most qualified individual, not necessarily a McCain. Harrison jotted down his thoughts on the issue in late 1985 in a memo to file. He feared that conflicts would inevitably surface in the next generation between those McCains who would become senior executives and those who would decide to remain non-executive shareholders. In a note to himself before circulating it to others he wrote "If, for example, one of Wallace's boys is made Chief Executive and makes his brother second in command, and they control the company and treat my kids as 'country cousins' who are supposed to be 'in the dark' about the company's business, and not in a position to understand the company's problems or to gauge how well the management is doing, *I am dissatisfied.* Likewise, if Allison, the most experienced member of the next generation, has the same role and he decides he doesn't need Wallace's boys in any area of high responsibility, *is Wallace satisfied?* I doubt it." He added,

"In summary, I am trying to point out that the company belongs to the shareholders of the next generation – not the Chief Executives – and we should deal with that problem now, and if we can't deal with it now, we will haemorrhage when we deal with it a few years from now."[18] He would be proven right.

Harrison and Wallace continued to exchange memos between themselves and later between their lawyers from the mid-1980s until the matter went before Justice Stevenson for arbitration. A number of possible solutions were advanced to resolve both the board's situation and the succession. On more than one occasion, it appeared that a solution was at hand.

A new board structure was mooted and at one time it looked as if Harrison and Wallace had agreed on its composition. Harrison even, albeit briefly, considered how to make a one-board structure work. No agreement was reached, however. Early on, Wallace had written to say that he was willing to accept the two-tier board system with some modifications. As we will see in the next chapter, that did not work out either.

IT'S ABOUT THE SUCCESSION

The succession issue was crucially tied to the unresolved issue of the board structure. Wallace wrote to Harrison in the late 1980s, reiterating that McCain Foods was a family business and a McCain should head the company. Harrison responded, "The proposal you gave me for immediate decision is the same proposal you have been making for two years, i.e., 1) Let's keep the company private; 2) We have to have a McCain run it; 3) It has to be Harrison's family or Wallace's family; 4) Michael has the most experience of the three McCains, Michael, Scott and Peter; 5) Therefore, Michael is named the new boss for McCain Foods 'in waiting' for his father or his uncle to die or quit. In summary, your formula just fits the decision you want to arrive at." Wallace knew that Michael stood a better chance of becoming CEO one day under a single board involving both shareholders and independent directors, while Harrison believed that all shareholders, through a two-tier board, should have the final say on all key decisions, including succession planning. If the two-tier board should decide that a non-McCain should become the next CEO, then it would be so.

Much as there was no turning back when Julius Caesar crossed the Rubicon, Wallace and Harrison's relationship would never be the same after October 1992. Harrison had consistently opposed Wallace's attempts to have Michael named head of US operations, convinced that he was not yet ready to take on the responsibility. Such was his concern that Harrison had a senior staff member in the United States report privately to him on Michael's performance. I am in no position to determine if the staff member fed Harrison what he thought Harrison wanted to hear or was providing the straight goods. Whatever the basis, Harrison did not like what he heard. In another note to himself, he wrote, "Michael has never made a nickel for us." Ignoring Harrison's opposition, Wallace struck the blow that would change the tension between the brothers into outright conflict. In October 1992, without consulting Harrison who in fact was heading off on a business trip to England, Wallace made a public announcement: his son, Michael, was now head of McCain Foods' US operations.

Harrison tried to get Wallace to rescind the appointment as soon as he heard of it. Wallace, however, would do no such thing. In any case, Wallace told Harrison, "It's too late, I can't rescind the appointment. It has been made and it has been made public."[19] Harrison told James Downey in his 2001 interview that "for his own family reasons he was obliged to support the promotion of his son Michael without my agreement. And I became highly incensed at that."

Justice Stevenson would later write that "the appointment of Michael to be CEO in the United States was the turning point in the relationship between Harrison McCain and Wallace McCain." He reminded both brothers that Harrison had appointed his nephew Allison to be managing director in England (albeit, a less exalted level than CEO) over Wallace's opposition. He added, "It is perhaps significant that friction occurred only when family members were the subject of the appointments."[20]

The easy relationship between Harrison and Wallace was now history. Friction now was simmering, including in their relationship as brothers. In 1990 Harrison was not only named CEO of the year by the *Financial Post*, he was the inaugural winner of the coveted business prize. Harrison called Wallace to say, "I realize we work together, but it's embarrassing to get out of it." Wallace shouted, "I don't care what you do," and slammed the phone down.[21]

Both Harrison and Wallace became increasingly sensitive to slights or perceived slights. Justice Stevenson, for example, provides a detailed account of an incident involving McDonald's restaurants which, by the early 1990s, had become McCain's biggest customer.

Harrison wrote to a senior McDonald's official on 30 July 1992 to explore how McCain could supply the fast-food chain more efficiently. Michael McCain, now head of the US operations, had also similarly been in contact with McDonald's. Wallace did not take kindly to Harrison's intervening directly in his sphere of responsibilities and wrote Harrison to complain that he did not even "have the courtesy to copy Michael or ask his advice" before writing to McDonald's.[22]

Michael, meanwhile, invited a number of McDonald's executives to a fishing camp in New Brunswick he had rented without informing head office in Florenceville. At about the same time, Harrison again telephoned McDonald's to arrange an appointment to "develop a plan for Global Purchasing, which could be useful to both of us." He was told that the officials he wanted to meet with would actually be in New Brunswick in a few days' time at the firm's rented fishing camp. Harrison did not react well to the news, as can be imagined. Michael insisted that no offence was intended in leaving Harrison out of the loop, but offence was taken.[23]

The Harrison-Wallace working arrangement as co-CEOs was breaking down quickly and as Justice Stevenson wrote, the McCains were now "working at cross purposes when they should have been working in concert in their relationships with the McDonald's organization."[24] McCain executives rightly became concerned that the competitors would take advantage of the dissension within the McCain family ranks and move in on their territory.

For too long, Harrison and Wallace had put off dealing with governance and now, with their relationship in tatters, they had no choice but to deal with the governance structure and the looming crisis in succession planning.

HEALTH IS NOT FOREVER

The McCain family has a history of heart and kidney problems. Recall that A.D. McCain had died of a sudden massive heart attack as he was preparing to leave for South America. In March 1992, as the war between the brothers was heating up, Harrison developed chest pains. He was too busy to worry about it at first, but he did tell his children and they pushed him hard to get it checked, as did Wallace.

Harrison flew to the Lahey Clinic in Boston where heart specialists performed emergency double bypass surgery. During the operation, Harrison suffered a heart attack and was placed in a medically induced coma by his doctors.

Harrison remained in a coma for ten days, Billie and his children at his bedside throughout. He gradually regained some strength, though he never fully recovered. On leaving hospital, he spent time at his Saint Andrews, New Brunswick, home recuperating.

Harrison, in frail health, faced the spectre of the governance structure breaking down at McCain Foods. Never a patient man, his brush with death determined him to bring the issue to a close, come what may. Justice Stevenson, who had known Harrison for years, told me that Harrison was never the same after his heart attack in 1992. His nephew Andrew, chair of the HOLDCO board and who worked closely with Harrison, said the same thing. He told me that his uncle had "less energy and less patience" after his first brush with death.

9

The Conflict

Harrison McCain was rarely one to speak disparagingly of others. Even when asked for his opinion of competitors or of politicians whose views he didn't share, a typical response was, "Good fella, good fella," and then he would go on to talk about his dealings with them. Only twice did I hear otherwise. Once when I mentioned an article in which a well-known Canadian businessman had referred to "his good friend Harrison McCain," Harrison replied, "A goddamn crook, a goddam crook." On another occasion, he unloaded on a businessman who, he believed, lacked integrity in his dealings with him, with others, and with his community. That was it. Harrison McCain was not one to bad-mouth others and certainly not his brother. When asked about Wallace once their disagreement became public, he was always courteous.

A Nova Scotia businessman said about the McCain conflict, "I can argue it both ways. But Harrison could have stopped it. He never told me, however, how." Another businessman, this time from New Brunswick, suggested that "there is enough blame there to go around. But, you know, Wallace and his family were more responsible for the mess than Harrison." He went on to maintain that "Harrison was the visionary, the driving force. He made what McCain Foods is today." My own view is that there was enough success to go around and that Harrison needed Wallace and Wallace needed Harrison as they grew McCain Foods. Trying to pinpoint which one is more responsible for the firm's success is a fool's game. McCain Foods remains a phenomenal success story and one can never overstate the contribution of either Harrison or Wallace, or, for that matter, of Robert, who convinced them in the first place to "bet the farm" on the future of frozen french fries.

It has been some twenty years since the dispute blew up in full public view. Neither Harrison nor Wallace is still with us. Though the clash between the brothers dominated the Canadian business media for several years, Harrison rarely discussed it or its fallout with me or with others I have spoken with, including his good friends Donald Trafford and Reuben Cohen. In his interview with James Downey he was clearly uncomfortable talking about that period of his life, even several years after it was behind him. If he had dark moments, he preferred to keep them to himself.

Harrison was distressed by one aspect of the media coverage of the dispute, and it had nothing to do with the business, but rather with how his wife Billie was portrayed as weak and that he was abusive towards her.[1] Everyone who knew Billie has only positive things to say about her inner strength. Donald Trafford, Harrison's lifelong friend, told me that they often went out as couples and at no point did Harrison ever show a lack of respect for Billie. Reuben Cohen wrote, "My wife and I were entertained on many occasions by Harrison and Billie and never did he show any disrespect towards Billie."[2] Jim Coutts spent time on holidays and socializing with Billie and Harrison. He told me, "No question, Harrison was deeply in love with Billie and he always showed great respect towards her." Dick O'Hagan and his wife Wanda also holidayed with Harrison and Billie, and Dick had the same response as Jim Coutts. Dick added that he always thought that "Harrison was totally in love with Billie." Terry Bird said, "Billie was one of the nicest women" he had ever met and "she had class." Gerald Regan told me that on one of their skiing trips, Billie fell and hurt herself. Harrison, he added, "doted on her, took care of her in a way that was quite remarkable." Sally Baxter, Billie's closest friend, told me that Harrison and Billie never stopped loving one another.

When Billie was diagnosed with ovarian cancer, Harrison left work and spent several weeks with her at the hospital while she was undergoing treatment.[3] As we will see later, he also missed some arbitration hearings to be by her side in her final days. Michael Campbell, vice-president and corporate secretary at McCain Foods, also told me that

Harrison stayed away from the office in mourning a lot longer than anyone expected after Billie died.

Billie died on 30 March 1994 and her funeral was held on Good Friday in the tiny Anglican Church in Florenceville. Wallace and his family attended the funeral, but only Wallace went to the reception. No one from Wallace's family was present for the graveside ceremony, though Harrison had asked them to come. Paul Waldie writes that Wallace had gone to the bishop before the funeral, seeking guidance. It was the bishop who had suggested that his family should attend the church service but not the reception or the graveside ceremony.[4]

As tension mounted, Wallace retained the services of a high-profile Ottawa lobbyist and communications expert, David MacNaughton, then CEO of Hill and Knowlton. His brief was to assist in portraying Wallace's version of events to the media. In the past Wallace had avoided media attention, but now he and his family gave interviews to journalists, outlining, as they saw it, the reasons for the breakdown in the relationship between the brothers. Their side of the story would be made public, come what may.

For years, Harrison had been the public face of McCain Foods and the go-to person for the media, but he was now reluctant to follow the route Wallace had taken. Then, as the media were feasting on just the one side of the quarrel, family, friends, and business associates persuaded Harrison that it was in his best interests to hire a public relations firm himself. The few times he met with its representatives confirmed his initial view; he could not see how they could possibly be helpful and told them as much. The thought of spinning his version of the conflict in order to counter Wallace's did not appeal. So he took the high road. Harrison and his children gave no interviews, on or off the record.

Harrison had been pondering the potential clash between family and business since the mid-1980s, and indeed had raised the issue with me more than once. However, he always spoke in general terms and with no reference to his own situation or to Wallace. He read widely on the topic, hoping to find guidelines as to how disharmony could be avoided over two generations, let alone three or four. On one occasion, he showed me a book on the subject he had just been reading. It, like the others he had consulted, had not led him to be optimistic. Harrison could not find the solution he sought. It was unusual, to say the least, for Harrison not to have answers.

It is, of course, not possible to tell the story of Harrison McCain without discussing the conflict with his brother Wallace. However, we should not forget Frank McKenna's words: "Reconciliation is the most important part of the story."[5] And, contrary to some media reports, there was indeed a reconciliation, which began at least one year before Harrison's death. As McKenna said on several occasions, Harrison and Wallace never stopped loving one another as brothers. Jim Coutts, who was close to Harrison, told me essentially the same thing, as did others.

I always felt that there was sadness in Harrison's eyes and voice rather than bitterness whenever the split with his brother came up in any discussion. He was reluctant to talk about it; however, the depth of the loss he felt was evident when he said, "You know, Wallace and I shared a bed until I was fifteen years old." That statement in itself speaks to the visceral affection Harrison held for his brother.

THE SPLIT

The news that Harrison and Wallace McCain had reached an impasse that would end their working relationship at McCain Foods shook the corporate world and, to be sure, New Brunswickers. The *New York Times* reported that the "McCain feud is Canada's answer to the recent dynastic spats in American business, like the fight within the Haft family, which owns Dart Drugs and Crown Books."[6] In Canada, the news was spread across the country, dissected, and examined. Paul Waldie, a well-known journalist with Toronto's *Globe and Mail*, wrote a book about it, as did Michael Woloschuk, then a journalist with the *Telegraph Journal* in St John, New Brunswick.[7]

Maritimers and, in particular, New Brunswickers were a good deal more than passive observers to the unfolding story. Apart from the McCains' having a special status in our region, the Maritime business community consists largely of family-owned businesses, so that Harrison and Wallace and McCain Foods had become role models to many of them. Indeed, one can easily list the Maritime businesses that are publicly traded.

When the split became public, Maritimers were deeply saddened by the news. Folks in Florenceville, meanwhile, were in disbelief. As Donald Trafford explains, many of them, in fact, were convinced that the brothers were as close as ever and that Harrison and Wallace had engineered the split for tax purposes.

It wasn't only Florenceville that thought this way. Bob Crossman, a well-known Moncton businessman who had worked in sales for McCain Foods for several years, told me that at first he thought "these McCain boys are some smart. This will now enable them to finish the job and acquire Maple Leaf Foods. They will be able to get around antitrust laws. I worked with Harrison and Wallace and these guys were tight, real tight. There was no way that they would fight like that."

In Florenceville, it was the talk of the town, in churches, stores, the local barber shop, and even in the schoolyard. John Doucet told me that Harrison came to his house to chat one Sunday afternoon and Doucet's six-year old son Ryan innocently asked Harrison, "Mr McCain, why are you fighting with your brother?"

Harrison calmly replied, "Do you have a sister?"

"Yes," said Ryan.

Harrison then asked, "Do you ever fight with your sister and then, after awhile, do you make up with her?"

Ryan nodded his head.

And Harrison said, "Well, that is the same between my brother and me."

HARRISON: TOP DOG

Despite Harrison and Wallace being joint CEOs of McCain Foods, there were subtle and not-so-subtle signs that Harrison was considered to be top dog. David O'Brien, a long-time executive with the firm, told me that he was interviewed for a senior management position by several people, including Harrison and Wallace. The final interviewer, the one who would also give the verdict, was Harrison. During this final interview, Harrison noticed that O'Brien appeared to be nervous and asked him why.

O'Brien replied, "Because I really want this job."

Harrison told him, "Relax, relax. Here, put your feet on my desk. Go ahead, go ahead. Relax, relax."

O'Brien never did put his feet on Harrison's desk, but he still got the job.

Harrison was the elder brother, the company's public face, and the chairman, while Wallace was president. Carl Morris, a long-serving McCain Foods executive, said, "Harrison was more than the older brother; we all knew that the buck stopped with him."[8]

Harrison, on the other hand, once said that "whoever was handy was boss"[9] at McCain Foods. The company's bylaws stated that Harrison and Wallace should have such powers and duties as the board might specifically determine. The board essentially decided what Harrison and Wallace decided. The bylaw also stated that the powers and duties "shall equally exercise general control over and supervision of the business and affairs of the company" and that "during the absence or disability of either, the other should assume his powers and duties."[10]

Justice Ronald C. Stevenson, in his arbitration report, wrote, "Both Harrison and Wallace McCain have strong wills and personalities. Harrison is the most assertive and was probably perceived by family members as a slightly stronger leader in the business."[11]

The perception that Harrison was top dog at McCain Foods was also widely held by the outside world. Not only was he the initial recipient of the CEO of the Year Award in 1990, he also received several honorary doctorates. (He turned down a few more.) He was made an Officer of the Order of Canada, and Companion of the Order in 1992. In 2004, he was made a Knight of the Legion of Honour of France. He was on the board of directors of the Bank of Nova Scotia, Petro Canada, and on several public service commissions. Wallace, meanwhile, was made an Officer of the Order of Canada in 1995 and Companion in 2007 and appointed to the Royal Bank board in 1986.

ALL IN THE FAMILY

As we have seen, the conflict between the brothers became public in 1993 but the seeds of the dispute were planted several years earlier. However, both Harrison and Wallace, at first, wanted to keep their disagreements private. As Harrison said, one advantage of having a private business is that you do not have to wash your dirty clothes in public. Or, as he put it even more succinctly to a journalist, "My business is not your business."

Any attempt to deal with the issue of succession fell squarely on the board structure at McCain Foods. Wallace McCain's lawyers argued before Justice Stevenson that "the discussions focussed on two issues: (1) how to begin involving the next generation of shareholders in the company at the board level; (2) how to deal with the question of succession to Harrison and Wallace after they had died or retired."[12]

Recall that the OPCO board was assembled at the time McCain Foods was established and HOLDCO, a holding company, was established for tax purposes in 1984 after Andrew McCain's death. Both boards met rarely and essentially were of no consequence in the running of the business.

This would change in 1985 when Harrison and Wallace started formally to discuss succession and the need to restructure the boards. Harrison wrote to Wallace in December of that year to say that they should stay as joint CEOs as long as their health would allow but, if necessary, rely on other, younger people to run the firm. A few months later, they discussed succession openly for the first time. Wallace wanted a McCain to run the company in future. Harrison was not convinced.

The second generation of McCains employed at the firm were all males, as we have seen. Of these sons and nephews, Wallace had his son Michael in mind as the next CEO, and Harrison had serious doubts as to Michael's abilities. Certainly, things had gone off the rails when Wallace unilaterally appointed Michael head of United States operations, much against Harrison's wishes.

BOARD EXPANSION PROPOSAL

Harrison wrote Roger Wilson, lawyer for McCain Foods, asking for advice in putting together a new board of directors. He had given the matter a great deal of thought, researching various structures tried in Europe and in the United States. Wilson responded three weeks later with options and recommendations. He wrote about a European-type board with a public board that would represent the shareholders and a management board consisting of senior officers, some family members, and outside directors. He suggested that HOLDCO could be the public board and OPCO the management board. He cautioned against a large single board that combined both the interests of the shareholders (the McCain families) and management.[13]

Harrison discussed restructuring the McCain boards in various exchanges with Wallace, but nothing came of it. Wallace was opposed to the two-board concept, as we saw earlier. He wanted a ten-member single board consisting of himself, Harrison, four outsiders, and four McCains representing the four families. He also stood firm on one point: he and Harrison, as the two co-CEOs, should make all major decisions and that they should decide the succession issue. Harrison remained convinced that Wallace wanted a single board for one reason only: it was the best route to secure Michael's elevation to CEO.

Harrison and Wallace were soon at an impasse. They looked at other options, keenly aware that failure to agree would result in the matter going before the courts, and thus their differences would be aired in full public view. They knew that if this happened, both the business and the family would pay a hefty price.

Going through Harrison's documents, one is struck by the variety and multitude of options both he and Wallace brought forward to resolve the impasse. At one point, Harrison suggested dividing McCain Foods into four segments – one with Allison, another with Scott, another with Michael, and yet another with his own son Peter. Wallace went further and proposed that McCain Foods be broken down into seven segments.

Later, Wallace wrote a note to Harrison with a series of new options: First, Harrison should select a family member as chief operations officer (COO) with the intent of making him CEO after several years. The second suggestion was to appoint a new single board along the lines that he had earlier proposed and let it appoint a COO for six months or so, with a view of making him CEO within a few years. He still saw the next CEO as coming from the McCain family. A third option was to divide McCain Foods by region and equity. Harrison would own two-thirds of one company and Wallace two-thirds of the other. This would, however, leave members of the other two McCain families in a weak minority position in both companies, at least weaker than the existing arrangement. A fourth option was simply to sell McCain Foods to the highest bidder and split the cash. This last option would have simply been unthinkable to either Harrison or Wallace only a few years earlier.

In the early 1990s, Harrison concentrated his thinking on reconstituting the two existing boards, while Wallace continued to focus on succession planning and his preferred single-board option. On virtually every issue, the two brothers were no longer on the same page. Harrison kept promoting his board expansion proposal (BEP), which would formally put in place the two-tier board system, to which Wallace was adamantly opposed. He asked that Harrison's proposal not go forward to shareholders until he and Harrison had sorted out several issues. In an attempt to solve the impasse, they consulted John Ward, one of the world's leading authorities on family business, but came away still at loggerheads.

Meanwhile, Harrison was in constant contact with shareholders, his nephews and nieces, about his proposal to expand the two boards. Some suggested revisions, while others had no difficulty with his proposal. When Harrison's proposal was put forward to the HOLDCO board, Wallace immediately informed shareholders that he would be bringing forward amendments. Wallace sought a firm mandatory retirement date for both himself and Harrison, which was accepted. The other amendments were not. He argued that a single board would provide a better overview of all the firm's activities and give minority shareholders a clearer insight into the running of McCain Foods, and that a two-board system would only give "a sheltered view" of how the business is run.

The BEP was put to a vote at the HOLDCO board. All shareholders were present or represented by proxy. The proposal sought to begin the transfer of ownership responsibility to the next generation of McCains and to establish a process to manage succession planning. It called for enlarging both HOLDCO's and OPCO's boards to seven directors, including four outside directors. The proposal also provided for a mandatory retirement age, which, as we have seen, accommodated one of Wallace's concerns. Both Harrison and Wallace would be ineligible to serve on either board after their seventy-fifth birthday.

The proposal envisaged the departure of either Harrison or Wallace as CO-CEOS, with the remaining brother continuing as the lead executive after the other retired. It would then turn responsibility for succession planning over to a management committee of OPCO. The committee would have the responsibility of identifying one or two individuals capable of becoming CEO at McCain Foods, for a recommendation to HOLDCO. The committee was to consist of four independent directors drawn from the OPCO board. HOLDCO would, however, continue to hold effective power in that it would have the final say on who would become CEO in the post–Harrison and Wallace era. Though OPCO was to be made responsible for managing the affairs of McCain Foods, HOLDCO could revoke all of OPCO's power and authority at the stroke of the pen. In brief, ultimate decision-making power would rest with the shareholders through HOLDCO, and that included selecting the new CEO.

HOLDCO approved Harrison's proposal. Wallace, however, was not about to throw in the towel. HOLDCO's approval was only the first step. Company by-laws had to be revised and all shareholders had to sign off again on the revisions. Wallace and his sons continued to marshal arguments against implementing the board's decision, but their efforts only delayed the inevitable, and formal approval to Harrison's plan was secured a few months later. Wallace, however, would not accept this as a *fait accompli*. Essentially, he saw McCain Foods as a partnership between himself and Harrison; thus the two partners, not HOLDCO, had to agree to all major changes to the governance of McCain Foods. He could always pursue the matter before the courts, but in the meantime Wallace had no choice but to work with the two-tier system he deplored.

THE NEW BOARDS

Harrison nominated his two sons, Mark and Peter, to the new HOLDCO board. Wallace put forward his two sons, Michael and Scott. Andrew, Robert's son, was named by his mother, and Andrew's son, Allison, was appointed to the board by his siblings. Andrew (Robert's son) was elected chair of the board. George McClure became the seventh board member, the one outsider on whom the McCain families could agree. Since Andrew was named chair of the board of HOLDCO, it now meant, if only in theory, that both Harrison and Wallace would report to him.

Harrison was to chair the OPCO board, while the members were to include Wallace, one nephew from HOLDCO, two senior McCain executives, and four outside directors from the private sector. These four were Arden Haynes, CEO at Imperial Oil; Kendall Cork, chief financial officer at Noranda; David Morton, CEO at Alcan; and Vic Young, CEO at Fishery Products International. Both Cork and Morton served with Harrison on the board of the Bank of Nova Scotia. It is important to stress once again that HOLDCO is the beneficial owner of all McCain Foods shares and that OPCO is subservient to HOLDCO.

The new board structure did nothing to solve the tension between Harrison and Wallace. If anything, it appears to have made it worse. Wallace remained convinced that it would give far too much power to the next generation of McCains, many of whom did not work with the company. He never wavered from his conviction that a McCain should lead the company when he and Harrison stepped down and believed that HOLDCO would stand in the way of this happening.

Wallace urged Harrison to name Michael, now a member of the HOLDCO board, to the OPCO board as well. Harrison rejected the suggestion, pointing out that Michael was also a senior manager with the company. Harrison pointedly asked, "Is Michael underemployed and is Michael in any worse position than any other McCain with the two-tier board concept?" Wallace, in turn, pointedly answered that all McCains now were "worse off." He added that Harrison got the two-tier board system approved, not through the strengths of the case or of his arguments, but by "cracking the whip," getting everybody, except himself and his family, to line up in support of Harrison's proposal. With this exchange, they reached the point of no return: both Harrison and Wallace knew that their business relationship was over.

THE PARTNERSHIP BREAKS DOWN

Harrison and Wallace were both indefatigable business-savvy entrepreneurs. They made certain that the business kept growing in good and bad economic times. McCain Foods, for example, sailed through the economic recession of the early 1980s. In short, they had been one of the best business tag teams of their era. Terry Bird said that at meetings Harrison sat at one end of the table, Wallace at the other, and that they took turns playing "good cop, bad cop." They were "quite impressive in how they handled meetings."[14]

Family slights or grievances were ignored or overlooked in these heady days. As accolades mounted for Harrison, Wallace was once asked how he felt working "for" Harrison. But that did not matter, not then. Wallace was too busy to concern himself about such trivial matters.

By 1993, McCain Foods generated $3 billion in revenues with a strong presence in every country that mattered. With the thriving business now on a solid footing, it was inevitable that past slights would come home to roost. Still, it seemed that the brothers now had breathing room to take stock and plan what the next steps should be. Wallace no doubt believed that he had every right to appoint his son Michael head of the United States operations. After all, he was responsible for the United States and he saw himself as a full and equal partner with Harrison in having built the business.

The crux of the problem was that Wallace saw McCain Foods as a partnership between himself and Harrison. Harrison did not deny this, but he also saw McCain Foods as a family business, owned by the shareholders. The partnership worked well when both partners agreed, but if an agreement between them was not possible, then Harrison believed strongly that it fell to all shareholders to come up with a solution or to find a compromise.

Harrison was convinced that a two-tier board system with shareholders holding effective power was the only way ahead. He also wanted the chair to be a shareholder from either Robert or Andrew's families, not from his or Wallace's family. Harrison won this battle, but the war was not over. What was once described as Canada's "feud of the century" would take a few more turns.

TURNING TO LAWYERS

Harrison worked closely with company lawyer Roger Wilson in designing the two-tier board system. Since the business relationship with Wallace was broken, he wanted to make certain that he was on solid legal grounds as he put together the revised structure. Wallace, as might be expected, also sought legal advice – in his case, to protect his own and his family's interests.

Wallace continued, through his lawyers, to explore avenues to find an acceptable compromise outside the two-tier board solution. He now documented his communications with Harrison in writing and retained the legal services of Jack Petch, from the top Toronto firm Osler, Hoskin and Harcourt. Wallace not only found the revised governance structure unacceptable and unworkable, he worried that it militated against Michael's getting a fair hearing in the succession planning. He wrote to Harrison to say that he would not allow him to manage the firm's succession because Harrison was biased against his son. Through it all, however, he still sought to keep his family relationship with Harrison separate from his business relationship. He told *Maclean's* when the conflict first became public, "Of course we're still talking to each other. He's my best friend. He's my brother."[15]

Nevertheless, Wallace and his lawyer served notice that the HOLDCO board did not have and should not have the authority to lead the firm's succession planning exercise. Wallace was convinced that HOLDCO would only do as it was told to do by Harrison. Wallace wanted OPCO's management resources committee, made up of the four outside directors and no McCain family members, to select the next CEO.

Harrison, on the other hand, continued to insist through the company's lawyers that HOLDCO should have final say on all things it wanted to decide. After all, HOLDCO represented all shareholders, the ultimate authority. He reminded Wallace and his legal advisors that OPCO could enjoy only the power that HOLDCO delegated to it. How could that be, Wallace countered, given that McCain Foods was a two-person partnership? Wallace maintained that the four families, all now represented on the HOLDCO board, were never intended to run the business and, in fact, never had done, and so why should they now be involved in such important decisions?

With no way out of the impasse, Harrison and Wallace, with their lawyers, met with the OPCO board on 29 October 1992. Harrison said that things could not go on and that it was much too difficult for everyone. Something had to give for the good of McCain Foods and of the four families. He wanted Michael McCain removed from his position as CEO of US operations, if only to clear the air, and start anew. Harrison also suggested splitting the US operations into two separate divisions and hiring an experienced executive from the potato industry to run the potato business. Wallace was incensed, declaring that Michael was the solution, not the problem, and that he had accomplished a great deal in only a few short years in the United States.

Things headed even further downhill from that moment. Harrison wanted to begin the process to identify a new CEO immediately. He argued that, given the impasse, Wallace should step down as president of McCain Foods and that he, in turn, would step down as chairman, once a new CEO had been chosen. His message could not have been more blunt: he could no longer work with Wallace, and Wallace had to go.

Allison McCain proposed a resolution before HOLDCO, seconded by Harrison's son Mark, that called for "an orderly transition of management from the present Chairman and President to the new Chief Executive Officer."[16] Wallace's sons Michael and Scott voted against the proposal, but it was carried five votes to two. Later, HOLDCO made it clear to the OPCO board that it would not agree if asked by OPCO to reappoint Harrison and Wallace as chairman and president of McCain Foods. George McClure, summed up the sorry situation by borrowing a sentence from Lord Durham: "We have two CEOs warring in the bosom of a single company and this is an untenable situation." He favoured asking OPCO's management resources committee to begin the search for a new CEO and finding appropriate non-executive roles for both Harrison and Wallace.[17]

Wallace saw these developments not only as the writing on the wall, but as a call to arms. He was being fired as co-CEO of McCain Foods, so he added another high-profile Toronto lawyer to his team, Alan Lenczner. The stage was being set to take the matter before the courts. Mr Lenczner wrote the secretary of OPCO, making it clear that "Wallace McCain is fulfilling and intends to continue to fulfil his role as President and Chief Executive Officer of McCain Foods Limited. There is no vacancy ... and it is inappropriate for the management resources committee (MRC) to proceed on the basis that there is or will be such a vacancy."[18] Several weeks later, the chair of the MRC, Arden Haynes, wrote to Wallace that his committee was not looking for a CEO but, rather, working towards an adequate succession plan.[19] Harrison was still hoping for a last-minute solution.

The on-again, off-again search for a new CEO continued to play out between late 1992 and the first few months of 1993. Wallace formally threatened litigation if HOLDCO or OPCO were to take the final step to remove him from his position at McCain Foods. In May 1993 he made an offer to all HOLDCO shareholders to purchase 17.5 per cent of the company's common shares at fifty-five dollars a share. If success- ful, this would have given Wallace majority control of McCain Foods and solve the problem, at least from his perspective. This offer made it clear, among other things, that, if accepted, Wallace would become the sole "Chief Executive Officer."

Shareholders considered the offer "hostile" and turned it down. They went further and signed an agreement not to sell shares without unanimous agreement to do so. Harrison too saw Wallace's offer as hostile and in turn offered to purchase all of Wallace's shares at $40.00. Wallace responded by resubmitting an offer to purchase "all" shares at $55.00. Later, Harrison said that he was prepared to recommend that McCain's buy out Wallace for $430 million or $53.91 per share.[20] Noth- ing came of these offers.

There would be no last-minute solution and on 17 August 1993 the HOLDCO board passed a resolution that read, "Wallace McCain is removed as President and co-Chief Executive Officer of McCain Foods. Harrison is appointed Chairman and sole Chief Executive Officer of McCain Foods until his successor is elected or appointed. Wallace is offered the position of non-Executive Vice-Chairman of McCain Foods, with such duties as may be determined by the Chief Executive Officer." OPCO's management resources committee was also directed to "commence the process of identifying a person ... for the position of Chief Executive Officer of McCain Foods."[21] The HOLDCO board passed the resolution, with Wallace's two sons, Michael and Scott, dissenting.

Within a week Wallace and his lawyers went before New Brunswick's court of Queen's Bench seeking an injunction to stop his dismissal. He could also use the media, and this he did. Michael Woloschuk writes, "Wallace's spin doctors went into overdrive," and some well-placed phone calls ensured that "the media would be all over the story."[22]

Wallace and Michael had already tested the waters several weeks earlier with stories in the *Financial Post* in Canada and *Forbes* in the United States. The *Forbes* article painted "Wallace's son as a whiz-kid." The two articles also suggested that Michael had what it took to be the next CEO at McCain Foods, but that Harrison stood in his way.[23] Michael and Scott presented a statement to the board of HOLDCO critical of Harrison for "exercising his influence over certain members of this board," implying that the other HOLDCO board members were too weak to make up their own minds on the matter.[24]

JUSTICE STEVENSON

The national and local TV and newspapers had a field day with the story. Harrison and a number of senior executives at McCain Foods became alarmed at the prospects that everything about the firm would be put out in full public view, including its financial and strategic business plans. Harrison also became concerned over the physical safety of his children, nephews, and nieces. The competition would have full access to the company's books, its production capacity, and its plans for locating new plants. Wallace also wanted to keep the company's books out of public view – hence the decision to go to arbitration. That said, within weeks of tabling it, Justice Stevenson's decision became widely available and many journalists have quoted it.[25]

Both sides had agreed to an arbitration before Justice Stevenson to resolve the matter. The McCains would assume all costs of the arbitration, except Stevenson's salary, and there would be no change to Wallace's status until the arbitration had reached a conclusion. Still, there was one immediate casualty. Arden Haynes, a member of OPCO and chair of the management resources committee, resigned. The succession process was now at a standstill and he saw no reason to continue as a member of the board.

The McCains rented the entire 166-room Wu Centre on the University of New Brunswick campus in Fredericton for the hearings. Harrison, his family, and legal advisors held court at the Lord Beaverbrook hotel in downtown Fredericton, next to the province's Legislative Assembly, while Wallace, his family, and legal advisors stayed at the Sheraton Hotel on the western outskirts of Fredericton. The exact cost to McCain Foods, and to Wallace and Harrison individually, will never be known, but one can easily speculate that it amounted to well in excess of $30 million.

Wallace argued that HOLDCO had no authority to dismiss him, that McCain Foods, when stripped to its basics, was a partnership between Harrison and himself and that he was being oppressed as a minority shareholder. He also argued through his lawyers that Harrison had made "misstatements" and "misrepresentations" that let the HOLDCO board take decisions that were beyond its authority. The objective was to have the 17 August 1993 decision to remove him as president and co-CEO declared invalid.[26]

Wallace's legal team again offered possible solutions. One was to divide the company in two with Wallace becoming CEO of half of the assets and Harrison the other half. Wallace would take over North America, Australia, and Thomas Equipment, and Harrison would have the rest. A second possibility was to implement a buy-sell arrangement between Harrison and Wallace, and a third was the sale of McCain Foods. Wallace's side came to the arbitration fully armed with financial reports that evaluated the book and market value of McCain Foods, prepared by some of the country's leading accountants. It was highly unlikely, however, that a New Brunswick judge would agree to divide McCain Foods into two companies.

Harrison and his team argued that HOLDCO, representing all shareholders, had every right to take decisions in their best interest. Harrison never denied that he and Wallace acted as partners in building McCain Foods, but pointed out that when the relationship broke down, the partnership model also broke down. He explained that the partnership worked "almost perfectly until the issue of succession arose."[27] He argued that the shareholders through HOLDCO had no choice but to deal with a difficult decision in the interest of McCain Foods. The impasse could not go on without bringing irreparable damage to McCain Foods and to the interests of its shareholders.

Harrison had another important, more difficult issue to attend to. His wife was dying of cancer as Justice Stevenson was going about his work. He spent as much time as he could by Billie's side while attending to matters with his legal team.

Justice Stevenson delivered his decision on time on 20 April 1994. He wrote, "There is no doubt that Harrison McCain and Wallace

McCain decided to jointly establish and jointly operate the business. They established the business with the corporate structure in which … they shared management … they held co-equal executive authority." However, he continued, "in recent years that undergirding collapsed." He then concluded, "On the facts as they now exist it is neither reasonable nor legitimate for Wallace McCain to expect to continue as a co-CEO with Harrison McCain … a decision to remove Wallace from the office of president and co-CEO, while retaining him as an OPCO director and continuing his employment contract, cannot be considered oppressive."[28] The basis for his conclusion was that "when relationships based on mutual expectations are brought to an end by changed circumstances the norm of majority rule takes over."[29] Justice Stevenson made it a point, however, of protecting Wallace's position as a director of OPCO and his employment agreement – salary, bonus, and pension rights, but not as co-CEO.[30] He also pointed to a legal oversight that HOLDCO had to correct: they must formally remove Wallace as co-CEO. HOLDCO quickly did so.

Undeterred, Wallace and his team still made other attempts to keep Wallace as co-CEO. Wallace's two sons, for example, made a final appeal to the HOLDCO board not to fire Wallace in light of the strong business success of McCain Foods and their father's contributions to it, but HOLDCO would not reverse its decision. Wallace then argued for a public share offering (IPO) of the company so that he could draw maximum economic benefits from his contribution to the firm, but again HOLDCO had no interest in an IPO. McCain Foods would remain a family business.

Justice Stevenson, in a personal letter to both Harrison and Wallace, suggested that the HOLDCO and OPCO boards be combined and that McCain Foods sell 20 per cent of its shares to the public. He explained why he wrote the letter, which was not legally binding, and which he recognized was unusual for a judge to do: "The importance of the McCain business to New Brunswick and my personal acquaintance with Harrison and Wallace justify what may be a departure from the normal rules of judicial conduct."[31] He added, "Unless some of my suggestions find favour with both there is little point in conveying my thoughts to the other parties."[32] They did not find favour with

Harrison, who never deviated from his position that McCain Foods was and should remain a family business.

Wallace and his legal team had one more card to play: they sought a court injunction to prevent HOLDCO's dismissing Wallace as CO-CEO. Justice Paul Creaghan from New Brunswick's court of Queen's Bench heard the case. He wrote that the HOLDCO board was well within its right to remove Wallace as co-CEO and that "the courts should not be interfering with corporate decision making."[33] So the case had run its course. The feud had officially come to a close, though the tension would linger on.

There was still one more drama to unfold. Shortly after the arbitration hearings, Wallace announced plans to purchase Maple Leaf Foods. Harrison quickly fired Michael and ordered the locks on Wallace and Michael's office doors to be changed. Harrison explained these measures in a memorandum to senior executives at McCain Foods. Michael had "declined to take my specific direction on various things I wanted done. I pressed but he declined to follow my directions. Wallace made an offer to buy Maple Leaf Foods. If successful … they will be a competitor with a French fry factory in Lethbridge, Alberta. Although I telephoned and congratulated Wallace, I took the French fry acquisition very seriously. After sending a message to Michael, he telephoned me and I asked him if he was part of the offer to buy Maple Leaf Foods and he said yes. Having thought over the whole matter carefully, I came to the conclusion that I should no longer accept this, so I wrote Michael saying I was discharging him."[34] Michael would in turn bring a wrongful dismissal suit against Harrison and McCain Foods, but nothing came of it.

LOOKING BACK

New Brunswickers rightly take great pride in the remarkable story that Harrison and Wallace McCain wrote between 1956 and 1994. In some ways, Harrison and Wallace were our success story too, not just theirs.

Maclean's once observed that "people who have chatted with Harrison, and that seems to be almost everyone in New Brunswick, remark on his energetic and usually good-natured conversation."[35] He was all of that and more. To many New Brunswickers, he was one of us. We not only admired his commitment to our province, we liked his unpretentious nature. And, as many of us had reason to know, his generosity was legendary.

Wallace was no less important to the success of McCain Foods than was Harrison. However, Wallace being more reticent in public, we did not know him as well as we did Harrison. Thus, when the conflict became public, the focus on the drama tended to detract from Wallace's substantial business accomplishments.

New Brunswickers watched as a once close-knit, highly successful family tore itself apart. As mentioned above, the New Brunswick business community is, at its core, a series of family businesses. They can be large firms, such as the Irvings and McCains, but mostly they are small manufacturing enterprises, and there are hundreds of them. They watched and wondered: if succession problems could break apart the McCain family and business, for all the brothers' acumen, could it also happen to any of them?

The split also meant that New Brunswick would be losing one of the most successful entrepreneurs in its history. Wallace would be moving to Toronto and Maple Leaf Foods. Going down the road is an all-too-familiar story in the Maritimes. But this was different. Wallace was not one of the countless young men who had given up on finding work at home. He was an icon of success and he was leaving.

Harrison and Wallace did reconnect towards the end. Harrison said many times that he never stopped loving his brother. But the magic, the bond, and the mutual trust and admiration between the two brothers could never be fully recaptured.

Still, there was a reconciliation between the two brothers, though the business relationship was irreparably damaged. In January 2003, as Harrison's health deteriorated, Wallace offered him his Jamaica winter home as a pleasant place to rest. Harrison accepted and greatly appreciated the gesture. A few months before he died, Harrison spent some weeks in Toronto to be close to his children. Harrison and Wallace visited one another during this time and chatted often on the phone.

But that lay in the future. To return to Justice Stevenson's decision, Harrison in 1992 would have to fly solo at McCain Foods. In a few short years, he had lost his wife and his business partner of thirty-seven years. His health was poor and he still had a thriving global firm to lead without Wallace by his side.

Some twenty years after the conflict erupted in full public view, the McCain family have turned the page. Harrison's children speak warmly of their Uncle Wallace. And Scott McCain, Wallace's son, takes satisfaction in telling me stories about his uncle. By all accounts, and from both sides, the conflict now belongs to the history books.

Andrew McCain, the chair of the HOLDCO board, told me in March 2013 that all family members on the board are now pushing in the same direction. Never, he reports, has the board worked as well as it does now. He should know, given that he has been chair of HOLDCO for more than twenty years. Scott McCain, a board member, agrees with Andrew's assessment, adding that he was pleased that someone was writing a book about how his uncle and his father, with the support of their two brothers, were able to build a world leader in the frozen food business.

The reasons for the conflict are gone and old wounds are healing. There are also no McCains on the horizon looking to become CEO.

Opening of UK plant. *Left to right*: Wallace, Andrew, Laura, Robert, and Harrison. (© McCain Foods Limited, all rights reserved)

Left to right: Harrison, Gillian and friend Linda Parfitt.

Family holiday in Jamaica. *Left to right*: Ann, Peter, Laura, Harrison, Billie, Mark, and Gillian.

Harrison and sons. *Left to right*: Peter, Harrison, and Mark.

The extended family. *Left to right*: Joyce holding John, Ann, Harrison holding Luke, Chris Evans, Peter, Billie, Mark, Laura, and Gillian.

Harrison and Mac McCarthy.

Official opening of the PEI plant, 1991. *Left to right*: Harrison, Premier Joe Ghiz, and Wallace.

Harrison and Wallace. (© McCain Foods Limited, all rights reserved)

Harrison and Peter.

Billie and Harrison.

Left to right: Tony van Leersum, Harrison, and George McClure. (© McCain Foods Limited, all rights reserved)

Left to right, front row: Marilyn Strong, Harrison, Gerda Hnatyshyn. *Middle row*: Sheila McCarthy. *Back row*: Laura Downey, Ray Hnatyshyn, Jim Downey, and Mac McCarthy.

Left to right: Reuben Cohen and Harrison.

Left to right: former New Brunswick Premier Louis J. Robichaud, Jim Coutts, and Harrison McCain.

Left to right: former New Brunswick premier Louis J. Robichaud, the author Donald J. Savoie, and Harrison.

Harrison McCain. (© McCain Foods Limited, all rights reserved)

Flying Solo

In his interview with James Downey, Harrison was asked, "Has the trajectory of McCain Foods been affected by the dispute with Wallace and the family?"

Harrison's reply was a brief no.

Downey persevered: "That has not had any serious affect at all?"

Harrison responded, "No. That doesn't mean that Wallace wasn't doing a lot of work and he's very effective too. He knows what he's doing and he's a smart guy."[1]

The growth of McCain Foods did not end in 1993–94. In fact, it continues to this day. The company generated $3 billion in 1993, and $5 billion in 1999. Today, revenues are over $6 billion a year and the *Globe and Mail* ranks it Canada's thirtieth-largest private company. It accounts for about one-third of the frozen french fries sold in the world and over 80 per cent of its revenues come from outside of Canada.[2]

In a speech in 2001, Harrison could claim that McCain Foods had acquired or built twelve new factories, including one in Eastern Europe in the 1990s. In 2000–01 alone, McCain Foods built or acquired seven plants, including two vegetable-processing plants in South Africa, the first time McCain Foods built or acquired plants in Africa. McCain Foods has continued on this trajectory ever since. In 2004 it started construction of a $43-million plant in northern China and a year later an $18-million plant in India. In 2008 it demolished the original plant in Florenceville and built a new state-of-the-art-plant (see Appendix C for developments at McCain Foods between 1994 and 2004).

Harrison told the Richard Ivey School of Business in 2001 that revenues grew at an annual rate of nearly 20 per cent, half organically and
half by acquisitions over the past five years. He outlined once again
his "drink the local wine" strategy and again invoked the right time,
right place, saying, "McCain Foods was in the right place with the right
products at the right time to ride the growth waves associated with the
international spread of supermarkets, convenience stores and quick
serving restaurants during the last forty years or so."[3]

LIFE GOES ON

Wallace and his sons, Michael and Scott, as we have seen, left Florenceville for Toronto, where they teamed up with the Ontario Teachers' Pension Plan to buy Maple Leaf Foods. This does not mean, however, that
they had nothing more to do with McCain Foods. Justice Stevenson's
decision had left Wallace with a non-executive title, a $3-million sal-
ary, and a seat on the OPCO board. His two sons also remained on the
HOLDCO board, though Michael recently resigned.

Wallace's legal team brought yet another court action over the partnership breakdown. This time Harrison and the family board decided
to go on the offensive and took Wallace to court to have the lawsuit
thrown out. The hearing was set for late January 1995 before Justice
Creaghan. He once again ruled in Harrison's favour.

For the first time since 1956, Harrison would fly solo as the CEO of
the firm. His health was not robust, but he was surrounded by a highly
competent team of executives and managers. Harrison also made good
on his commitment to have OPCO's management resources committee
search for his replacement as CEO.

In 1995, the committee of four outsiders of the OPCO board put forward a candidate recommending an outsider, British-born Howard
Mann, to succeed Harrison as CEO. Before his appointment, Mann
had been the managing director of the food products division at Rank
Hovis McDougall, the large UK food conglomerate. He came on board
in June 1995, and at first he took over McCain Foods in North America, Australia, and New Zealand, while Harrison continued to look
after Europe and Japan. In time, Mann took over all operations and
Harrison remained as chairman of OPCO and of McCain Foods.

Things, however, would never be the same. The ashtrays linking Harrison and Wallace's office were gone. No more evening chats
between the two about developments in the firm, or just winding
down together over a Scotch. Harrison must have had many lonely
feelings driving past Wallace's now empty house, just two doors from
his, when going back and forth to the office. Harrison's home was also
empty. Billie had died and his children had all left home, though they
returned often to visit with their father and to attend board meetings.
It was on their separate visits home that I met the children.

Terry, Harrison's cook-housekeeper, looked after the house and the
meals. He was quiet, friendly, discreet, and always there whenever I
visited Harrison, as was his long-time assistant Marilyn Strong, whose
loyalty was nothing short of remarkable. Frank McKenna, in his eulogy
at Harrison's funeral, said, "Any discussion of loved ones would not
be complete without talking about Marilyn Strong. She is one of the
most competent, unselfish and devoted people that I have ever met.
No man had a more faithful companion. She was his rock of Gibraltar.
He needed her."[4] Harrison trusted her implicitly and relied on her. He
once told me, in her presence, and with a sparkle in his eyes, "You
know, Donald, she is a Tory, a Carleton County Tory."

I met Marilyn on numerous occasions and when I interviewed her
for this book, she handed me a two-page handwritten letter which
said, "Harrison McCain was an icon, leader, power house. In personal
life he was more quiet. But when Harrison went into a room, he was
the room. At large gatherings, people would stop talking and gather
around him to hear his stories. I've seen it happen."

AT McCAIN FOODS

Slowly but surely, Harrison withdrew from day-to-day operations.
He stopped going to the office every day in the early 2000s. Howard
Mann, after a year or so, took over as CEO for all of McCain Foods. It
was during this period that I spent more and more time with Harrison,
in his Florenceville home or in Saint Andrews. Although curtailing
his days at the office, Harrison had an office set up at his Florenceville home, with its floor-to-ceiling window, from which he could look
down the valley and to his beloved Florenceville.

Harrison continued to keep a close watch on the company, jotting down facts and ideas in his little black books. Howard Mann was now in charge of operations and the details of the day, but Harrison still had his hands on the wheel and pointed the way for McCain Foods.

He took a keen interest in the company's five-year plans. His personal papers reveal that he carefully read everything that was put to him and never failed to offer comments in the margins, responding in considerable detail to all proposals submitted for his consideration.

He also kept a close watch on both the HOLDCO and OPCO boards. His nephew Andrew continued to chair the HOLDCO board and Harrison himself chaired OPCO. He carefully managed all new board appointments. Among others, he invited Jacques Bougie, CEO at Alcan; Paul Tellier, former clerk of the Privy Council and secretary to the Cabinet under Brian Mulroney; and Vic Young, CEO at Fishery Products International, to become OPCO members. All three accepted and continue to serve on the board.

Three matters were at the front of Harrison's mind as he moved from being CEO to full-time chairman. First was the appointment of senior executives. Second was the company's growth, its margins and profits. Third, he sought to anchor as much of McCain Foods in Florenceville as he could.

MANAGING GROWTH

Harrison took great pride in the fact that ever since McCain Foods was established, equity had always come strictly from retained earnings. Growth, he argued, had to be carefully managed. Betting the farm had been fine for the early years, but only for the early years.

Harrison would go over every proposal to build or acquire a new plant with a fine-tooth comb. He always applied the same criteria: the plant had to be competitive at the international level, not just nationally. It also had to be part of a broader plan to diversify, to establish McCain Foods in strategic locations in order to reduce both business risks and the threat of crop failure.

In March 1997, Harrison signed off on a major expansion in the United States market. McCain Foods now had both the financial and human resources to take on the big American companies. It bought out one of its main United States rivals, Ore-Ida's food service division, from H.J. Heinz for $500 million.

The purchase immediately vaulted McCain Foods to the number two position in the frozen appetizer sales in the United States. The acquisition added nine plants and some 5,500 employees to McCain Foods. The plants were also in strategic centres around the United States.[5]

Purchasing Ore-Ida was a bold move that required an implementation strategy, given the size of the acquisition. Harrison told the *Financial Post* in December 1998 that he and McCain Foods had to "behave until the Ore-Ida integration is complete."[6] To be sure, the acquisition was not easy to digest. At the time, McCain Foods had annual sales of $325 million in the United States while Ore-Ida had $550 million. Thus, McCain Foods–United States was absorbing a business larger than itself. But that was not all. McCain Foods had to "extricate" the business from the engrained Heinz corporate culture. This forced McCain to upgrade all of its systems, from financial reporting to human resources, to accommodate new demands. David Sanchez, a former CFO at McCain Foods, explained, "Our systems and processes were extremely weak. It was an around-the-clock fight for four to five months just to do the basic shipping of products and collecting money. In the meantime, the factories got completely out of control, and we ended up with three hundred million pounds of inventory, most of which we did not need."[7]

The plants on the whole met Harrison's criteria of being competitive internationally. The challenge was to marry McCain's management style and information requirements to the new operations. Another senior McCain employee, Frank van Schaayk, said that the merger "was almost a catastrophe. There were so many things that had not been understood and anticipated as large issues. People were just overwhelmed."[8]

It was also necessary to merge two different cultures. McCain Foods brought a number of Ore-Ida managers to Florenceville for a briefing. Harrison spoke "passionately" to the group about McCain Foods and its future, and his talk had an immediate impact. Randy Myles, CFO at McCain–United States, observed, "I think the people at Ore-Ida were surprised at the roll-up-your-sleeves attitude at McCain and the involvement of senior management in all aspects of the business." Most of the Ore-Ida officials who went on that trip to Florenceville were still with McCain Foods ten years later.[9]

For Harrison, the fact that McCain Foods could successfully manage the integration in a few short years was further proof that it was better that the company be privately held. No need to wash dirty linen in public, as he often said, and decision-making did not have to go through the kind of checks and balances and transparency requirements that publicly traded firms had to manoeuvre.

Harrison's dream that McCain Foods would one day be a major player in the United States had come to pass. McCain could now compete successfully everywhere it went in the world. Mission accomplished. Tom Albrecht, vice-president of purchasing at McDonald's, remarked that McCain Foods has "Americanized its business."[10]

Within a year, McCain Foods was well on its way to accomplishing the merger, and the company was again on the building and acquisition trail. Under Harrison's careful watch, the company built a new $78-million plant in Poland, an $82-million expansion of its Portage la Prairie, Manitoba, plant, and a new $94-million plant in Alberta. In 1999 it acquired the assets of the French firm Farscheure d'Europe, and in 2001 it struck another deal with Heinz to acquire its frozen food companies in South Africa and Australia.

Harrison could also put things in reverse when he felt that it made business sense. He told the *Financial Post* in November 1998 that he was taking a strong look at the highly competitive orange juice business, and he made it clear to his senior executives that it had to produce a profit "or else." McCains sold frozen orange juice under four brands: Kent, McCain, Picnic, and Niagara.[11] Harrison opted for the "or else" and sold the American frozen orange juice business at a handsome profit and McCain Foods also sold its Canadian frozen orange juice business in early 2013.

The development of genetically modified plants (GM) has been highly controversial. Some researchers claim that they are as safe to eat as foods modified by traditional methods of plant breeding, if not safer. They also argue that GM can help solve the challenge of food supply in the developing world. Others, however, believe that not enough research has been carried out to know the full impact of GM, both on the health of individuals and on the world's ecosystem.[12]

After pondering the issue for several months, Harrison decided in November 1999 to refuse to purchase genetically modified potatoes: "We think that genetically modified material is very good science but at the moment it is generating very bad public relations." He went on, "We have too many people worried about eating the product and we are in the business of giving our customers what they want, not what we think they should have."[13]

As for the discord between Harrison and his brother, things were not improving. Wallace had his own challenges in leading Maple Leaf Foods but he remained a major shareholder of McCain Foods and a member of the board of OPCO. Although Wallace chose to continue to sit on OPCO, Paul Waldie reports that he did not feel welcome there.[14]

Wallace made life difficult for Harrison and the HOLDCO board. He had never seen any merit in the two-tier solution and he often referred to HOLDCO as "the kiddie board," making it obvious that he preferred working with the outside directors on the board rather than with the family members.

Wallace also continually criticized Harrison's decisions, at times publicly. He slammed the deal with Heinz, claiming that the $500-million price tag was much too high. A senior McCain executive told me in December 2012 that, in hindsight, the acquisition was a very wise decision and that McCain Foods was able to repay the investment in about three years.

Harrison's papers contain many exchanges with Wallace about the direction of McCain Foods. Wallace argued at times that management was too heavy-handed in certain areas, but not enough in others. He insisted, for example, that the company's pension plan should be driven by "a committee of outside directors and not insiders." At other times, he argued that Harrison was paying insufficient attention to key issues. He wrote Harrison to say that Howard Mann, as CEO, was not getting the kind of support "that he had earned and that there was no one in the firm that was ready to move into the CEO's office if Mann should leave." Harrison responded in March 2003, "You are pretty hard on our organization considering our results and your statement that none of our people are capable of being President of McCain Foods even with an experienced Chairman and a Founding Chairman not far away. Please reply to my home," and gave the

telephone number. There is no indication in Harrison's papers that
Wallace responded.

FLORENCEVILLE

Harrison, as we have noted, kept a careful watch on McCain Foods'
operations to make sure that Florenceville remained the centre of its
activities. He agreed, with some reservations, when Howard Mann
decided to establish his own office in Toronto. Mann explained that
he had no intention of sitting on his backside and that he would, more
often than not, be on the road, given that McCain Foods was now a
global firm. Toronto, he pointed out, was far more accessible to Europe, Australia, and the United States than was Florenceville. Harrison,
however, "ferociously resisted any suggestion that the head office
should be moved to Toronto." Indeed, he continued to pile "everything
he could into New Brunswick."[15]

Not everyone, however, agreed with Harrison on this matter.
Wallace certainly did not, arguing that it was easier to attract top talent
to Toronto than to Florenceville. Nor was Wallace alone in making this
case. Senior executives would, from time to time, raise with Harrison
the possibility of moving various activities to Toronto. One told me
of a colleague who had suggested moving some responsibilities to
Toronto: "He walked in with a smile, walked out without one, and that
matter was never raised again by him, at least as long as Harrison was
chairman."

Harrison would simply not give up on Florenceville. I recall well
his deep sense of pride whenever he talked about the firm's data and
technology centres being located in Florenceville and Centreville,
respectively. The centre attracted IT workers from many countries
and provided services to McCain offices around the world. The centre
is housed in a beautiful state-of-the-art, 1500-square-metre building
built in 1999 at a cost of $2.4 million. To attract and retain IT talent,
the company provides housing at low cost. The centre, which employs
about 250 IT staff representing many nationalities, has squash courts,
saunas, a room for the exclusive use of chess players, and a gym.
According to a McCain Foods publication, "Their presence makes
Florenceville perhaps the most multicultural rural community in
Canada."[16]

The centre's first director, Anil Rastogi, tells how he went to Harrison shortly after he arrived to press for a new IT building: "Nobody thought that he would approve it, but he did."[17] The centre processes over 95 per cent of McCain Foods' worldwide transactions and connects some eight thousand computers, all from little Florenceville.

Harrison also told me with obvious satisfaction that some of the best IT workers were a product of the Computer Science Department at the University of New Brunswick (UNB). At every opportunity he would remind people that UNB was the first Canadian university to establish a computer science department.

Harrison also decided that McCain's Potato Technology Centre should find a home in Centreville. The centre, which undertakes leading-edge research on food processing, product development, and experimental development of new products and processes, attracts scientists from across Europe and North America. It is housed in a large, handsome, two-story building, just on the edge of the town. Harrison took me to the site several times when it was under construction, and once I asked him, "Any chance that you will see a good return on your investment?" "Christ, Donald, do you have any idea how many potatoes we process in an hour? Imagine if we could shave a tiny, tiny slice of more material from a potato. We could produce a lot of cash in no time. Good move, good move, no question." This technology centre, like the IT centre, has been able to attract and retain the accomplished and the gifted from Europe and elsewhere to work in Florenceville.

Harrison also made a substantial personal contribution to the construction of a potato museum in Florenceville, which tells the story of the central importance of the potato to New Brunswick's early settlers. Harrison went further and met with provincial officials to secure their support for the museum. He also urged them not to locate the province's new four-lane highway away from small communities like Florenceville. Otherwise, tourists would just barrel through the province on their way to Prince Edward Island and Nova Scotia. He has been proven right.

GOING PUBLIC

Harrison had reluctantly pondered taking McCain Foods public, but not for very long. Wallace had pushed to have an IPO of McCain shares shortly after Justice Stevenson brought the feud to a close, but then he too had a change of mind. Later, the financial press, and even some of the local newspapers, wrote about the advantages to McCain's going public, arguing that its growth was slowing and profits were not as strong as they once were or could be. They believed an IPO could reverse this situation.

To be sure, going public would have been one solution when the partnership broke down. Early on, Wallace tried to buy company shares from other family members. It will also be recalled that at one point he tried to have Harrison and other McCain families buy his shares or, failing that, to sell them to the public. He wanted full market value, which was not easily established. By the mid-1990s, however, Wallace declared that his shares were "not for sale."[18]

Harrison did not react well to the financial writers' suggestion that McCain Foods should offer some shares to the public. Along with his consistent position that the firm should remain private, he also feared that going public would lead inevitably to Florenceville becoming yet another branch plant.

Both Harrison and Howard Mann wrote letters to the newspapers in which they presented McCain Foods as a family business that continued to thrive in a highly competitive environment. Harrison wrote to the editor of the *Telegraph Journal*,

> Your news story remind me of a story I heard from my former employer, the late K.C. Irving. He said that at one time when he was operating a very large Ford Dealership in Saint John, one of his competitors advertised in a negative way that his company was outselling everyone in Saint John and that no one else amounted to much and made some other ragged comments, much the same as your pejorative story regarding me and our Company. Mr Irving told me that his reply was to buy a page in the local Saint John paper quoting his unit sales of new cars for the last year and the competitor's lower unit sales, and underneath those figures he had inscribed, "And the dogs barked but the caravan rolled on." I think that his story rather fits our situation."

He continued, "McCain Foods continues to dominate the global French fried potato business. We are the world's largest producer by a substantial margin. In the last two years, after the departure of Wallace and sons, we have had our highest sales and highest profits ever. Will you kindly stop that barking."[19] The Irving family owns the *Telegraph Journal*.

Harrison's desire to keep much of head office functions in Florence-ville was unbending, and this loyalty extended to the province itself. Allison McCain tells about being in Toronto when he ran into his uncle. Harrison was off to a meeting with Price Waterhouse Coopers (PWC) – who had audited McCain Foods since its beginnings in 1956 – and asked Allison to accompany him.

PWC made a presentation, outlining new services and informing Harrison and Allison that they were assigning a top accountant from their Toronto office to look after the McCain account. They explained that they were having a difficult time finding first-class people for their New Brunswick office in Saint John, and Harrison wasted no time in responding. He reminded them that McCain Foods had been with PWC since day one, and warned them, "You close your Saint John office and we will put our audit work out to tender." He said that he would not be around forever, which is why he had brought Allison along. He added, "He will remember what we talked about today." PWC to this day has an office in Saint John.

DETERIORATING HEALTH

Harrison never fully recovered from his 1992 heart attack. His personal papers contain numerous exchanges with Boston's Lahey Clinic, both on the state of his health and his medication. Soon, however, he also had to deal with serious kidney problems. Some even suggest that he underwent a personality change after his 1992 heart attack. From that moment on, everything had a sense of urgency for Harrison, even more so than in previous years.

Harrison went into cardiac arrest on 25 September 2000 while in Regina, where he was attending meetings as chair of the National Art Gallery Board of Trustees. He collapsed on the sidewalk while walking back to the hotel with fellow board members and Marilyn Strong. As fate would have it, a nurse was driving by and understood quickly what was happening. She ran to Harrison and wasted no time in applying chest compression and mouth-to-mouth resuscitation. She saved Harrison's life.

Harrison's four children flew to Regina to be by his side. They were able to locate the nurse through the hospital Human Resources Department. As she arrived in the hospital waiting room, there was not a dry eye in the room. Ann called it "a roomful of tears." She later accompanied her father in an air ambulance to the Lahey Clinic, where he slowly improved. Harrison would forever call the nurse his guardian angel. She accepted his invitation to spend time at his Florenceville home, and Marilyn Strong tells me that Harrison made a generous donation to the Regina hospital.

Harrison's second heart attack left him very weak, and soon his failing kidneys required him to be on a dialysis machine three to four times every week. By 2001, he sensed that the end was near but he still kept fighting. Though he loathed the dialysis regime, he never once gave up on the battle; to do so was simply not in his nature.

Harrison spent his final months in Toronto, visiting his children. When, near death, he left Toronto, he told his driver on his way to the airport, "I'm very tired. I want to go home."[20]

Home was always Florenceville. Harrison spent his last days with his close friends, Donald Trafford and John Doucet. Trafford drove him to the Anglican church service on Sundays, but he himself never went in, despite Harrison's urging. He waited outside in a reserved parking spot, close to the church. Trafford was, however, a pallbearer at Harrison's funeral. Sitting in a front pew, he looked at the coffin and said to himself, Harrison, you win again, you finally got me inside a church.

In early March 2004, Allison McCain left his office and drove to Harrison's house for a chat about the company. They had a drink and a good discussion. Harrison was now "founding chairman," with Allison replacing him as chairman. Allison left, telling Harrison that he would be back to continue the chat, but the promised visit never happened.[21] In the afternoon of 16 March 2004, Harrison's niece, Heather Sutherland, came with her three children to visit Harrison at his home, then joined Harrison and his daughter Ann for dinner. Harrison collapsed early the next morning and was immediately flown to the Lahey Clinic, where he died the following day.

NOT THE SAME

McCain Foods became a different company the day Harrison died. To be sure, many things have changed since 2004. The global economy suffered a near-death experience in 2008, and the frozen food industry is considerably more competitive than it has ever been. Not surprisingly, McCain Foods' growth rate has slowed since Harrison's death.

McCain Foods, however, remains the world's leader in the frozen french fries business. The sector is mature, so growth can never equal that of the early years. Andrew McCain, HOLDCO 's chair, maintains that the company has never been as strong as it is today, competing successfully in all corners of the globe, having become what Harrison and Wallace believed that it could be.

Florenceville has, however, lost its place in the sun. The ever-vigilant watchdog is no longer there to look after its interests. Dale Morrison replaced Howard Mann as CEO in 2004 and he accelerated the shift of head office functions away from Florenceville. Today the corporate head office is, for all practical purposes, in Toronto, which houses virtually all executive responsibilities. Florenceville remains home to the company's global head office, but the formal title cannot mask the fact that most of the real action is elsewhere.

Dale Morrison made a pitch to OPCO and later to HOLDCO that the firm's accounting function be outsourced to India. OPCO had little difficulty with the recommendation. Family members of HOLDCO, however, had serious reservations about moving accounting out of Florenceville, despite the cost saving. Morrison snapped at the HOLDCO board, "If I hear the word *Florenceville* once more, I'm going to quit." If Harrison had been in the room, Morrison would not have had to quit.

In his biography of Lord Beaverbrook, another son of New Brunswick, David Adams Richards writes that Beaverbrook did not look from the bottom up for very long. John Stairs, a highly successful Halifax financier, took him under his wing and gave him a view of the business world from the top down. Harrison McCain knew the business world from both ends. In the early years he at times worked on the production line, sold products to restaurants throughout the Maritime provinces, and helped load trucks. By the 1980s, however, he had also mastered the art of viewing the business world from the top down as well.

Like Beaverbrook, Harrison had one weapon that worked, whether looking at the business world from top or bottom: "brash self-confidence."[22] Harrison, however, differed from Beaverbrook in one crucial way. Beaverbrook was known as a good "starter" but not as a "sticker." Harrison was both. He stuck it out until the very end with both McCain Foods and Florenceville. He never became bored with either.

LOOKING BACK

There is a French expression, *rien à son épreuve*, roughly translated "nothing stops him," that defines Harrison McCain. McCain Foods' motto under his watch, "One world, one fry," may sound overly ambitious to many, but not to Harrison McCain. He was wired for ambition, inspiring everyone in his orbit to meet goals that were seemingly out of reach; he always relished a good fight.

Harrison had the ability to compartmentalize, to put things in boxes, each separate from the other in his mind. Thus, the feud with his brother Wallace was all about business. Into its box it went. Family was a different matter. He never stopped loving Wallace as his brother; family had a box of its own.

Yet another box was reserved for Harrison's heartfelt attachment to Florenceville, to its potato farmers, and to New Brunswick. They had been loyal to him and he was loyal to them to the end.

In the following chapters, we look at Harrison's interest in politics, public policy, his community, his province, and his country. We also look at Harrison and his family and friends. Finally we seek to answer the question, Could there be another Harrison McCain?

At McCain Foods and in the country's business community, Harrison will be remembered as a builder, leader, sticker, and leading entrepreneur of his generation. He promoted entrepreneurship at every turn and he took great pride in building, with his brother Wallace, McCain Foods into a highly successful global firm. His ability to focus, to inspire people with his vision of what McCain Foods could be and his incredible attention to details are his legacy.

Harrison was always willing to share lessons learned in business with business associates, family, and friends. Many of those I interviewed for this book had stories to tell about nuggets of wisdom they learned from Harrison. Harrison, they report, was always available to offer advice.

Jim Pattison told me that one lesson he learned from Harrison was to "always be positive, always be enthusiastic about the business, always be aggressive, but always be respectful of others." Scott McCain said that his uncle once told him, "There is no shame in hiring the wrong person, but there is shame in keeping him." Scott added that he learned from his father and his uncle the importance of accountability and the need to measure. He explained, "They wanted and they did measure everything. You always knew where you stood with them."

Andrew McCain reports that Harrison often had him over to the house for "a drink and a chat" and adds that he learned "a lot about business from these chats." One time, they talked about someone who always talked a good line but could never make a decision. Harrison told him, "Andrew, Andrew, when facing a problem, make a decision quickly, don't hem and haw. You will get it right 50 per cent of the time and you will always learn something from the other 50 per cent."

Harrison once summed up how to grow McCain Foods. His thinking applies not just to McCain Foods but to entrepreneurs and businesses wishing to go global. Given his willingness to share lessons learned, it is only appropriate that we would conclude our discussions on Harrison McCain and McCain Foods by reproducing, in his own words, his seven-point business strategy:

1   The continuing strategy of McCain Foods is to pursue profitable growth. Not just profit, not just growth – both!
2   Our principal goal is to lead the global frozen processed potato business. This is our largest business and our first priority.
3   The McCain brand is our most important asset. We will increase its value by advertising support, outstanding marketing, improved quality, and cost reduction.
4   We plan to develop new products and enter new product sectors that complement our brand and utilize our manufacturing, sales, and distribution skills. We will participate in categories only where we believe we can win the number one or number two market share positions.

5   We will search out and develop new geographic markets. Priorities
    will be the profitability of building production facilities at an early
    date and/or better-than-average gross profits.
6   The construction of new factories and the upgrading of existing
    ones will lead to the lowest possible costs. We will not build or buy
    a factory that is not or cannot become internationally competitive
    without tariff protection.
7   We will increase our investment in more and better potato
    processing technologies and new potato products. By better
    efficiencies and improved process technology, we aim for larger
    market shares globally.[23]

EXPANDING BUSINESS SUCCESS

It is relatively easy to document Harrison's business success. This book
and other publications document the growth of McCain Foods from
its early days.[24] The many honours and awards also speak to Harrison's
business accomplishments, but it is more difficult to explain how the
success was generated. At the risk of sounding repetitive, both Harrison
and Wallace contributed to the firm's business success.

Harrison often summed up the reasons for his business success in a
phrase: "Right place, right time." To be sure, launching a frozen food
business at a time when fast food restaurants and eating out came into
fashion with two-income families was fortuitous timing. The decision
by all three levels of governments in Canada to provide cash grants
and loan guarantees to support job creation was serendipitous as well.
Governments have done away with many of these incentives.

But that hardly tells the whole story. Dick Currie, a leading Canadian
businessman of his generation, once told Harrison that he was asked
for one word that best describes business success. His answer, "Cash."
Harrison responded, "A good answer but a better one is tenacity."

Harrison was tenacious. Business success never follows a straight
line, as entrepreneurs know full well. Harrison and Wallace met their
share of challenges, notably in the early years when they were trying,
with limited financial resources, to make a frozen food processing
business work. But there were other obstacles. Recall Bodine, getting
farmers to grow new species of potatoes, putting in place a transporta-

tion system, and the list goes on. More than one former executive at McCain Foods told me that he would walk in Harrison's office with what looked like an unsolvable problem and walked out thinking that they could make things work.

Students of business may wish to take note of Harrison's approach to management. He made a point of reading the business management literature, no matter how busy he may have been. And he learned at the feet of one of Canada's leading industrialists – K.C. Irving.

He learned several lessons from Irving. He knew how to delegate responsibility, believed in management by suggestions, was tolerant of errors (provided that they were not repeated), pushed the envelope in securing new business opportunities, and was always readily accessible to his senior executives and managers, much like K.C. Irving was. Like Irving, he was quick to strike a decision and, once it was made, he could be counted on to stay the course.

Harrison made measurement the central focus of his management style. He measured everything and held his managers to account on these measurements. Salary increases and promotion were tied to performance, based on an easily accessible management information system.

He had an easy relationship with senior executives that was often informal. However, he could be impatient and, in the words of one senior manager, "Harrison could blow a gasket or two every once in awhile."

One former senior executive told me that whenever he had a difficult issue to discuss with Harrison, he would call his assistant Marilyn Strong and ask "How is Harrison today?" She knew what I meant and I would go in to see Harrison, he added, "When the time was ripe for a tough discussion." He went on, "But, you know, Harrison's impatience made us impatient and push harder and perform better."

Politics and Public Policy

Percy Mockler, a rookie Tory member of the New Brunswick Legislative Assembly, received a telephone call from Harrison McCain shortly after the 1982 election. Mockler knew, of course, that McCain Foods was the region's dominant employer, but he had never met Harrison. Nervously, Mockler took the call.

Harrison was calling to congratulate him and to say that since Mockler was representing the region, they would likely be working together. Mockler thanked him for the call and said, "Look, I have just run an election campaign and met a lot of potato farmers. I know a great deal about the potato industry and I think that I can help you." Quick as a whip, Harrison answered, "Christ, I thought that I knew everything I needed to know about the potato industry. What can you tell me that I don't know?" Uncharacteristically, Mockler was at a loss for words.

As Harrison had foreseen, the two men in time forged a productive relationship with each other. For example, one of Mockler's constituents, a potato farmer, came to him with a serious problem. The bank was closing in on his farm and he had over 2,500 barrels of potatoes that he could not sell because the market had temporarily collapsed. Mockler called Harrison and explained the situation.

Harrison asked, "Where does the farmer usually sell his potatoes?"

Mockler answered, "I'll ask, he is sitting in front of me."

The farmer answered, "On the open market."

Next question from Harrison, "Where does he usually buy his fertilizer?"

The farmer's answer, "From now on, from Harrison McCain."

Harrison bought the potatoes, and the farmer kept his farm.

Harrison was not one to sit back and wait for politicians to come calling. Gerald Regan, the former Nova Scotia premier, told me that shortly after he was elected in 1970, Harrison and Wallace walked into his office uninvited and unannounced. Harrison had said to Regan's assistant, "We are here to see the premier. Can you show us the way?" She did, and on walking into Regan's office, Harrison simply said, "We decided that we should know you, and here we are." Regan and Harrison subsequently became fast friends.

POLITICIANS

Harrison knew how to work with politicians from all parties. He had politics in his blood. His grandfather served two terms in the New Brunswick legislature, his father was a leading Liberal figure in Carleton County, and his brother Bob ran unsuccessfully for the provincial Liberal party in the 1960 election. Harrison liked to say that he was a Liberal who sometimes voted Tory.

He had no problem showing his partisan colours. After he had just been awarded Canada's CEO of the Year award, he said in an interview with the *Financial Post*, "I don't see any reason not to declare one's politics, even though I don't always vote that way. I'm a Liberal, a middle-of-the-road hair-to-the-left-of-centre Liberal. I believe in social justice and taxes." He added that he had no problem paying taxes for Canada's extensive social programs because "it's uncivilized to live in a place where the quality of health care is conditioned by the ability to pay."[1]

Harrison believed that politics was the key ingredient to a stable well-functioning society and he contributed both time and money to the political process. I came across many copies of letters to politicians in Harrison's personal papers, and the great majority of them had included a financial contribution to help them pay election expenses. It may come as a surprise to some politicians, particularly Liberals, to hear that he contributed to all the major parties. He also contributed to candidates in leadership campaigns who had no chance of winning. They asked and he gave. I found no evidence in any of the documents that he expected any political favours in return or that any favour was given.

Harrison enjoyed the company of politicians and he was close to several of them. He was sporadically active in the Liberal party. When he did become directly involved, it was to win, as in business. He decided to support Robert Higgins for the leadership of the provincial Liberal party in 1971. It was a tight race and Harrison arrived the night before the weekend convention. There were five candidates but the fight was between the top three: Higgins, John Bryden, and Norbert Thériault. Harrison wasted no time meeting with key Higgins organizers and proceeded to lay down the winning strategy: Harrison's brother Andrew would be appointed treasurer of the party, and someone should talk to Thériault to say that they would like him to become president of the party – a position that came with a modest salary. Thériault had enough votes to be the kingmaker and decide who would become leader – Higgins or Bryden. Shortly before the vote, Thériault withdrew from the race and lent his support to Higgins, who won. Thériault became president.

Harrison also wanted his brother Andrew to become party treasurer. Arthur Doyle, who was in the room, told me that someone reminded him that Senator Nelson Rattenbury was the party treasurer and that he had served the party well. Harrison responded, "Well, does Rattenbury want to continue as party treasurer?" No one knew the answer. Harrison immediately picked up the phone and called Rattenbury to ask whether he wanted to stay on as treasurer. "No" came the answer. Andrew McCain became Liberal party treasurer.[2] Job done for Harrison McCain. He was off on the Sunday afternoon on a business trip to Europe.

Harrison had a special regard for New Brunswick's former premier Louis J. Robichaud. I was a friend to both and the summer before Harrison died, I arranged a get-together for them at Harrison's summer home in Saint Andrews. It was Canada Day 2003. We had lunch and chatted for several hours. It was a magical day, one that will always live with me. Two titans – one in politics, the other in business – spent the afternoon comparing notes and talking about the battles they had fought. The mutual esteem was palpable.

Harrison had told me several times that he had nothing but admiration for Robichaud. He proudly displayed a photo of Robichaud in his office. He also told me that he had never campaigned door-to-door for any politician – except for Robichaud. For his part, Robichaud told me that he had asked Harrison to run for his Liberal party in the 1967 provincial campaign but that Harrison had declined, on the grounds that he was not comfortable with public speaking. Harrison's version was rather different. He was "too busy building the business and making money."

Louis J. Robichaud led New Brunswick kicking and screaming into the modern era. His Equal Opportunity Program touched virtually every aspect of the province's society. As I have mentioned, Robichaud and I became very close friends and, shortly before his death, he gave me the sad task of organizing his funeral. I invited a dozen people to be ·honorary pallbearers, including Wallace McCain. Harrison had died the year before.

Robichaud's impact on New Brunswick is legendary. He established the Université de Moncton, abolished county councils, overhauled the province's social services and education programs, redesigned the taxation system, and introduced an Official Languages Act, making New Brunswick officially bilingual. The legislative agenda was astounding: a total of 130 bills were brought before the Legislative Assembly. The *Canadian Encyclopedia* described the Robichaud reforms "as rapid and fundamental as to be called revolutionary."[3]

Robichaud's reform package unleashed a firestorm of protest. Some anglophone business leaders, the economically strong urban areas, and the English-language media went at Robichaud with all the determination and venom they could muster. The *Telegraph Journal* happily published a letter to the editor saying that Robichaud's plan was a plot to "rob Peter to pay Pierre."[4] The Fredericton *Daily Gleaner* produced a series of cartoons against the plan, including one which depicted Robichaud as Louis XIV with rats crawling out from underneath his robe.

The 1967 provincial election was a critical moment for Robichaud's plan. If he won, he would be able to implement the ambitious program. If he lost, the plan was doomed. The province's largest private sector firms were joined against Robichaud. They financed the return of flamboyant, fluently bilingual, fiery orator and high-profile Tory politician J.C. Van Horne in one of the most hard-fought campaigns in the province's history. Harrison McCain stood tall for Robichaud.

He contributed money to his campaign and spoke out publicly in his behalf, never hesitating to raise his head above the parapet during the tumultuous campaign. Robichaud won thirty-two seats, Van Horne twenty-six.

New Brunswick author David Adams Richards spoke for many in the province when he said that Robichaud "was our greatest premier."[5] In his interview with Harrison, James Downey asked who stood out "among the other political leaders that you've known." Harrison's replied, "Oh, well, Louis Robichaud is an outstanding politician. Outstanding, very, very good. Everybody was calling him everything. The newspapers, led by the Saint John *Telegraph*. They were threatening. They even talked of assassination. Just called him everything they could lay their tongue to. I remember very well sitting down one day and writing a letter to Robichaud saying, 'You're not alone, you're not alone. You're doing just exactly the right thing and tell them to go to hell.' Smart and tough. A great friend of mine. Still is."[6]

Harrison and Robichaud stayed in touch after Robichaud left politics. I discovered in Harrison's personal papers that year after year he had quietly sent Robichaud two season tickets for the Montreal Canadiens. Robichaud was by then in no position to return the favour. This was simply Harrison's way of saying thank you for a job well done.

PIERRE ELLIOTT TRUDEAU

Harrison liked to say that he was the first to come out in support of Pierre E. Trudeau for the leadership of the federal Liberal party. I asked Jim Coutts, Trudeau's chief of staff and a close friend of Harrison, if this was true. Coutts said, "Well, he was there but you know there were also a lot of others. Many supported Trudeau in the early days." However, in a letter to the journalist Nancy Southam, Harrison wrote, "I heard Pierre Trudeau say in public – Harrison McCain was the first political supporter I had."[7]

He also told Southam that when Trudeau came to Florenceville in his first national election campaign, he had taken him around to various churches and Legion Halls to meet with people and to give short speeches. In his interview with Downey, Harrison continued with the story:

On one occasion, I was taking him to a hall to speak and I told him on the way that the place I was taking him to was notoriously Conservative and the ladies who would be there wouldn't be very sympathetic to a Liberal candidate and he should be forewarned. When we got to the hall, there was a crowd, mostly ladies, sitting around the perimeter of the hall, scowling. Mr Trudeau spoke from the centre. His first words were, "I suppose you ladies don't know I am the Minister of Justice for Canada, and I suppose you don't realize I know that besides quilting you are playing cards for money in the basement of this building. If I weren't in a good mood I would do something about that because it is illegal." The ladies were stunned, then broke into loud laughter with good humour.

Harrison tells James Downey that he thought highly of Trudeau from the time he was justice minister in the Pearson government: "I admired him before I knew him – just from his speeches, from hearing him speak and reading his speeches. He just made such eminent good sense. When the Liberals needed a leader, he was a leader. Without even having met Trudeau in my life, I selected Trudeau."

Typically, Harrison got down to business. Several times he called Trudeau's office but was never able to get through to him. After a few attempts, he called Premier Robichaud and told him, "I want to support Trudeau and I can't even get him on the telephone. Can you arrange that for me?" Robichaud said he would, but added that he himself was supporting Allan J. MacEachen or Bob Winters, because "MacEachen and Winters were Maritimers and they would look after the Maritimes." Robichaud later told me that in fact he had favoured Trudeau and was very close to him, but that it would be best for an Acadian premier to be seen supporting MacEachen and Winters. He went on to say that he had a long discussion with Trudeau to explain his decision and that Trudeau had understood. Robichaud also made it clear to everyone that he was with MacEachen or Winters only on the first ballot and that he would be with Trudeau the rest of the way.[8] Trudeau called Harrison immediately after speaking with Robichaud, or in Harrison's words, "the same day."

Harrison told Trudeau that he admired his speeches, particularly on social justice and Quebec's place in Confederation. He offered his support, financial and otherwise. As a result, Harrison became chairman of Trudeau's leadership campaign for New Brunswick and, together with Wallace, chief fund raiser in the province. Trudeau and Harrison became good friends, and their friendship lasted until Trudeau's death in 2000.[9]

They met frequently. Harrison told me that he was likely the only Canadian who saw Trudeau getting dressed. They were going to a social event in Ottawa and Harrison had gone to meet him at 24 Sussex. Pressed for time but wanting to carry on his conversation with Harrison, Trudeau invited him to his bedroom where they talked while he was putting on his tuxedo.

In a letter to his daughter Ann on 20 July 1976, Harrison wrote that he had had a good chat with the prime minister at the Queen's reception in Halifax and that Trudeau had invited him to join him at the Montreal Olympics the following week. He added that Trudeau introduced him to "Margaret, whom I had a nice chat with. She is good-looking, very friendly and smoking 8-inch thin cigars! No kidding! No doubt, like some of the rest of us, she wants to be the centre of attention."

In the mid-1970s, Trudeau offered Harrison a Senate appointment, but Harrison declined because he "had too damn much to do" and "couldn't even take that job in my spare time." According to Harrison, in his interview with Downey, Trudeau replied, "Don't worry," suggesting that he would not have much to do in the Senate and so could still attend to his business responsibilities. Harrison was convinced that Trudeau simply wanted to do "a favour to an old friend, that's all." Downey asked, "But you were not tempted?" Harrison replied, "No, no. Making money, Jim, is the only game in town."[10] Harrison asked Marilyn Strong, "What would I do sitting around in the Senate all day doing nothing?"

FRANK McKENNA

Harrison also counted Frank McKenna among his close personal friends. Always the man to get things done efficiently, Harrison carefully planned his own funeral. He selected the pallbearers, went through the guest list, and asked McKenna to give the eulogy in the tiny Anglican Church in Florenceville.

Harrison had happily contributed to McKenna's election campaigns and supported him in his successful bid to lead the provincial Liberal party. He also helped McKenna establish new contacts in both the political and business communities.

He wrote federal Liberal leader John Turner on 7 May 1985 to say that he believed that New Brunswick "has a big winner in Frank McKenna." He went on to say that there "is a high degree of certainty that we can push Richard [Hatfield] out of office in the next election." He was right. McKenna's Liberal party won every seat in New Brunswick in the 1987 general election, the largest electoral outcome in Canadian history. To Turner, Harrison said about McKenna, "Like most of us country boys, he is a little rough around the edges and unsophisticated, but will improve and, more importantly, he is a man of substantial energy with a genuine desire to do something for our people."[11]

McKenna did indeed improve. He became a highly sought-after speaker, Canada's ambassador to the United States, and a business titan in his own right on Bay Street. If Robichaud was New Brunswick's greatest premier, Frank McKenna was a close second.

McKenna pursued economic development for New Brunswick with a missionary zeal and met with considerable success. He led the province through some difficult times, most notably the sharp recession of the early 1990s and the substantial reductions to federal transfer payments resulting from the Chrétien-Martin program review. He also had a major impact on New Brunswickers' view of themselves by bringing industry and jobs to the province and by his own "can do" attitude.[12]

Harrison said to James Downey, "McKenna had a reasonably good flair for business. McKenna definitely has a business bent. He can do business and does do business. And he's able." He gave McKenna his seal of approval: "Good fella, good fella."[13]

Harrison also stood by other Liberals through thick and thin. He was there not only to provide funding but also an encouraging word when needed. After Camille Thériault took over from Frank McKenna as Liberal leader and premier in 1998, his short-lived government went down to defeat at the hands of Bernard Lord and his Progressive Conservative party.

The day after his defeat, some senior Liberals asked for Thériault's immediate resignation as party leader, with a few even suggesting that he leave the province. Thériault did not know Harrison well and he was surprised to get a telephone call from him a few days later. Harrison told him, "Ignore those bullshitters. They do not know what they are talking about. Stay as long as you want. You have my support."[14]

TORIES

Harrison counted Tories among his political friends. He became quite close with Ray Hnatyshyn, former governor general, whom he first met when he served on the advisory committee of the Order of Canada. Harrison often invited the Hnatyshyns to join him on holiday or at his summer home in Saint Andrews. He told me that Hnatyshyn was a very nice man, whose company he thoroughly enjoyed.

Dave Kearney, one of Harrison's pilots, recalls flying Harrison and Ray Hnatyshyn from Ottawa to Florenceville. When they arrived, Harrison asked Kearney if he would give them a lift because he did not have his car at the hangar. Kearney said, "Look, I only have my old Toyota truck that I take hunting and fishing, and it's not in good shape." "No problem," Harrison replied, and turning to Hnatyshyn, said, "Let's jump in the back of the truck." Kearney drove them to Harrison's house with "Harrison and the governor general chatting away in the back of my old truck." He added "Oh! I only wish that I had had my camera."[15]

Both Harrison and Billie were close to New Brunswick premier Richard Hatfield, though Harrison fought hard to defeat him in the 1987 election. Harrison's capacity to put things in separate boxes came to the fore again. Friendship belonged in one box, business in another, and partisan politics in yet another. That said, Harrison did vote for Richard Hatfield twice and Hugh John Flemming once, likely the only times he voted Tory. To paraphrase Winston Churchill, Harrison "loved the rider but disliked the horse."

Hatfield, another Carleton County politician, would frequently drop by Harrison's for dinner. He and Billie became close friends and Harrison said of him, "A good fellow, I always liked him." He tells a fine Hatfield story:

Well, one day he called and invited himself for dinner that night. And he said that he'd be coming up in the government plane and landing at the airport and he told me the time to pick him up. And the plane was going on to Montreal to some event that was going to take an hour or two, and then returning, and would pick him up on the way back. This was in the winter time. Well, at least it was cold out. He got into the sauce in very, very good style. We both had several drinks before dinner and then some wine. Then he got out the brandy. And I, my common sense had finally shut me off the brandy, I knew that was deadly stuff. He laid the brandy right to him and he really did have a snoot full. Now in the meantime, the government plane had returned and circled around Florenceville three or four times to make sure he could hear it, so he'd go to the airport. And I reminded him of that.

He said, "No, they're perfectly all right. Don't pay any attention at all Harrison, they're perfectly all right."

Well then the captain arrived at the door and spoke to him and said, "You know, it's cold up there. We can't run the heater in the airplane while it's just sitting and we're not flying. And we can't get in the hangar, the hangar's locked. And I didn't have any key to it; I couldn't let them in the hangar. And so, you know, we're freezing to death, we've got to get going."

He said, "Yeah fine. I'm not going for now." And he came back and he said, "Well, Harrison, I think I'll have another drink before I go." So he downed another cognac, he had another cognac or two.

And anyway, when it finally came time for him to go, I suppose it was half past 10 or 11 o'clock at night and at that time he'd be the best part of an hour late getting up to the airport. He had a lot to drink. I drove him up to the airport. I really didn't know what to do. The ground was slippery and I wasn't at all sure that he could make it to the plane. But I didn't feel I could take him by the arm because there was a good big crowd there.

There was a good, big crowd there of Florencevillites because they heard the plane circling around the village three or four times and so they immediately said, "Something is wrong, you know. Harrison and Wallace are trying to get in here somehow and can't get in. There's something badly wrong here."

So they had all collected around the hangar in Florenceville. There must have been twenty-five people there or maybe more, maybe even fifty people around there. And he had to walk by them to get to the plane. And I didn't know if he could or not. But I didn't feel I should really take him by the arm because that would be a dead giveaway that he was drunk. So I was caught between a rock and a hard place. So I just crossed my fingers, and he made a beeline for the plane door. He just said, "Hello," and he kept on walking. He didn't stop to talk to anybody but he kept on going very straight. He got up the steps.

And I said, "Thank God."[16]

Harrison maintained that Hatfield was "no more conservative than I am. He was a Liberal just masquerading as a conservative, time and again." He added that Hatfield had little interest in the management of government but he had the "right attitude towards the federal government [i.e. Trudeau's Liberal government] and the French."[17]

Hatfield was soundly defeated in the 1987 election. His party lost every seat, including his own, so he was out of a job and had little money. Harrison arranged to have him appointed chairman of the Beaverbrook Art Gallery, quietly providing funding to the gallery so that it could pay Hatfield a $25,000 salary.

Harrison also enjoyed Brian Mulroney's company, though he said, "Women almost universally said, 'Oh that blabbermouth, that bullshitter.'" He was "too slick, he worried them to death. But," he added, "I like him enormously, I like him great. He's got a wonderful personality, got a wonderful personality, very easy to talk to, gregarious, and I like him great."[18] Harrison, however, had a strong disagreement with both Mulroney and McKenna on one policy issue – the Canada-US Free Trade Agreement, as we will see later.

Bud Bird was the federal member of Parliament for Fredericton between 1988 and 1993, having served as minister of natural resources in Hatfield's government from 1978 until he resigned in 1982. Bird owned a construction supply company, which ran into financial difficulties during this time. He resigned from Cabinet and the Legislative Assembly so as to concentrate on salvaging his business. One of the first calls he received was from Harrison McCain, whom he knew only slightly. They belonged to different political parties and their paths had not crossed often.

Harrison asked, "Bud, how much shit are you in?"

Bird, in his *Family History*, has a chapter titled "Saving the Business," in which he gives substantial credit to Harrison McCain: "In his usual blunt and aggressive fashion, Harrison said 'Even though we are on the opposite side of the political fence, Bud, we thought you were a damn good minister and it's a shame that you had to leave the government. Just what the hell is wrong with your company and what do you need to do to fix it?'"[19]

Bud outlined the problems, which included a number of sizeable accounts payable.

Harrison then presented a game plan: "Bud, here is what you should do. You should call every one of your suppliers and remind them of how much business you have given their firms over the history of your company. Tell them you need their help now. Ask them to take the debts you owe them and set them aside for at least a year or even longer. There is no reason why you should go out of business and you tell them to call me if they want to discuss the matter further."

Bird answered, "Well, Harrison, I owe one of your companies about $50,000."

Harrison promptly replied, "We will freeze that account indefinitely ... And I will send you a letter today to that effect. You can use that letter to show other suppliers and the bank."

Bird did precisely that and within a few years he had his business back on its feet. He writes, "Thanks almost entirely to the initiative that Harrison McCain had taken in calling me and to the advice and assistance he provided, I was able to stop the bleeding and give the business a fighting chance to come back."[20]

PUBLIC POLICY

Harrison McCain took an active interest in public policy and often welcomed an opportunity to engage in a debate or shape public policies. He had strong views on trade, economic development, and taxation policies, as one would expect. But he also had a keen interest in national unity and social policies.

Harrison jumped into the Canada-US free trade debate with both feet. Frank McKenna, a strong proponent of free trade, remembers the "knock down, drag out battle with Harrison and Wallace." Harrison called McKenna early on in the debate to say, "Mr Premier, you're doing a great job. We like you. We like you a lot. You're a great fella but on this free trade issue, you're dead wrong and we're going to do everything that we can, everything, everything, to destroy you." In recalling this conversation, McKenna mused, "Gee, I thought to myself, I'm glad he likes me."[21]

Harrison did his homework and remained in constant contact with both senior federal and provincial government officials throughout the debate. His files contain numerous documents and letters that he sent to both Mulroney and McKenna on the issue. In one instance, he stressed that "in general" he supported free trade and lowered tariffs. However, he wrote that McCain Foods had responsibilities to its employees and shareholders. Here, he maintained, there was cause for considerable concern for them and for New Brunswickers.

He reminded McKenna that there were 120 people working at the McCain pizza factory in Grand Falls and that it was an unlikely place to have a pizza plant to serve the Canadian market. Only McCain would build it in New Brunswick, but nobody, even the McCains, would have built it in the province to serve the entire North American market.

He elaborated: "Under the Free Trade Agreement, frozen pizza will come into Canada duty free, and that will make us non-competitive because we are forced to buy cheese (the largest cost factor) from Milk Marketing Boards at about 40 percent more than the American price." He added, "We have tried hard to get Ottawa to do something about this and your people know our concern, but apparently there is no relief." He concluded, "I seriously doubt the ability of that plant to continue its operations in Grand Falls, and it probably should be relocated to Niagara Falls, New York."[22]

He reminded McKenna and others that New Brunswick's climate does not compare well with much of the United States, at least for growing vegetables. He insisted that McCain Foods and job creation in New Brunswick would be hurt by the proposed free trade deal. He put the question to policy-makers, "What companies in New Brunswick can flatly state that with free trade they will expand their business and hire people? Who are they?"[23]

Harrison and his staff kept a close watch on the free trade negotiations as they came to a close. He put forward proposals to both orders of government to deal with specific concerns at the company. Among them:

1 Further processed products containing 10% or more of Supply Managed Ingredients go on the Import Control List. In this context, we mean the total weight of supply managed ingredients, for example, eggs, cheese, poultry, not to exceed 10% in total.
2 The proposed guidelines for fresh fruit and vegetables allow a 20 year right of intervention by our Federal Government under a certain now-agreed formula. We ask that *processed* fruits and vegetables be included in this section under exactly the same rights because the same reasons apply for 12 months, not three months![24]

Some of his concerns were accommodated, but many were not.

The Canada-US Free Trade Agreement came into force on 1 January 1989, and the result was substantially increased trade between the two countries. Trade with the United States today accounts for over 40 per cent of Canada's GDP, compared with about 25 per cent prior to the agreement being struck. Implementation of the agreement was to be carried out over a ten-year period to enable businesses to adjust to the new economic realities. This, and a particularly weak Canadian dollar, generated new economic activities for Canadian firms.[25] The McCain pizza plant is still in business and McCain Foods has hardly been hurt by the agreement. Harrison admitted later that he had been wrong about the agreement's impact on McCain Foods and New Brunswick. He once said, "Looking back on it, it was exactly the right thing to do."[26]

Harrison kept a close watch on all government policies that had an impact on the company. He did a lot of the legwork himself and had an aversion to hiring lobbyists. He insisted that no one should need a middle-man to talk to government officials. As he wrote in 1985 to Prime Minister Mulroney, Finance Minister Michael Wilson, Agriculture Minister John Wise, and his Member of Parliament Fred McCain (a Tory and a distant cousin),

I am advised that the Department of Agriculture is about to levy a charge of 43 cents per 100 lbs on frozen foods exported from Canada. I believe we are Canada's largest exporter of frozen foods and so the matter is of particular importance to us. Over the last three years that fee would have cost us 470,000 dollars. The export business is tough. We don't want any extra costs whatsoever so I strongly recommend as follows:

1   Forget those charges. It is the wrong place to add costs.
2   Allow us to ship our goods declaring Canadian standards basic scores taken by our own quality control department who give continuous inspection to all this merchandise anyway. In short, we absolutely don't need a government inspector so you save the cost and we save the fee.
3   We would happily pay the fee anytime we have a buyer requiring a Canadian government inspection certificate. I look forward to your comments at your earliest convenience.

Regards,
H. Harrison McCain

There is no evidence to suggest that Harrison either won or lost his point.

PROMOTING ECONOMIC DEVELOPMENT

Harrison had a strong interest in economic development in his province, often putting forward ideas to the government or others with an interest in public policy. He knew of my academic interest in regional development and claimed to have read one of my books and my report to Prime Minister Brian Mulroney on the establishment of the Atlantic Canada Opportunities Agency. In one of our conversations, he told me, "You know, we could solve this regional development problem. Here is what you do. Just abolish all corporate income tax in the four Atlantic provinces. That would work. That would work. No question. It would bring in tons of new investments."

He wrote McKenna and his senior staff on a number of occasions with specific suggestions, such as when he urged them to hire smart

MBA types who "can think, talk, and get going." He prompted them
to identify five or six industries that could be as "logically" located in
New Brunswick as they could in Toronto or Boston, and pursue an
opportunity rather than "simply waiting for good fortune."

He suggested a few possibilities, such as high-tech manufacturers,
because New Brunswick had plenty of labour, and freight was not an
obstacle. He believed that they should look to Japan for new investments. He also suggested that they go after data processing firms,
including credit cards companies, since data processing could be done
anywhere and New Brunswick could do it more cheaply than Toronto
or New York. How about the insurance industry?, he asked. The sole
fixed assets are a building and desks, and the principal asset is trained
staff. New Brunswick with its universities and colleges could be asked
to provide the necessary training.

He also urged policy-makers to seek out corporations with a "record of good corporate citizenship" and cited IBM as an example. Good
corporate citizenship can take many forms. Instead of giving money
to charity, why not talk to the CEOs of large firms with a track record
of good corporate citizenship and say to them, "You want to do something good for your country or for communities? Locate some of your
activities to New Brunswick." He suggested they make the case that "a
donation of effort would pay much better rewards than donations to
charities." The premier should make such a pitch and explain that it
would also be profitable for the companies because New Brunswick
has excellent workers. He identified a number of possible firms – IBM,
Merck, Imasco, Moore Corp., General Motors, Ford and Canadian
Marconi."[27]

RELATIONS WITH THE UNIVERSITIES

Harrison had something of a "love/hate relationship" with universities.
Given my own position, I was often the butt of his teasing. Nevertheless, he was financially generous to universities, especially those in the
Maritimes. University presidents came calling for one "special" project
or another – some expensive, others less so – but all asking for money.
Harrison gave. He also stayed in close communication with a number
of university officials and faculty.

Harrison's frustration with universities involved their role in research and development. He called for a "national industrial focus" and a comprehensive economic development plan tied to R&D. He asked for targets so that progress could be measured, the goal being to produce "innovative world-class products." Here, he argued, the universities had "a super important role" but that they were not living up to expectations.

Harrison also believed that linkages between universities, the private sector, and government were not as strong as they should be. In his view, all three were operating far too much in isolation. Closer collaboration was essential, he argued, if Canada was to prosper. His prescription: "Basic research should be linked more closely to applied research, and applied research should be linked to a Canadian application, and, if we can't see a strong linkage in the last two, and some linkage with the first one, we shouldn't do it." He told a McGill University convocation in 1991, "I doubt that research work should be administered or managed by scientists. I seriously doubt that. Businessmen are not much on molecular structure. I do not believe that scientists are much on cash flows."[28]

NATIONAL UNITY

Harrison was a strong proponent of national unity. In the immediate aftermath of the failure of the Meech Lake Accord, he joined the Group of 22, a collection of politicians and business leaders who met to ponder Canada's future as a nation. They produced a report with David Cameron, the political science professor from the University of Toronto, holding the pen. Cameron said of Harrison's participation, "He was clearly sufficiently concerned about it to spend a big chunk of his time working on it ... His whole impulse is to action. It's 'let do it' ... He didn't try to dominate the discussions. He would ask pointed questions. Nobody could be unaware that he was in the room."[29]

I too became concerned when the Meech Lake Accord collapsed. I feared that the Maritime provinces would be left on the outside looking in as Canada's future was being played out elsewhere. The West had the Reform Party, Quebec had the Bélanger-Campeau Commission looking into the political and constitutional status of Quebec, and Ontario had its powerful political, economic, and financial infrastructure.

I contacted a number of high-profile Maritimers to see if we could put together a group that would bring a Maritime perspective to the debate. I called it the Northumberland Group, after the Northumberland Strait, which links the three Maritime provinces. A dozen people signed on, representing various sectors of society. From politics came Louis J. Robichaud and Robert L. Stanfield; from the business community, Harrison McCain, Allan Shaw of Shaw Industries, Derek Oland, president of Moosehead Breweries, my brother Claude Savoie, a Moncton entrepreneur, and Regis Duffy, a well-known businessman from Prince Edward Island; from the academic community, President Howard Clark of Dalhousie University; and from the arts community, the artist Alex Colville, singer Rita MacNeil from Cape Breton, and lastly, Harvey Webber, founder of Atlantic Canada Plus.

Recently in going through my old files for this book I was reminded that three people in particular played a very active role in the Northumberland Group. I have a number of letters and notes, some of them handwritten, from Robert Stanfield, Harrison McCain, and Alex Colville. McCain pushed hard for the group to endorse an equal and elected Senate, but Stanfield was strongly opposed to the idea, feeling that the time was not ripe to talk about Senate reform. I had several telephone conversations with Harrison, suggesting that we should find a middle ground. At first Harrison was not convinced. He said, "Donald, Donald, we need someone in Ottawa to speak for the Maritimes. Christ, other countries like the United States and Australia have it, why not us? We can't win with how things work in Ottawa."

In my search for a middle ground, I suggested that we should have an independent review of the merits of an elected Senate. Harrison relented and finally agreed to go with my suggestion. "Stanfield is a good fellow and I will defer to him for now," he said. If I could turn back the clock, knowing what I do now, I would have stood firm with Harrison. He had it right. The voice of the regions will never be properly heard in Ottawa if the status quo in our national political institutions is allowed to continue.

GIVEN TO THE COMMUNITY

Harrison was on the board of one publicly traded firm – the Bank of Nova Scotia. He was asked to join a number of others but declined. He did, however, agree to serve on the board of Petro Canada, a Crown corporation with modest director's fees, because "I believe in what they're trying to do."[30]

Harrison was also chairman of the National Gallery's board of trustees from 1999 until 2002. The gallery reports that it "thrived" during the period, mounting a series of exhibitions, including one devoted to the work of Alex Colville.[31] Harrison served because he felt that it was his public service duty to do so, but also to honour his wife, Billie, who had a lifelong interest in fine arts.

Harrison encouraged others at McCain Foods to serve the community. David O'Brien, a McCain executive, tells me that he went to his office one day, exhausted. The pressure of work was one thing, but he also spent long hours in his role as chair of the Board of Governors at the University of New Brunswick. Harrison took him aside and told him that he "had" to take time off for himself and his family. He said that he should count the hours he devoted to the university as hours at work. "David," he explained, "we all have a responsibility to give back to the community. It is part of being a good corporate citizen."[32]

Often without fanfare, Harrison contributed funds to many causes. His papers reveal that he gave regularly to the universities, health-care facilities, churches, political campaigns, and the arts and culture community. On numerous occasions, he would ask that his identity not be revealed to the recipients. Another New Brunswick businessman, well known for not opening his wallet, suddenly started to support some causes. I mentioned to Harrison that this man had obviously had a change of heart. "No, Donald," came his response, "he had a change of mind. Big difference, big difference." As for the people of Florenceville, Harrison was often first on the scene with help, be it someone whose house was destroyed by fire or someone else who had incurred steep medical bills after having gone outside the province for treatment.

Bob Brown, a McCain Foods pilot, reports that Harrison and Wallace always had a plane on call to go on a moment's notice. He tells me that the McCain brothers had "a quiet agreement with the local medical community that a plane would be made available in case of an emergency. There was no cost involved. The medical community understood not to abuse the favour."

Brown recalls that Harrison called one time asking him if he could fly that evening. Brown said that he could be at the terminal in fifteen minutes or so and have the plane in the air in forty-five. Harrison responded, "See you there in fifteen minutes." Harrison told Brown that the local doctor had called him to say that he had just been told that a local farmer was eligible for a kidney transplant, provided that he be in Halifax in a few hours. Harrison explained that he knew the farmer and that he was of very "meagre means" and that "he had probably never left New Brunswick before." Harrison gave Brown taxi money and asked him to look after him in Halifax. He left before the farmer arrived at the terminal because he did not want to be seen doing him a favour.

On another occasion, Harrison called Brown on a New Year's Eve, asking if he could fly to Halifax a forty-year-old potato farmer with a serious heart condition that required immediate attention. After the farmer returned home, he went to Harrison's house to say that he wanted to pay him for the flight. Harrison told the farmer that the flight "cost a lot but there would be no cost to him," asking "to forget about it." The farmer never did and he left a basket full of table potatoes on Harrison's doorstep once a week, for several years. Brown told me that Harrison always insisted on "no publicity."

Harrison not only gave a substantial amount of his own money to various New Brunswick causes, he was also the "go-to-guy" for many New Brunswick institutions. Arthur Doyle, then with the University of New Brunswick, asked Harrison if he would call the CEOs of the six major Canadian banks to raise funds for a university construction project whose costs had been underestimated and in consequence the university was in "a bit of a bind."

Harrison asked how much the university needed.

Doyle said, "$25,000 from each of the six banks would do it and we have a one-month time line."

Harrison responded, "What the hell do you mean, a one-month timeline? I don't have a month. We are going to get it done today."

He called in Marilyn Strong and asked her to get the six CEOs on the line. The first call was to the CEO of the Bank of Nova Scotia, no problem, given that Harrison served on its board of directors. The second was to the CEO of the Bank of Montreal, who said that he would happily take the request to the "committee." Harrison was quick to respond, "Take it to a committee? What the hell is that about? Who runs the bank, you or a committee?" By the time the conversation ended, Harrison had a firm $25,000 commitment. The third CEO asked Harrison about the nature of the project and why there was a cost overrun. Harrison told him, "Why in Christ are you cross-examining me? Last month, you called me to ask for a contribution to a cause you were supporting. I didn't cross-examine you about it and I said yes." Harrison got the $25,000, and by the end of the day he had secured commitments from five of the six CEOs.

Harrison did not always wait to be asked to help, often taking the initiative, as his personal papers reveal. One such instance involved the serious drought in the southeastern United States in 1988–89. When he read that farmers were struggling to keep their livestock fed, Harrison decided to organize a "trainload" of hay to be shipped to farmers in the affected states. He called a number of friends to solicit their help, and within a few weeks, he was able to deliver the hay. I note again that he did not want any publicity about this initiative.

During the water shortage in New York City in the mid-1980s, Mayor Ed Koch urged residents to conserve water, postponing the opening of a new water fountain in Central Park to underline the importance of water conservation.[33] Harrison McCain called Koch to offer a few truckloads of water to enable the city to open the fountain, explaining that his trucks were bringing up orange juice but often going back south empty. The mayor accepted the offer and the fountain was formally opened, with considerable publicity.

Harvey Gilmour, a friend of Harrison's and at the time head of development at Mount Allison University, read about the initiative and sent a fax to Harrison saying, "We are running out of money at Mount Allison. Could you send a truckload of cash?" The next day, Gilmour came home from work to see one hundred pounds of potatoes on his front lawn with a note from Harrison, "No cash, but we do have potatoes."

LOOKING BACK

Harrison McCain believed in giving back to society and to his community. He was once asked by a journalist what he found most rewarding about his work. Harrison responded without hesitation, "Seeing new cars in our parking lots, and solid roofs over the heads of the fellas who drive them. I like the fact that we are able to provide jobs for thousands of hard-working people."[34]

He saw merit in partisan politics and had little patience for cynicism. He had respect for those entering the political arena, whether they were Liberals or not. To be sure, it was a different era, a less cynical age. However, Harrison did more than his peers. He played an active role in politics and also never hesitated to roll up his sleeves and contribute to shaping public policy.

Harrison also demonstrated real courage. The 1960s was a tumultuous decade in New Brunswick. The national media, preoccupied as they always are with Ontario and Quebec, hardly noticed, but New Brunswick too was having a revolution, one that was more daring, more dislocating, more controversial, and more disquieting than Quebec's Quiet Revolution. In publicly supporting Robichaud's program of equal opportunity, he set himself against many in the anglophone business community, of which he was a part, and who were ferociously opposed to the program.

Harrison never hesitated to speak out on issues that he believed in. If someone had to speak truth to the provincial or federal governments on ways to promote economic growth or to Ottawa on national unity or to the universities on research and development, Harrison was the man for the job.

Family and Friends

A wise elderly Acadian woman once remarked to me that there is only so much oxygen in any room and that some people consume more oxygen than others. Harrison McCain was one of them. He had presence in the way a great actor has presence. He could hold sway in a room by the sheer force of his personality. Bob Crossman told me that this could be intimidating, and David O'Brien said, "If you put twenty people in a room who had never met each other before and Harrison was one of them, within an hour, there would be a consensus that he was the leader to show them out of the room."

Harrison was anything but a loner. He was gregarious, needing to be around people. He once wrote to Richard Hatfield summoning him to join a party of friends at a chalet he and Billie had rented in Switzerland. His reason? He needed "a Tory" to balance the group that would otherwise consist only of Liberals. He enjoyed the company of friends from business, politics, academe, and Carleton County.

FAMILY

The family home was Billie's domain, since Harrison was so frequently away. The children remember her special pleasure, and theirs, in decorating the house for Christmas, putting up the tree, or planning for Halloween. She was a gentle woman who had a talent for defusing her husband's temper if he came home frustrated by something that had gone off the rails. Her close friend Sally Baxter told me that Billie "was shy" but that she "had incredible inner strength."

Laura recalls her mother teasing Harrison, who was always out of the house and on his way to work by eight in the morning. "Who," she would ask, "is at the office with a whip, making sure that you are the first one in?" Harrison "would laugh, jump into his Cadillac and gun it down the road as fast as he could." Gillian, the youngest, remarked that despite her father's whirlwind departure for the office, he still made the time every few weeks to bring her mother breakfast in bed. It was always the same menu: "cereal, a muffin, coffee, and a flower in a vase." Before leaving home, said Gillian, her father would tune into the radio "farm report" at such a volume that it woke the whole house. When at home in the evening, he would religiously listen to both the six and ten o'clock national news and occasionally watch a movie in between, although sometimes he jumped out of his chair to record on his Dicta-phone the next day's instructions for his assistant. The movies they watched had to be comedies, since no one should ever want to watch a sad movie. Gillian explains that "my dad had a happy gene."

Students in Carleton County had a school "potato break" in the fall so that they could stay home and help with the harvest. Laura would go to her friend's place, about two kilometres from her house, and stay for much of the week to help with the harvest. She recalls that they would get up at 6:30 a.m. and be in the potato fields by 7:00, ready to work. Pickers were each allocated a space and they had to keep up. Laura, as a youngster, could not keep up, and within an hour or so she would be on the phone to her father asking for help. Harrison would leave the office, drive over to the potato farm several kilometres away, and help Laura pick potatoes. It would take only ten minutes or so before she was caught up, and Harrison would then chat with the farmer and return to the office.

Mark, like his sisters, remembers Billie as the anchor of the family. He has happy memories of childhood summer holidays in Prince Edward Island and family ski trips, first to Mars Hill just across the border in Maine, from which they graduated to Sugar Loaf in Maine, Mont-Sainte-Anne in Quebec, and eventually to Sun Valley, Idaho. Harrison described himself as not "a great skier but a brave one."

Mark attended a private school in Ontario's Muskoka region. On one occasion he flew to Fredericton to see a girlfriend without letting his family know. While there, he called home as he often did. When

Harrison asked, "Where are you?," Mark replied, "In the phone booth at school." "How could that be?," Harrison asked, "given that school officials called to say that the school burnt down yesterday, but that you were OK, since you were not at school?" The next thing Harrison heard was a click.

Harrison strongly encouraged all his children to read. Mark remembers his father taking him to buy comic books, on the sensible grounds that you have to start somewhere. Reading anything, including comic books, was always better than not reading at all. Harrison himself, who could rarely sit still, always found time to read.

Ann remembers her father being supportive and willing to see his children spread their own wings. She said that he may have had reservations but he was always careful not to show it. At the age of nineteen, Ann informed her parents that she decided to go to Addis Ababa, Ethiopia, in 1976 to work for Canadian Crossroads International. The organization's goal was to promote greater cross-cultural understanding between Canada and the developing world. Nervously, Harrison and Billie gave their blessings.

Harrison was not one to brood. But if he had one regret about the past, as he told me a few years before his death, it was that he wished he had spent more time at home as his children were growing up. He never mentioned it again; it was a rare instance of introspection, and I know that it was heartfelt. No one in the family, however, resented his long absences. "It was his passion. He loved what he was doing and we were all 100 per cent behind him," said Laura.

In Frank McKenna's eulogy at Harrison's funeral, he recalled, "He was devoted to and talked incessantly about Mark, Peter, Ann, Laura, and Gillian. They and their spouses were the centre of his universe. He glowed with pride at their accomplishments. His grandchildren bedazzled him."[1] The *Spud*, the newsletter of the New Brunswick potato industry, wrote, "A family man, Harrison loved his family. They were the most important part of his life. The challenges which hurt Harrison most deeply and from which he never recovered were the losses of his beloved wife and son [more on the tragic death of Peter McCain, below]. He was very proud of his children and would tell you about them if given any opportunity at all."[2] Two years after Billie's death, Harrison told his friend Reuben Cohen, "I loved my wife and I love her still," and he never remarried. Cohen wrote that when Harrison "lay ill in Boston, I phoned Billie, or she me, almost every evening, and no wife could have shown more care and concern."[3]

Except for Peter, all Harrison's children eventually moved away from Florenceville. But they were frequent visitors, coming to see their dad, separately and together.

As the children grew older, Harrison wrote letters to them when they were abroad, chatty letters giving them the local news and telling them what their siblings and their mother were up to. He also wrote them "notes," in which he offered "free advice": "If you agree with it, that's fine. If you don't agree with it, just ignore it." His notes ranged over a variety of topics from life in general to running a business.

Like many wealthy parents, Harrison wanted his children to sign pre-nuptial agreements. He wrote them all to say, "None of you are engaged to marry, so I cannot be accused of picking on an intended spouse." However, "because of the frequency of divorces in our society, now as common as dirt, I would like to have a proper legal marriage contract signed which says – should we separate, you don't owe me anything nor do I owe you anything." He was thus no less direct with his children than he was with others. He wrote, "Bluntly, it is not my intention to financially support any ex-spouses of yours in any way." He reminded them that "living with a partner for any length of time and not marrying can have the same legal implications as marriage." Harrison always paid attention to detail, whether in business or in personal affairs.

His personal papers also contain a number of documents and magazine articles on the "do's" and "don'ts" of leaving wealth to children. Harrison looked to others to see how they transferred financial resources to their children to capture the best lessons learned.

In giving his "free advice" to his children, Harrison always signed the notes, "Love, Dad." He told them that he had learned some of life's lessons the hard way and that he wanted to share his experience with them so as to spare them the pitfalls. Much more often than not, the advice was about business: how to evaluate a business, how to manage accounts receivable, how to make cold calls on potential customers. They make for a fascinating read for students of economic development and business.

On 11 August 1986, he said on assessing the value of a business,

When I am trying to find a company, the first thing the man says is, "You tell me what this business is worth." I reply, "Not the least bit confidential, I will tell you how I am going to value it and I will show you the figures. I will probably pick the lowest value and you will probably pick the highest one; and who knows, somewhere in the middle we may do a deal!" Here is how we value the purchase of a business:

a) *Multiplier of earnings* – It is used to be 8 times earnings, today it is about 12 × earnings because of higher stock prices. If the company is really growth, maybe you would pay 14 times earnings if you thought earnings would go up so it would only be 10 times earnings in a couple of years. By earnings, I mean full tax paid earnings.

b) *Book value* – Most companies are purchased at more than their book value, and you understand that book value means total equity or capital investment in the business plus earnings retained in the business. Each of these descriptions means "the value of the company according to its own books." Although you have to pay more than book value, the question is what is the real value of the company if you had to break it up?

c) *Book value after appraisal* – If some of the properties are old but the land values have gone up and/or factories that are worth more than their depreciated value, an appraisal may mean that the value of the assets is higher than shown on the company accounts. Therefore, the book value would go up and the seller is entitled to that.

d) *The multiplier of tax paid cash flow* – Tax paid cash flow is the net profit after tax plus depreciation, and this is the kind of extra cash you have at the end of every year to pay your bills, to expand the business, to buy equipment, etc. We used to think that a business was worth 5.5 to 7 times cash flow, but today's market would be higher than that – perhaps 7 to 9.

In a P.S. to this letter Harrison added a long checklist covering such matters as quality of management, rate of growth of business, prospects for new products, etc. "That is of strong interest to determine whether or not we want to buy the business, but the above four points will tell you pretty closely how much to pay for it."

On accounts receivable, Harrison told his children that the best way to measure them is not just by the amount (the gross exposure you have to the bank) but rather receivables to your sales. "If a company has sales of $100,000 per month, you definitely shouldn't have receivables of more than $100,000 per month. That would be called '30 days' sales in the receivables.' Hopefully, they can be less than that."

If the company is owed money more than 30 days, it may well mean that there is a claim or a dispute about the invoice, and it doesn't necessarily mean the man won't pay. It should be investigated promptly on the basis of "You owe this money, it is overdue. *Why* haven't you paid?" If your company offers a cash discount, and the customer doesn't take it – be careful, the customer either doesn't know what he is doing, or is running out of money, and maybe you shouldn't sell to him, even if he pays you in 30 days.

On cash flow, he wrote,

A company making $100,000 is worth possibly multiplier of 10 or $1 million to purchase. However, often overlooked is the fact that two companies each making $100,000 each, one of them may have a depreciation on the fixed assets of $10,000 and the other one may have a depreciation of $100,000.

It is obvious that the company that has a cash flow made up of $100,000 profit plus $100,000 depreciation of $200,000 a year is worth more to the new buyer than a company that has a $100,000 profit and $10,000 depreciation or $110,000 profit.

In the first company, if you take all the cash flow and pay it against your purchase price you would own the company in 5 years, but in the second one it would take you 9 years to pay for the company. That's the reason it is important to know the *cash flow* of a business in addition to its profit, and some tries to arrive at the earnings of the company, it's wise to say, I'll invest in a company on a multiplier of earnings of 10 or 12, but when I multiply the cash flow by the price I don't want to pay more than 6 times the cash flow.

He urged his children to bear in mind that "you can go broke in a business while you're still making a profit! You can simply run out of cash, and if you have a small profit but you're making large expenditures, you still can find yourself in a place where you can't pay the bills.[4]

On learning to say no, he suggested, "It seems to me the people in business who have the hardest time to get things done are those who can't bring themselves to say 'no.' They can say 'maybe,' they can say 'I'll see,' they can say 'later,' all of which are reasonable answers under some circumstances, but sometimes there is only one answer, and it is a simple, straightforward 'no.' When you can't say no, people come back and ask you the same question again, or give you the same problem again, and you find yourself apologizing for not doing something different. *You* are then on the defensive. It is difficult to look someone right in the eye and say 'no,' but all it takes is practice. It is very difficult the first time, it is not so difficult the third time, and after the fifth time you can say it anytime it needs to be said."[5]

Later, he wrote a note labelled "Chutzpah" to his five children, reminding them of his earlier caution on the importance of being able to say no when circumstances demand it. This time he wanted them to learn not to be afraid when someone else says no to them. "Chutzpah," he wrote, "is a Yiddish word that can best be summarized as a disregard for the possibility of getting a negative reply."[6] It was important for Harrison that his children develop an attitude that enabled them to think "it won't cost me anything to ask, but if he says 'no,' I really don't give a damn. I would rather try and hear no than not try at all." He told them that this attitude "pays big results in personal satisfaction and in accomplishment."[7] It was an attitude that worked for him and he strongly recommended it.

Harrison encouraged his children to go into business. He stood by Laura as she got into the seafood business in Halifax, and he had a strong word of encouragement for Ann when she decided to launch a business in Montreal. He urged her to become fluent in French, as "doing business in Montreal in English only is just as passé as high-button shoes, and if you don't want to learn French, then you should move to a town where you don't need it."[8] Peter meanwhile worked in the family business, as did Mark.

Harrison's son Peter died in the early hours on 4 February 1997. At the time, he was head of international sales at McCain Foods in Florenceville and separated from his wife, Joyce, who lived with their two sons a few doors down from Harrison. Peter had taken up residence next door to his father, in one of the two guest cottages on Harrison's property.

Harrison's neighbour reported that he heard Peter leave on a snowmobile at about midnight. The temperature was -20°C. Peter headed for the McCain airstrip behind Harrison's house. Driving at great speed, he failed to stop at the southern end of the strip and hit a high snowbank. The snowmobile flew an estimated thirty-five metres before it hit ground again, bounced some ten metres, then another ten before it came to a stop. Peter was wearing light clothing for the time of year. Still, there was evidence that he attempted to walk towards the safety of a nearby house with a bright outdoor light.

Next morning, Harrison waited for Peter to join him for breakfast, which was an established routine whenever both were in Florenceville. When he didn't show up, Harrison went to work and inquired about Peter. He then drove to the hangar and airstrip, knowing that Peter might be in the area. Not finding him, he called his good friend John Doucet to see if he would drive around and help to look for Peter. He was found dead from exposure at eleven that morning.

Dave Kearney recalls Harrison kneeling by his frozen son a short distance from the runway. He got up and, "weeping like a child," asked Kearney to take the plane, "go to Toronto to get Ann and the others. They need to be here. I will call them."

Harrison carried that pain with him until he died. Soon Joyce left Florenceville for her native Newfoundland with the two boys Luke and John, then six and eight years old. Harrison was very close to his grandsons, much as his father-in-law John McNair had become once he was no longer premier of the province. Harrison tried to persuade Joyce to stay on in Florenceville or, failing that, to move to Halifax or Toronto so the boys could be close to their aunts, uncles, and cousins on the McCain side, but he was not successful, and that only compounded the pain. A few weeks after Peter's funeral, he said, "They say I'm a billionaire. I don't know about that, but whatever I have, I'd give away every cent of it to have Peter back."[9]

Gillian stayed with Harrison at home for several months after Peter died. Though Harrison was not one to cry, she vividly recalls him breaking down in tears for weeks after Peter passed away.

FRIENDS

Harrison had friends from all walks of life. He enjoyed the company of politicians, business leaders, artists, academics, and, perhaps above all, potato farmers. His two closest friends were Mac McCarthy and Donald Trafford, not only a potato farmer but a friend from grade one. Amongst a host of other good friends he counted James Downey, George McClure, Jim Coutts, Reuben Cohen, Jim Pattison, Dick O'Hagan, Cedric Ritchie, Don Young, and Tony Van Leersum.

Harrison had charisma. He attracted people. My daughter can attest to that. My wife, Linda, and I were invited to attend the installation of fellow Acadian and lifelong friend Roméo LeBlanc as governor general. Linda suggested that instead of her I take Margaux, our fifteen-year-old daughter, along, thinking it would be a memorable experience for her.

After the ceremony, we mingled with the other guests. When I saw Pierre Trudeau standing alone, I went over for a word and introduced him to Margaux. He asked how the Université de Moncton was doing. He was always very fond of my university, a francophone university outside Quebec, and one of the very first universities to give him an honorary doctorate. Then at one point he asked Margaux how she spelled her name. Trudeau took her program, wrote a note, and signed it. We then spoke briefly with Roméo LeBlanc, and a few former Cabinet ministers whom I had met over the years. We had a good chat with Louis J. Robichaud.

Harrison McCain was also a guest, and I spotted him in conversation with several people. I waited my turn and introduced him to Margaux. He asked her about school, when she was going to get her driver's licence, and what kind of car she wanted to buy some day. She asked him about his french fries. Like the great majority of New Brunswickers, I suspect, McCain's were the only french fries that ever entered our house. Harrison told her, "They are the best, the very, very best."

On our drive home, I asked Margaux of all the people she had met today which had she enjoyed the most? Without a second's hesitation, she said, "Harrison McCain."[10] I thought she would have chosen Trudeau, but Harrison won the day with Margaux simply by being himself, relaxed, interested in what she had to say, and sharing a joke with her.

Harrison always enjoyed a good joke, convinced that laughter was the shortest distance between two people.[11] He was loyal to his friends and they were loyal to him. In James Downey's toast to Harrison at his seventieth birthday party, he said, "Though the storms and stress of sorrow of recent years, that centre of compassion and courage has held for Harrison. What has also held are the love and loyalty of friends. It is not hard for the gifted and successful to get respect. It is not hard for the generous to get gratitude. But it is only the rarest of birds who elicit such admiring and protective affection as Harrison McCain's friends feel towards him."[12] Harrison was that bird.

His long-time friend Jim Coutts remarks that Harrison has "lots and lots of friends everywhere. Remember, he did business in some forty countries and it did not take him long to make a new friend. Harrison made friends easily and he needed friends around him. He always kept in close contact with friends wherever they were. One thing I can tell you for sure, Harrison was loyal to his friends." He added that Harrison stayed loyal even when a friend screwed up badly. Indeed, I saw in his personal papers that Harrison had contributed to more than one legal fund in support of friends facing legal challenges.

As we know, Harrison had the habit of inviting friends to join him and his family on skiing trips. When I asked Coutts how Harrison was as a skier, he had a one-word reply: "Dramatic." Harrison did everything with enthusiasm – he worked with enthusiasm, he ate with enthusiasm, he partied with enthusiasm, and shared a laugh with enthusiasm. As Coutts would have it, "He even walked down the street with enthusiasm."

Après ski for Harrison was as much fun as skiing. One story speaks to several facets of Harrison's personality – his enthusiasm, his zest for life, his pleasure in taking on any competition, and his will to win.

Harrison, Billie and a party of friends were in a dining hall at a Sun
Valley ski resort. As Harrison told it,

So, we were sitting down there talking away and drinking and I
think awaiting dinner. And this man and woman walked by, and
she really was the most striking looking girl I'd ever seen in my
life. She wasn't just good looking, she was smashing, absolutely
smashing, and all of us at the table agreed, including the women,
that she was a very, very attractive-looking woman. She returned
to her seat back up on the dais, right on the edge. Could see her
quite clearly. And we were talking about what a remarkably good-
looking woman she was.

And I said to Coutts, "Coutts, I've a good mind to go up and kiss
her."

He said, "Kiss her! Harrison, are you crazy? You're going to start
a fight."

I said, "Four hundred bucks says I can kiss her."

He said, "It's a deal." There was no money put on the table, but
the 400 dollars was bet.

So I approached the table, and I approached up the lower level so
I was down at essentially a lower level than her. And she bent over
some and I spoke to her.

I said, "Look, tell me. Are you here with your husband, or your
boyfriend?"

She said, "Yes, I'm here with my husband, and he's the man
sitting right fair across the table from me."

I said, "Fine." So I then went up on the mezzanine and went
around to his side of the table where I squatted down on my
haunches till I was at his height, and told him my name, and I said,
"My wife is down at the table sitting just down below. You can see
her. I think if you look hard you'll see she's glaring at me." But I
said, "I have a friendly bet with a guy at my table, guy at my table,
for 400 bucks that I can't kiss your wife." And I said, "It's important
that I win this bet. It's very important that I win this bet. Now could
we do a deal? I'd be glad to supply all the wine for your table for the
evening if I get a chance to kiss your wife."

He said, "It's no trouble at all. Sally, come here a minute. Come
here a minute Sally."

So he stood up and grabbed me by the arm and got Sally over, who was his wife. And I kissed her right on the lips, right on the lips. And my God, she responded, she responded cheerfully. She wasn't the least bit embarrassed. She wasn't the least bit embarrassed or shaken up by it all. So that was over with. And I suppose half the restaurant saw this. Anyway, my wife was cheesed off at me. And Jimmy said he'd pay later. And he hasn't paid since.[13]

I have it on good authority that Coutts did eventually honour the bet.

Harrison was available to friends whenever they asked for business advice. In some instances, as in the case of Bud Bird, he took the initiative. Jim Coutts recalled calling Harrison to say that one of his plants in Ontario was performing "under capacity." Harrison replied, "Jim, Jim, there is no such thing as under capacity. There is no such thing as under capacity in business. Just increase your prices, problem solved."

Harrison was asked by James Downey, "Among your peers in the business world, and you've known a lot of them over a long time, who do you admire most?"

He replied, "Jimmy Pattison on the West Coast is a guy that I admire a lot. He's a brilliant entrepreneur and good, very good businessman. Very hard worker. Honest, straightforward, high-class guy."[14] Harrison's high regard for Pattison was based on his having started at the bottom, selling cars. He then moved into the real estate market and then, according to Harrison, moved into "everything in sight." Harrison also admired Pattison's generosity, including his willingness to devote time and energy as head of Vancouver's Expo '86.

Harrison and Pattison often saw each other socially. Harrison once told me that he thoroughly enjoyed a weekend he spent at Pattison's compound in Rancho Mirage in California. The fact that Pattison had bought the compound from Frank Sinatra was a smash hit with Harrison. Pattison told me, "Above all, Harrison was a loyal friend," and added that Harrison always called him on Christmas Day. Pattison also made a point of telling me that "Harrison always told you exactly what was on his mind. You never had to guess what Harrison was thinking."

Though they were not close, Harrison also enjoyed the company of Robert Campeau, the high-profile Canadian entrepreneur. Like Jimmy Pattison, Campeau also started with nothing. His first job was as a construction labourer, then he became a carpenter, and later still a general contractor. He was highly successful in the real estate market and in the 1980s launched a series of leveraged buyouts, starting with Royal Trust, now part of the Royal Bank of Canada. He met his Waterloo, however, when he purchased Federated Department Stores, owner of Bloomingdale's. He had overreached his financial resources and the debt load brought him down. He came under heavy criticism both in the United States and at home in Canada for his business decisions. Harrison stood by his friend for trying, and wrote to him, "I hope you will take comfort in the saying of a famous New Brunswicker – old dogs for the road and the pups for the sidewalk."[15]

Harrison and Billie were close to Dick O'Hagan and his wife, Wanda. Dick, originally from nearby Woodstock, served as head of Communications in the Prime Minister's Office under Trudeau before becoming senior vice-president with the Bank of Montreal. The O'Hagans often joined Harrison and Billie on holiday. O'Hagan told me that Harrison had an "incredible capacity" when on holiday to turn off the business switch and focus exclusively on family and friends. This, once again, speaks to Harrison's capacity to keep things in separate compartments. I note, however, that cellphones, iPads, and BlackBerrys had yet to make their presence felt when Harrison was in the thick of things at McCain Foods.

Harrison and New Brunswick–born business leader Dick Currie were life-long friends. Harrison tried but failed to get Currie to work with McCain Foods. However, Currie did go into the food business and became head of Loblaws, later serving as chair of the board of Bell enterprises and member of other boards of leading Canadian businesses.

In his tribute to Harrison when he was named CEO of the Year, Currie said that wherever Harrison "went in the world, he took New Brunswick with him." He went on, "Perhaps his most admirable quality" was that "he truly believed that no one ever built himself up by running someone else down."[16]

Currie tells a story that speaks to Harrison's integrity. A McCain Foods marketing employee heard through the grapevine that Coca-Cola was planning to introduce a mixture of five citrus juices that already had success in the US market, so he decided to register the trademark "5 Alive" in Canada. Several months later, the president of Coca-Cola contacted Wallace McCain to purchase the trademark. When Wallace raised the matter with Harrison, Harrison told him, "Sell it to them for one dollar. We are not goddamn crooks. This is not the way for us to do business."

Harrison and Currie decided that they would do something memorable every year, something that they would do only once in their lifetime. The only criterion was that it had to be a non-business event. One year, they went to the Derby at Epsom Downs in England, another to the Indy 500, and yet another to the Belmont Stakes.

Harrison did mix business and friendship at least once. He and long-time McCain Foods employee George McClure struck up a close friendship. McClure has many Harrison stories, one of which I reproduce here, verbatim:

In the fall of 1988, Harrison and I were in Hanover, Lower Saxony, in what was then West Germany. We were having a cursory look at potatoes, acreages, and growers. On a free Sunday morning, Harrison said, "Let's do something different, let's go to East Germany." I reminded him that the Iron Curtain still stood between the West and the East. We had a large black Mercedes sedan, which I insisted on driving for obvious reasons. We were dressed in our usual dark business suits, white shirts, and formal ties. After a short drive, we reached the fortified East German frontier at Helmstedt. I spoke "rough" German and decided that I needed a story for the frontier guards. At the barrier they asked for passports and said that we needed visas to enter East Germany. We had no visas so I quickly make up a story. I said that we had very recently heard a report on BBC International that relations were warming between West and East, and as a sign of this, visas were no longer required by Westerners to enter East Germany. Needless to say, the frontier guard had not heard of this (because I had made it up, to Harrison's great amusement). He referred us up the line to his sergeant and then to his lieutenant. In the meantime, the traffic lineup behind us was building. The lieutenant was perplexed but came up with a solution. He would issue the two smartly dressed, dark-suited Canadian businessmen a two-day visa for camping in

East Germany. We drove on into East Germany, stopped at a work-
ingman's pub where Harrison bought beer for everyone. We had a
great time and a great laugh about going to East Germany on our
Sunday off. We were both terrible show-offs and played off each
other.[17]

Harrison had a very strong aversion to pretentious people and what
he labelled "bullshitters" or, in more polite company, someone who
was "full of beans." He was genuinely fond of Carleton County potato
farmers. When I went for walks or drives around Florenceville with
him, he was always on the lookout for neighbours and friends. He
would wave and at times stop to have a friendly chat.

Donald Trafford, perhaps Harrison's closest friend was, as already
mentioned, a Carleton County potato farmer. I spent an hour and a
half talking with him in his home and I understood Harrison's affection for the man. He sat in his chair, upright, eyes fixed on me and
answered every question with a remarkable level of honesty. He has
wide shoulders, strong arms, and large hands that take only one quick
glimpse to see that they have worked the soil for a lifetime.

He has friendly eyes and a warm smile. There was never a hint of
envy at the phenomenal success of his friend Harrison. Quite the
contrary, he was extremely proud of Harrison's achievements. At
one point, he stopped talking, let his head droop, and started to cry.
He said, "I'm very sorry, but Harrison was my friend and I loved
him."

Harrison often dropped by unannounced to see Trafford. They
talked about politics, business, potato farming, their families, whatever
came to mind. I have no doubt that Harrison's visits to his old friend
also served as a blessed antidote to the bullshitters he encountered in
the wider world.

SIZING PEOPLE UP

A journalist once asked Harrison, "Why do you stay put in Florenceville?"

His answer, "Because I like it here."

The journalist pushed. "Why do you stay here – is it the scenery?"

Harrison repeated, "I like it here." He then went on to point out that the McCains had been here since the 1820s.[18] Roots mattered a great deal to Harrison McCain, as they do to many Maritimers.

The New Brunswick potato industry's newsletter writes that "Harrison genuinely liked farmers and farming." It adds, "A McCain employee tells of Harrison's ongoing interest in watching the crop being planted and harvested. Harrison would often stop his car, watch the process, and then speak to at least one or two of the employees he knew best, to tell them what a great job they were doing and thank them."[19] Potato farmers, to Harrison McCain, were the salt of the earth and potato farming was real economics, a real product that you could plant, grow, process, and sell, something that could not be duplicated in the financial markets, in government, or even in the service sector.

Harrison's presence was also felt in the local business community. He was among friends and commanded respect. But he could always keep business and friendship separate. Joe Palmer, head of Day and Ross, ran into some financial difficulties in 1986. The local bank did not want to issue a new loan unless someone endorsed the note, so Harrison did and was able to secure the loan for Palmer under favourable terms. He wrote to Palmer, "I am endorsing this loan because of my long friendship with you. As you know, the bank does not think it is a very good proposition, but I believe that you can pull it off. However, I am not going to renegotiate this deal or postpone payments or take any change whatsoever in this deal, and I don't want you to ask me. All this was discussed by telephone and is clearly understood." Harrison was right – the loan was repaid. One also had to try very hard to misunderstand Harrison. His thoughts and communications were always clear.

Joe Palmer would say of his friend, "Harrison is the most disciplined man I've ever met. In his world, there's a time and place for everything." He added, "He has a fantastic memory and his memory is just as good when a deal goes against him as when it goes for him. When he loses a deal he pays the bill and keeps going, and he has been in deals when he dropped one or two million. When he wins on a deal he expects everybody else to play by the same rules."[20] Harrison's credo was simple – if he owed you a dime he would pay you and if you owed him a dime he expected to be paid.

Harrison told a journalist, "I can't think of one person in the world today that I despise, not one. That's not because I'm sanctimonious, or of very high moral character. I just think it's the greatest waste of energy in the world to hate somebody ... Now, I can erupt, blow up and say lots of things, but I can't think of anyone I hate."[21]

Harrison admitted that some of his success, "not all of it, has to be at somebody else's expense and I'm sure some of the people don't like it."[22] Many potato farmers did a great deal better after McCain Foods was established than they had before. However, some farmers did not prosper and, rather than look in the mirror, they blamed McCain Foods. That said, Harrison negotiated hard on behalf of McCain Foods with everyone, including farmers. Farmers did not have the skills and ability to go toe-to-toe with Harrison McCain.

To be sure, Walter Stewart's *Hard to Swallow* did not paint a positive profile of McCain Foods, nor did Adrienne Clarkson's *Fifth Estate* interview with Harrison, discussed earlier. Stewart devoted a full chapter to McCain Foods, pointing to it as the villain in the growth of the modern agribusiness.[23] He argued that McCain Foods was forcing farmers off their land in the pursuit of bigger and larger farms. But Stewart neglected to mention that the trend to larger farms was hardly a New Brunswick–only phenomenon. Even by the mid-1970s, the traditional family farm was disappearing from the Canadian (and American) landscape. Many local farmers and provincial government officials jumped to McCain's defence in the immediate aftermath of the Stewart book and the Clarkson interview. James Pattison of the Western New Brunswick potato agency and the minister of agriculture, Mac MacLeod, both maintained that the presence of McCain Foods had in fact slowed the exodus from the land in Carleton County.[24]

Harrison claimed that it was "not a big job to size people up. It doesn't take a long-term study. If you listen to somebody talk for an hour or two, or spend a day or two with them, you've got a pretty good idea what makes them tick and what their values are and how far they look ahead and what their habits are."[25] He employed this approach at work and at play.

However, he was hardly infallible in sizing people up. He told his nephew Scott, "There is no shame in hiring the wrong person. There is, however, shame in keeping him." Scott adds that this is one of many reasons why his uncle and his father Wallace attached a great deal of importance to measuring performance.

LOOKING BACK

Harrison needed to be around people. He was a devoted husband and father. If anything, he was over-protective of his children, and later in life he regretted being away so much when his children were growing up. It's never easy to be the child of a high achiever, and it must have been daunting for the five children to measure up to their father's expectations. Fortunately, Billie was Harrison's rudder in the family home. Reserved and quiet, so unlike her husband, she had the inner strength to steer the children through their growing years and to keep things in proper perspective.

Friends mattered to Harrison and he had many from various places and walks of life. He was loyal to his friends through thick and thin. He enjoyed a good chat, a good laugh, and a good drink or two of Scotch. His anchor was always Florenceville, and he particularly enjoyed the company of potato farmers. His son Mark tells of the great satisfaction his father would get from driving around, pointing at newly repaired and repainted houses, with a new car in the driveway. Before McCain Foods, he would say, the houses around Florenceville were "leaning." No more. People now had jobs and income. Homes around Florenceville had stopped leaning.

13

Could There Be Another Harrison McCain?

Of course not, and you shouldn't even be asking this question.

Marilyn Strong

Harrison's stock response when asked for the secret of his success was that it was no secret at all: "Right time, right place, good luck." When pressed by friends, however, he was willing to elaborate. He told James Downey, "The first requirement to be successful, in my opinion, is single-mindedness of purpose. And I don't think the professors that teach kids who want to be a great success in their field point it out to them with enough vigour and say, 'Do you understand? You have to sacrifice. You have to make difficult choices and say, "Goddamn it, I said I was going to do it, I'm going to do it. I'm going to do it if it kills me." And you'll win. You'll beat up the other guy who doesn't have that single-mindedness of purpose."[1]

Harrison McCain had clarity of purpose and of thought. He had a strong bias for action and was willing to take calculated risks. He also had a remarkable ability to see through the mist, grab the essential points, and sort out what mattered and what did not. Harrison believed that any obstacles could be overcome through will, work, and tenacity. Those who failed, he also believed, were undone by a tendency to complicate things unnecessarily, to look for reasons why something couldn't work, rather than how it could be made to work. To his mind, success boiled down to singleness of purpose. It was that simple. Harrison often told his senior executives, "Don't give me your problems, give me your solutions."

Carl Morris said that Harrison McCain "could see things that we could not, he could look into the future and spot potential markets and see who our competitors would be."[2] Donald Young said, "Harrison had an incredible memory. You told him something about a minor issue or detail over lunch and four years later he would bring it back to your attention." He added, "Harrison inspired incredible loyalty from employees. He was special."[3] Terry Bird, who worked closely with McCain Foods, said that Harrison was the most curious man he had ever met.[4] Ken Cossaboom, who also worked closely with Harrison, meanwhile maintains that Harrison was the most "brilliant" man he had ever met.[5]

Harrison of course was not so much the single-minded entrepreneur that he lacked a human side. Far from it. He had his cherished family, scores of friends. He suffered greatly when first his wife and then his son died. Many of his close friends told me that he never fully recovered from this double blow. He was sensitive to criticism and was deeply hurt whenever anyone criticized his wife or his children. His public image was of a man brimming with self-confidence – yet this same man had been subject to panic attacks in the early years of McCain Foods. In building his business, Harrison lived by the rules of the market – except when it came to Florenceville and New Brunswick. Where they were concerned, he made up his own rules and happily pulled against gravity to protect his community's interest, whether or not it made business sense.

I set out in this chapter to answer a theoretical question: could there be another Harrison McCain? Accordingly, it may well strike the reader as somewhat out of character from previous chapters. But Harrison's business accomplishments contain many lessons learned, including some for rural Canada, the Maritime provinces, national political institutions, and shaping public policy. I conclude the chapter with Harrison's own words on entrepreneurship and business development.

SO, COULD THERE BE ANOTHER HARRISON McCAIN?

The easy answer is yes. Successful entrepreneurs are born every day and new billionaires crop up every year – Bill Gates, Steve Jobs, Mark Zuckerberg, Jim Pattison, Guy Laliberté, to name a few. Harrison was also not the only generous billionaire benefactor, though he was that and became known as New Brunswick's "pre-eminent philanthropist."[6]

In many ways, however, Harrison was unique. Certainly, he was driven, he had a dominating personality, but he also had a wonderful smile that would light up a room, an endearing sense of humour, and an unbending loyalty to his family, friends, community, region, province, and country, in that order. Could there be someone, somewhere with similar characteristics and personality traits as Harrison McCain? Perhaps.

But could there be another Harrison McCain spring from rural New Brunswick or indeed from anywhere in rural Canada? I would argue that the chances are slim.

THE WORLD HAS CHANGED

Think back to 1956. Canada then had many viable rural communities, governments were viewed as positive economic actors, and the shift towards favouring the attributes of the individual over those of the community had yet to begin. The local bank manager was able to take certain decisions without referring to head office, and the wave of new Canadians from Asia and India had yet to arrive. Today, the public sector does not enjoy the credibility that it once had, the attributes of individuals have been on the ascendancy for thirty years, the local bank manager has been stripped of most decision-making authority, and new Canadians go to large urban centres, not to small towns.

National economies are not nearly as self-contained as they once were. Forty years ago, China held that foreign trade was akin to treason, while today it is open for business and has become an economic powerhouse. Forty years ago, the Soviet Union dominated Eastern Europe, where communist ideology reigned supreme. Today, some of the world's wealthiest individuals are Russian. Forty years ago, Canada had an agency with a mandate to control the flow of investment dollars coming into the country. Today, Canada has an agency with a mandate to do the exact opposite – to attract foreign investments. Forty years ago, the government of Canada had a clear priority to promote economic development in slow-growth regions. Today, every postal code in Canada, including those on Bay Street, has access to a federal regional economic development agency. Today, large firms such as the auto industry are too big for governments to let fail, while small communities now appear to be too small to survive.

As the economy becomes increasingly global and interconnected, there is little concern for slow-growth regions. The global economy is tied largely to the voice of the market. One consequence of globalization has been the "de-attachment of money from territorial space."[7] It is now widely accepted that national governments that do not adjust to the requirements of the global economy will suffer. The rewards for getting it right or, conversely, the consequences for getting it wrong in the global economy are far greater than in years past. In short, globalization has de-territorialized economic power.

In theory, at least, market forces should determine winners and losers, distinguish strong regions from weak ones. But national governments, even to this day, are not in the habit of sitting idly by and letting the market call the adjustment tune. They will intervene, as the 2008 financial crisis so clearly demonstrated. But governments no longer intervene as they once did. The intervention has taken a different focus.[8] The aim now is to create or protect jobs in highly populated and high-profile sectors that are concentrated in urban areas – for example, the automobile and financial industries, the arts and culture sectors, and research and development. In short, national governments, and Canada is no exception, still promote regional economic development. The focus, however, is no longer on slow-growth, peripheral regions.[9] The rationale is that economic development should centre on regions that already enjoy economic strengths to enable the national economy to compete in the global economy.

Harrison McCain played by the rules of the market. Yet, as we have seen, he was willing to sidestep those rules when it came to his community and his region. His view on fiddleheads sums up his position. There would be no market test for frozen fiddleheads for the simple reason that they are a vegetable from his province. As well, he situated a good number of McCain Foods' business activities in New Brunswick when others would have chosen large cities in other provinces. Similarly, he insisted that the company's data centre and its potato technology centre be built in Florenceville. When the federal government official who worked on a McCain Foods proposal to build a frozen pizza plant in Grand Falls, New Brunswick, asked, "Why Grand Falls?," he got this answer from Harrison: "Because I'm from Florenceville."

John Doucet, long-time Day and Ross CEO and a close friend of Harrison, suggests that things changed radically after Harrison died. Florenceville is no longer the nerve centre for either McCain Foods or Day and Ross, as they were under Harrison. "Everything of significance and everything new" is moving to Toronto or elsewhere. Harrison would not be happy. Gordon Pitts writes that Harrison "served as a kind of ballast – as long as he was living in Florenceville, the soul of the company resided there."[10]

Harrison's commitment to New Brunswick was heartfelt in all things. To be sure, he was a generous man. There was one constant theme in his philanthropy – it was to be directed to his region. Frank McKenna tells us, "Nowhere but nowhere was that hometown loyalty more pronounced than in charitable giving. He recognized an inescapable reality that when it came to giving, New Brunswick might be 1000 miles from Toronto but Toronto was 5000 miles from New Brunswick."[11] McKenna, Reuben Cohen, and Howard Clark, former Dalhousie University president, among others, pressed Harrison to make a donation to establish a chair at Oxford University, and Harrison replied, "Oxford, great university, great university. My father-in-law went there, but they will have to stand in line behind our universities here at home. They don't have a lot of people to count on."[12]

WHERE IT ALL BEGAN

The first sentence in Donald Akenson's brilliant biography of the Irish politician, public servant, and academic Conor Cruise O'Brien, reads, "The most important events in any of our lives occurred before we were born."[13] Harrison McCain was a fourth-generation Canadian. His great-grandfather left Ireland to begin a new life in the new world. He set his sights on Florenceville.

It made sense for Andrew McCain to go to rural New Brunswick to start a new life. Western Canada was virtually empty and far from Ireland, the industrial era was still on the horizon, urban Canada was just then taking shape, and agriculture still drove economic development in both the Old and New Worlds. Andrew McCain quickly demonstrated an entrepreneurial flair, acquiring land and turning it into productive acreage. Harrison's grandfather, H.H. McCain, and his father, A.D. McCain, inherited Andrew's entrepreneurial spirit. And, of course, so did Harrison. An entrepreneurial spirit and business acumen were in Harrison's blood.

Immigrants or new Canadians bring vitality and a strong desire to create new economic opportunities for themselves and their families. Leaving aside those seeking refugee status, it is the main reason why immigrants decide to pick up and move to Canada.[14] New Canadians, however, almost invariably go to the cities in search of a better life, not to small towns. Under the category "economic class," 51,403 new Canadians went to Ontario in 2011, another 36,102 to Quebec, and 21,904 to British Columbia. Only 1,474 went to New Brunswick.[15]

The city is the draw for most of them. In Ontario, in 2010, for example, 92,185 of new Canadians from all categories went to Toronto from a total of 118,114. In New Brunswick, in the same year, all but 483 new Canadians out of a total of 2,125 went to three cities: Moncton, Fredericton, and Saint John.[16] Rural New Brunswick in turn confronts daunting challenges in attracting new Canadians when compared with, say, Halifax. Harrison McCain recognized the challenge when he observed, "Extra-nationals don't settle very well in rural areas."[17] Data from the latest census reveal that things have not improved – one-fifth of Canadians today are foreign-born and few look to rural regions to start a new life. The household survey also reveals that "more than six in ten immigrants who arrived in Canada between 2006 and 2011 opted to settle in one of Canada's three big metropolitan areas."[18]

A study on the interprovincial mobility of immigrants to Canada between provinces of nomination versus provinces of residence based on the 2005 data point to another worrisome trend for Atlantic Canada. About one in three new Canadians to Atlantic Canada is found in another province within a few years. The study concludes that the outflow of new Canadians from Atlantic Canada far "outpaces inflow."[19]

It is hardly possible to overstate the importance of the immigrant-entrepreneur to economic development. The *Economist* magazine reports, "Fully 18 percent of the Fortune 500 list of 2010 were founded by immigrants, among others, AT&T, DuPont, eBay, Google, Kraft, Heinz and Procter & Gamble." It goes on to point out that if one includes the children of immigrants, the figure is 40 per cent. It adds that immigrants founded a quarter of successful high-tech and engineering companies 1995 and 2005 and that they "obtain patents at twice the rate of American-born people with the same educational credentials."[20]

The fact is that the successful entrepreneurs able to hit the billion-dollar mark in net worth in the next two generations are very likely to be the sons and daughters of new Canadians who moved to a large urban centre. Even the agricultural sector is now dominated more and more by large corporate farms. The aspiring entrepreneur-farmer today has to compete with large well-resourced and well-managed farms in a sector where scale of land holdings, equipment, and quality of machinery matter.

None of this, of course, is a uniquely Canadian phenomenon. Urban centres comprise only 2 per cent of the world's surface but consume 60 to 80 per cent of the global energy. We have reached the point where less than 10 per cent of the world's rural workforce is employed in agriculture, producing less than 6 per cent of gross value added in agricultural regions. The world's urban population growth, meanwhile, has continued to outpace rural areas by a wide margin, and every hour the world's urban population grows by roughly eight thousand people.[21] The natural resources sector that gave birth to so many rural communities in Canada can now be exploited with fewer workers because of advanced mechanization.

As Canada's population continues to concentrate in large urban areas, Canadians will increasingly ask why they should be concerned about rural Canada. Why should governments be concerned with rural Atlantic Canada? Why should they be concerned if national policies do not apply well in rural Canada, so long as they strengthen the national economy? Why should Atlantic Canadians be concerned if provincial policies do not apply well in rural areas, so long as they strengthen provincial economies in their region? Without suggesting for a moment that they agree with the implied premise of the question, Mario Polèse and Richard Shearmur have asked, "Why not simply let market forces do their work and allow doomed regions to gradually fade away, and when the process is complete perhaps turn them into national parks or nature reserves? Let the last person to leave turn out the light and close the church door."[22]

It is hardly original to write that economic development in future will be driven by productive and creative workers. Creative people tend to go to university, and university graduates tend to locate in urban areas. Richard Florida, in a seminal book in the economic development literature, wrote about the importance of cities and mega-regions driving economic growth.[23] Creative people tend to go where other creative people are, much like new Canadians go where new Canadians are. Gillian McCain, one of Harrison's daughters, has taken her creative talent to New York, where she has met with success as a poet and author.[24]

PULLING AGAINST GRAVITY

Harrison McCain rarely pointed publicly to national policies to explain our region's underdevelopment but it was a different matter in private. Harrison strongly favoured a triple-E Senate – elected, effective, and equal – and he often made his views known both in public and in private. It is revealing that the government of New Brunswick also favours a triple-E Senate, the government of Ontario wants to abolish the Senate altogether, and the government of Quebec has made it clear that it would take the government of Canada to court if it seeks to reform the Senate.

Harrison clearly saw what many Maritimers have seen down the years – a national government politically dominated by the large heavily populated provinces. There is no need to go over the impact of the national policy on Canada's history of economic development. It has been well documented elsewhere. Suffice to note here that the "Maritimers could legitimately claim that there was no place for them in the National Policy."[25]

Things have not improved since 1879. *Globe and Mail* columnist John Ibbitson went to the heart of the matter when he wrote, "After the Second World War, Queen's Park and Ottawa collaborated to ensure that the rest of the federation served the interests of the economic heartland." He pointed, as just one example, to the construction of the Saint Lawrence Seaway where "the railroads and Halifax paid the price. Ontario reaped the benefits."[26]

He could have pointed to many more examples – the Canada-US auto pact is one. In 1964 only 7 per cent of the automobiles built in

Canada were sold in the United States, but the proportion jumped to 60 per cent by 1968. The pact created thousands of jobs in Ontario, but all it did for the Maritimes was to make the purchase of a car more expensive. He could have also pointed to the thirty-two Crown corporations created to assist the war effort in the early 1940s. They would later provide the basis for Canada's manufacturing sector. Not a single Crown corporation was established in the Maritimes – all were set up in central Canada.

Ontario's auto sector has been to Ottawa since 2001, cap in hand, asking and receiving assistance in various forms. But from an Ottawa perspective, assistance to the automobile sector comes under a national policy, while that for McCain Foods came under its regional policy.

The federal government decided in the 1960s to try to rectify the situation with an ambitious regional development policy. McCain Foods, as we saw, benefitted greatly from it. But even that policy has now been turned on its head. The federal regional development agency for the Atlantic provinces (the Atlantic Canada Opportunity Agency) is one of five federal agencies that cover "all" of Canada. The federal government is also now less present in the Maritime provinces than it once was, having relocated a number of units to Ottawa.

The government's presence in the region has also taken a different form. It will be recalled that it was a federal public servant, Donald Young, who invented the Shepody potato, which transformed the frozen french fry business first in Canada, then in Europe. Federal public servants are more risk-averse and more likely to write reports about the state of the agricultural sector than undertake "practical" research.[27] Researchers at Agriculture Canada are more engaged in "upstream" or "fundamental" research rather than working with private sector firms to solve a specific problem.[28]

We are unlikely to see in future Donald Young types working with entrepreneurs or aspiring entrepreneurs to come up with new products. The federal government is shutting down a number of laboratories at Agriculture and Agri-Food Canada, where Donald Young worked and helped create economic engines like McCain Foods.[29] It takes only a moment's reflection to appreciate the potential impact on rural Canada.

Maritimers have come to recognize that *national policy* is little more than a code term for the economic interest of Ontario and Quebec. The tap is turned on when Ontario's economy is in recession or when national unity is threatened in Quebec. The number of seats from Ontario and Quebec in the House of Commons with no counterbalancing force in the Senate to speak for the other regions defines what is of national importance and what is merely regional. It is interesting to note that we have heard less and less the plea that Western Canada "wants in" since Stephen Harper became prime minister and as the population shift to Western provinces has increased its representation in the House of Commons.

Harrison McCain knew better than anyone that market forces alone do not explain Canada's spatial pattern in economic development. The country's national political and administrative institutions have also contributed to it. He travelled the world and saw where other federations have an effective upper house, be it the United States or Germany. He saw that Australia, which, like Canada, has a Westminster-style parliamentary system, also has an effective upper house. He noticed that the United States had a more balanced pattern of economic development as between regions. He saw that, unlike Canada, each state has two elected senators, that state and regional interests are all equally defended in a Senate with actual political clout, whether or not there is a federal agency charged with promoting regional economic development. He likely concluded that the ability of the United States government to spread military installations, military procurements, and government operations around the country did not occur by chance. In the United States, fewer than 20 per cent of federal public servants are located in Washington. In Canada, over 40 per cent of public servants are located in the National Capital Region.[30]

Alex Campbell, former premier of Prince Edward Island, went to the heart of the matter in a private letter he wrote on 7 November 1972 to Prime Minister Pierre E. Trudeau, "In government there is a tendency to centralize. Those individuals, in a position to advise and recommend, who do have roots in a particular region have a particular difficulty to overcome. The influence of Ottawa can be debilitating. It is the unique individual who can overcome the pervading influence of Ottawa and continue, over a long period of time, to understand and reflect a regional point of view ... some method must be sought to allow for a more meaningful input from the various regions of Canada into National thought, interpretation and eventual policy."[31]

What has changed since 1972? The tendency to centralize in government has only grown, as I documented in my *Governing from the Centre: The Concentration of Power in Canadian Politics*. As for the rest, everything is the same. The Senate remains a politically appointed body unable to express or uninterested in giving voice to the regional dimension in shaping national policies. There is even less appetite today in Ottawa or in the heavily populated provinces for Alex Campbell's message than there was in 1972. There is a tendency to dismiss such concerns out of hand by labelling them simply as "Maritimers whining."

Harrison McCain likely shook his head at the inability of Canadian policy-makers to view the country's economic development from a historical perspective. The mantra by which slow-growth regions are simply told to pull themselves up by their own bootstraps does not cut much ice in Florenceville.

It's fine for the federal government to pick winners in Ontario and Quebec, to invest in the auto, IT, aerospace, and the pharmaceutical sectors, but it is a different story when it comes to the Maritimes. Here, the old stereotype kicks in – throwing good money after bad and distorting market forces. I have heard, time and again in the media and even in the academic literature, references to government assistance to the failed Clairtone plant in Nova Scotia.[32] I have very rarely seen, however, any mention of the federal assistance to McCain Foods under its regional development program. Yet McCain Foods is a success story that equals or betters any other in Canadian economic history.

I have, in my own work, referred to Ottawa's regional development efforts and transfer payments to the Maritime provinces as guilt money. Various royal commissions, starting with Rowell-Sirois in 1940, have looked at Canada's economic development prospects and recognized that national political institutions and national policies have had an influence in the location of economic activities. Their solution – and that of successive governments in Ottawa – does not disturb where wealth is created but finds ways to assist slow-growth regions. Rowell-Sirois recommended that "the wealth produced nationally should be taxed nationally and redistributed on a national basis, instead of being taxed in the main by the central provinces for the benefit of the central provinces."[33]

Guilt money began to flow our way in 1957 and it continues to this day. In the process, it has created a dependency syndrome. Transfer payments have sapped energy and, in the words of Prime Minister Stephen Harper, created "a culture of defeat" in Atlantic Canada. Observers and other politicians neglect to mention that Harper's full quote reads, "Because of what happened in the decades following Confederation, there is a culture of defeat that we have to overcome."[34]

Federal transfer payments, or guilt money, I have argued elsewhere, have not only inhibited self-sustaining economic development, they have also given the Atlantic provinces a bad image. The government of Ontario, various research groups, and the national media now simply add up all federal government dollars spent in Atlantic Canada, compare it with Ontario on a per capita basis, and claim that the Atlantic region benefits more from federal spending than other regions. Their calculations imply that a dollar spent on Employment Insurance or under the Equalization Program equals a dollar spent on R&D, the automobile sector, or the IT sector in Ontario. It takes only a moment's reflection to appreciate that this is comparing apples to oranges, at least from an economic development perspective.

The national media – concentrated as they are in Toronto, Ottawa, and Montreal – also tend to define national issues from an Ontario-Quebec perspective and deplore federal transfer payments going to the Maritime provinces. Ottawa-based officials read the *Globe and Mail*, the *Toronto Star*, and the *Ottawa Citizen*, and, if they should happen to be bilingual, perhaps *Le Devoir* or *La Presse*. They do not as a rule read the *Cape Breton Post*, the *Saint John Telegraph Journal*, *L'Acadie nouvelle*, or the *Winnipeg Free Press*. The media regard Trudeau, Mulroney, Chrétien, and Martin as national politicians, while Diefenbaker, Harper, and Manning were and are described as regional politicians. As Stephen Tomblin writes, "Regional stereotypes have drawn national attention to peripheral regions, rather than to Central Canada."[35] Ontario Member of Parliament David McGuinty, albeit perhaps unwittingly, spoke to the problem when he said of Alberta MPs, "They are national legislators with a national responsibility, but they come across as very small 'p' provincial individuals who are jealously guarding one industrial sector, picking the fossil-fuel business and the oil sands business."[36] For McGuinty and MPs of like mind from Ontario, the fossil-fuel business or the fishery sector are regional matters, but the automobile sector is national. Yet the automobile sector is essentially located only in Ontario.

One would be hard-pressed to find a positive stereotype in the national media in recent years about the Maritime provinces. Harry Bruce's *Down Home* documents the "cultural imperialism" of CBC Toronto and the "insistence" that stories from the Maritimes deal with "Anne of Green Gables, Highland games, national parks, and fishermen in rubber boots."[37] Jeffrey Simpson, one of Canada's most widely read columnists, writes, "Atlantic Canada has a bit of an image problem. It's been down, economically speaking, for so long that people in the rest of Canada think of the region as nothing more than four provinces full of friendly people looking for handouts. You know the image. Unemployment insurance. Seasonal workers. Make-work projects. Regional development agencies. Pork-barrel politics. Equalization."[38] As Robert Young explains, "There can also be comfort in the old images of politics in the Maritimes – the snake-oil salesmanship, the rival cliques fighting for the spoils of office, and the politicians who stride across small stages like petty princelings – for these images elicit, especially among Upper Canadians and the more jaded elements of the regional society, that soothing sense of bemused condescension so gratifying to those who can afford to be above the fray."[39]

What the national media report about the Maritime provinces matters for two reasons. Media stereotypes are like codes that give the reader a ready understanding of a region or a group of people. Stereotypes can also become realities in the eyes of the region itself and of policy-makers. As Edith Robb explains, "Stereotyping can impact on a region's self-image. We start to think that if this is the way others see us, then perhaps that is the way we are. The confidence to trust yourself when others doubt you is not in great supply."[40]

One of Frank McKenna's most important contributions to economic development in New Brunswick during his term as premier was to instil in New Brunswickers a sense of self-worth and a "can-do attitude." McKenna had asked an outside firm to assess New Brunswickers' views of themselves and their province and to get a feel for the perceptions other Canadians had of New Brunswick. The report found that New Brunswickers' pride focused on their local community, their cultural heritage, and on being Canadians, while pride in their province trailed well behind the others. Perceptions of New Brunswick in the rest of Canada were dominated by the "have-not" image. Except for those who had a personal connection with the province, the rest of Canada, the wealthier provinces in particular, viewed New Brunswick as a place they had to subsidize.[41]

To sum up, Ontario and Quebec interests dominate the national political and economic agenda because the two provinces are key to securing political power in Canada. There is no second house in our national political institutions to give voice to the smaller provinces. It is hardly possible to appease the demands of those wishing to assist Canada's economic engine to compete in the global economy and with the United States or of Quebec federalists in Ottawa wishing to make the federal government more relevant in Quebec. Our national political administrative institutions by design give weight to these two appetites, appetites that are rarely satisfied.

I once attended a meeting in Ottawa when Gordon Osbaldeston, former clerk of the Privy Council and secretary to the Cabinet said about economic development in the Maritimes, "Every once in awhile, you see someone from the Maritimes getting a breakaway and scoring big." McCain Foods was one such and it scored a hugely impressive win. Given changes to the political and economic worlds over the past thirty years or so, we may well see fewer and fewer breakaways from the Maritimes.

OTHER CHALLENGES

The workings of financial institutions have also changed over the past forty years. They – combined with the federal unwillingness to provide cash grants or subsidies to businesses, entrepreneurs, and aspiring entrepreneurs in the Maritime provinces – have substantially changed the landscape from when Harrison and Wallace set out to establish McCain Foods. A young Harrison McCain from rural New Brunswick could not now access the kind of government assistance McCain Foods received in its early years. Government subsidies designed for slow-growth regions now have a bad reputation and most have been eliminated.

The Halifax *Chronicle Herald* ran an editorial on 12 October 2012, dealing with the difficulty in finding local equity for entrepreneurs in the Maritime provinces to assist them in starting up a business or growing one. It also spoke of the "problems associated with going down the road to venture capitalists who don't know the region," and that has "long frustrated entrepreneurs."[42]

A long-serving employee of the National Bank of Canada compares the responsibility of a bank manager today versus when she was first appointed branch manager. Twenty years ago, she had delegated authority to approve mortgages or loans up to $300,000. Today, the local bank manager has virtually no authority to make any loans. All loan requests are sent to the risk assessment centre at head office for review and decision. The local branch manager is, of course, free to make a recommendation, but it is the centre that takes the decision. The centre, in turn, relies almost exclusively on Equifax's formula to establish a credit score to arrive at its decisions.[43]

"What," I asked, "do branch managers now do to keep busy?" Her answer: "They manage staff, pay close attention to clients, and do a great deal of public relations activities." She laments the passing of the old way of doing things, saying that it made for much better decisions and management: "You knew the client, and the client knew that it was you who made the decision. You met clients at social gatherings, at the grocery store, and you felt that they did not want to let you or anyone down. Today, things are different."[44] In other words, the client felt responsible to the local bank manager who approved the loan. It is much easier to let down a process, a formula, or a distant risk-assessment centre than it is to let down your local bank manager. Harrison knew the local bank manager.

A senior official with another Canadian bank has a similar take: "All decisions are now hard-wired into computers. We now have one manager managing three or four branches, making sure part-time workers are on time, the windows clean, and things like that. They are not much different than managers of fast-food outlets like McDonald's. Communities no longer recognize them or value their presence because today they simply have no power."[45]

Harrison McCain became critical of financial institutions, particularly as banks began to move away from their more traditional responsibilities to investment banking. In his speech at the Canadian Business Hall of Fame dinner, he said, "In the last decade great financial reward has not occurred to those who manufactured things and sold them. Rather, the best profits have gone to those involved in financial engineering such as leveraged buyouts paid for with junk bonds and often only successful at the expense of thousands of workers and managers."[46]

Harrison, however, did not dwell, at least publicly, on what was wrong with Canada's national political institutions and the workings of financial institutions. He was the classic indefatigable entrepreneur. He had a vision, knew when and how to take risks, and joined forces with another indefatigable entrepreneur, his brother Wallace, to write one of the greatest business stories ever to come out of Canada. Harrison had the chutzpah, the intelligence, and an unparalleled ability to focus on details, as his hundreds of little black books reveal. He could have grown a business wherever he may have been from.

Rural New Brunswick is increasingly being described as a curse, a serious impediment to the province's economic development prospects. I have in my own work underlined the point that the Maritime provinces are substantially more rural than other regions. While Ontario is only 13 per cent rural, the Maritime region remains close to 50 per cent rural. Urban regions have a higher standard of living than rural areas as measured by per capita income and GDP per capita.[47]

Don Mills, a Halifax-based pollster, recently observed, "One of the problems we have in this region is that we're too rural for our own good." He added, "It makes it difficult to be successful economically because we have people living in communities that can't support them from an economic point of view." Michael Haan, a professor of population and social policy at the University of New Brunswick, argues that government investment in infrastructure "needs to follow people," and adds that "people need to live where the employment opportunities are."[48]

Rural communities have been transformed by stealth since McCain Foods was founded in Florenceville in 1956. To be sure, the fact that decisions on business loans have been taken out of the hands of local bank managers and are now hard-wired to computers in head office is a factor.

Related or not to this development, the local proprietors class is not what it once was. I grew up in a small New Brunswick rural community. There, in Bouctouche, small local proprietors owned the grocery store, the pharmacy, the restaurant, and the local jewellery store. They and other small proprietors earned their own living and hired a few employees. Today national drug store chains, McDonald's, and online shopping have pushed small proprietors aside.[49] The local proprietor class that once provided community leaders in small towns and villages across the country and role models for aspiring entrepreneurs has now all but faded away.

Could there be another Harrison McCain from a small Maritime community or from rural Canada? The very nature of entrepreneurs makes it impossible to predict with any degree of accuracy future breakaways from the Maritime provinces. K.C. Irving, Harrison and Wallace McCain, and John Bragg speak eloquently to this point.

That said, the odds of another Harrison McCain coming from rural New Brunswick are not strong – possible, but highly improbable. Consider this: Harrison never turned his back on Florenceville, insisting on having many of the firm's activities centred there, even when he was told that it made more business sense to locate them elsewhere. At the same time, he saw the potential in globalization before most of his peers did. He said publicly that he considered it important that he pay his fair share of taxes. He was satisfied to live in the family home and have one summer home. He gave millions to causes in his home province, mostly in education and health care. He approved of partisan politics and contributed to shaping public policy; he financially helped the campaigns of politicians from various parties, not just the one he supported; and he remained deeply loyal to his family, his friends, his employees, and to New Brunswickers.

Harrison was truly one of a kind. There was something special, something different about him. He saw what he could be and became what he saw. He left a high-profile and well-paying executive position with arguably Canada's leading businessman of the last century to pursue his dream.

His goal was not to accumulate wealth, to own the biggest home, the most expensive car, or to flaunt possessions. He was a classic entrepreneur and loved the chase or, as he often put it, "the game." In business, you compete and you negotiate to win, and he won big. He did not win only for himself. He won for his family, his community, his province, and his country. He travelled the world and made friends with world leaders. But he never forgot his roots and the likes of Donald Trafford.

Senior Heinz officials met Harrison on several different occasions with generous offers to buy McCain Foods. This would have allowed him to walk away as one of Canada's wealthiest men with no responsibility. Harrison always turned them down. Accumulating wealth was not his purpose in life. He understood that the key to real success was to devote oneself to creating something that gives purpose and meaning and to care deeply about your community.

Harrison had the tenacity to pull against gravity and build with his brother a highly successful global firm from a small community. History and the human spirit have taught us that no one can predict from where the next Harrison McCain will emerge. That is one of the strengths of a free market economy, where one can pull against gravity and succeed. Entrepreneurs with a single-minded purpose are key to business success, and nowhere is this more necessary than in slow-growth regions. Harrison McCain showed us the way and we can only hope that others will follow.

A FINAL WORD

Harrison McCain wanted to write a book about entrepreneurship, business development, and marketing, and how to grow a business. Sadly, he never got around to it, with his failing health no doubt a factor. In going through his personal papers, I came across an undated note that he had written to himself, headed "Characteristics of the Entrepreneur." I have no way of knowing if this was intended to be the basis for his book. He listed six characteristics. It is only fitting that I give the last word to Harrison. The note reads:

· The entrepreneur keeps himself operating on the threshold of excellence because he fears mediocrity.
· The entrepreneur has learned to dig for facts. The first explanation given does not include all the facts. Once the facts are found the necessary action is clear.

- The entrepreneur has a sixth sense of what will work and what will not work – by adjusting experience and knowledge.
- The entrepreneur tenaciously grasps every opportunity to meet goals using the art of human relations (some say it is a science), the laws of the marketplace, and excellent management of manpower, money, and machines or resources.
- The entrepreneur knows that he must delegate responsibility but he never sacrifices his knowledge of the details.
- The main difference between the entrepreneur and the manager is attitude!

APPENDICES

Interviews

Sally Baxter	27 February 2013
Bud Bird	29 January 2013
Terry Bird	14 February 2013
John Bragg	12 October 2012
Bob Brown	20 February 2013
Michael Campbell	Various dates
Jim Casey	19 November 2012
Reuben Cohen	13 October 2012
Jimmy Coutts	30 January 2013
Paul S. Creaghan	26 February 2013
Bob Crossman	16 January 2013
John Doucet	12 December 2012
James Downey	15 November 2012
Arthur Doyle	14 February 2013
Chris Evans	29 February 2013
Harry Gilmour	18 March 2013
David Hay	14 December 2012
Arthur Irving	17 December 2012
Dave Kearney	15 February 2013
Tyler Langdon	10 December 2012
Astrid Lundrigan	13 October 2012
Elmer Mackay	22 January 2013
Mitch MacLean	14 January 2013
Allison McCain	Various dates
Andrew McCain	Various dates

Ann McCain	Various dates
Gillian McCain	15 February 2013
Laura McCain	15 February 2013
Mark McCain	29 January 2013
Scott McCain	7 March 2013
Steve McCain	11 December 2012
Mark McCauley	11 December 2012
Nancy McCauley	11 December 2012
George McClure	Various dates
Frank McKenna	4 February 2013
Percy Mockler	9 January 2013
Carl Morris	12 February 2013
Christine Morris	13 December 2012
Dick O'Hagan	1 February 2013
Jim Pattison	1 March 2013
Ghislain Pelletier	30 January 2013
Carole Regan	5 February 2013
Gerald Regan	Various dates
Janet Scarfe	3 December 2012
David Smith	26 February 2013
Ronald Stevenson	5 March 2013
Marilyn Strong	Various dates
Camille Thériault	30 January 2013
Donald Trafford	11 December 2012
Donald Young	14 February 2013

McCain Foods Chronology
(1956–1993)

1956   McCain Foods Limited became incorporated, 24 May

1957   First production at Florenceville plant

1958   Cold storage addition

1959   Cold storage addition

1963   Cold storage addition

1965   McCain products enter the British market

1966   Cold storage addition

1968   Sales organization established in Australia

       McCain International Limited established in the United Kingdom

1969   First entry into US market

       Opening of french fry plant in Scarborough, England

1970   Australian french fry plant purchased and expanded

1971   Start-up of Grand Falls french fry plant

       Completion of Prepared Foods plant in Florenceville

1972   Scarborough, England, plant doubles production capacity

       French fry plant purchased in Werkendam, Netherlands

1973   Cold storage addition in Grand Falls

       Second french fry plant purchased in Lewedorp, Netherlands

1974   Pizza production starts in Florenceville

1975   New french fry plant starts up in Ballarat, Australia

       French fry plant acquired in Washburn, Maine

1976   Pizza plant starts up in Grand Falls

       French fry plant purchased in Easton, Maine

       Second french fry plant opened in Whittlesey, England

1978   Third french fry plant acquired in Hoofddorp,
        Netherlands
        Major expansion of Prepared Foods plant completed in
        Florenceville
1979   New french fry plant completed in Portage la Prairie,
        Manitoba
        New pizza plants opened in Ballarat, Australia, and
        Scarborough, England
1980   Sunny Orange Ltd Juice plant acquired/purchased in Toronto,
        Ontario
        Major expansion of Florenceville plant and cold storage
        completed
1981   New french fry plant completed in Harnes, France
1982   Third French fry plant acquired in Grantham, England
        Cheese plant purchased in Oakville, Ontario
1983   New pizza brand purchased (Gusto Pizza)
        New juice plant completed in Grand Falls, New
        Brunswick
1984   Major vegetable-processing plant purchased in Smithton,
        Tasmania
        Cheese plant purchased in Tavistock, Ontario
        Potato-based animal food plant purchased in Presque Isle,
        Maine (Tater Meal Inc.)
        Cheese plant purchased in Harrowsmith, Ontario
        Fish-processing plant purchased in Hull, England (Britfish
        Limited)
1985   Expansion of Easton cold storage – new cold storage and
        plant improvement totalling $5.5 million initiated in Easton,
        Maine
        Construction of dehydrated potato products line begun in
        Portage la Prairie, Manitoba
        $3.5 million expansion of french fry plant in Ballarat,
        Australia
        Major American juice-processing plant purchased in
        Chicago, Illinois Company renamed McCain OJ Inc., later
        McCain Citrus Inc.

1986   Major Belgian frozen food company purchased in Ostende,
        Belgium (McCain Frima N.V.)
        Purchase of french fry and potato flake manufacturing
        company in Bethune, France (Beau Marais SARL)
        Purchase of juice-processing plant located in Taunton,
        Massachusetts (McCain Citrus Inc.)
        Announcement of the establishment of a juice plant in
        Calgary, Alberta
        Announcement of the construction of a $13 million potato-
        processing plant in Smithton, Tasmania (McCain Foods
        [Aust] Pty Ltd)

1987   Acquisition of Chalet Foods by McCain Foods (Aust) Pty Ltd
        Purchase of major potato-processing facility in Presque Isle,
        Maine (J.R. Simplot Company)

1988   Acquisition of Dell Products Corp., Hillside, N.J., by McCain
        Citrus Inc.
        Acquisition of Dansco Dairy Products Ltd, Loanhead,
        Midlothian, near Edinburgh, and Tolona Pizza Products Ltd.,
        East Pimbo, Skelmersdale, near Liverpool, by McCain Foods
        (GB) Limited

1990   A Canadian $25-million reconstruction initiated at McCain
        in Florenceville, New Brunswick, after a fire on 31 December
        1989 damages the facilities
        McCain announces the construction of a Canadian
        $36-million potato-processing facility in Borden-Carleton,
        Prince Edward Island, for the production of specially potato
        products
        Construction of Canadian $2.4 million McCain Group Data
        Centre begun in Florenceville
        McCain acquires New Zealand Alpine Foods Ltd, a vegetable
        processor in Timaru, New Zealand, renamed McCain Foods
        (NZ) Ltd

1991   McCain acquires the assets of the former Polder Food
        Products plant in Lelystad, Netherlands, by McCain Foods
        (Holland) BV

1992   McCain acquires Safries Pty Ltd in Penola, Australia

1993   McCain announces a major expansion of its plant in Timaru, New Zealand

1993   McCain announced a $35-million expansion of its potato-processing plant in Othello, Washington

McCain Foods Chronology
(1994–2004)

1994   Plans announced to build a potato processing facility in
        Balcarce, Argentina

1995   McCain announces an $82-million expansion to its french fry
        facility in Portage la Prairie, Manitoba

1996   McCain purchases Everest Foods plc in Wombourne,
        England
        McCain's plant in Balcarce, Argentina, begins operations
        McCain acquires Growers Foods Ltd in Hastings, New
        Zealand

1997   McCain purchases the Ore-Ida foodservice frozen french fry
        and appetizers business in the US for $500 million
        McCain begins a $41-million expansion of its french fry line
        in Leltstad, Netherlands

1998   McCain announces plans to expand production into Eastern
        Europe with the construction of a $78.6-million french fry
        production facility in Wroclaw, Poland
        Plans announced to construct an $84.2-million french fry
        plant in Matougues, France
        Plans announced for a $93.9 million potato processing plant
        to be built in Coaldale, Alberta
        McCain announces a $70.8-million expansion of its french
        fry processing facility in Easton, Maine, to more than double
        its production capacity

1999   McCain more than doubles the size of its Balcarce, Argentina,
        potato-processing facility with a $68.4-million expansion

McCain announces a $2.4-million, 1,500-square-metre expansion to its Group Data Centre in Florenceville, renaming it the McCain Global Technology Centre

2000   McCain purchases Aloro Foods Inc. in Mississauga, Ontario, manufacturer of frozen pizza product as well as a french fry plant

McCain purchases vegetable-production facilities in South Africa from Irvin and Johnson

McCain purchases new potato-processing plant in Coaldale, Alberta

McCain announces the construction of a $7.2-million Potato Processing Technology Centre near Florenceville

2001   McCain acquires Heinz Frozen Foods (SA) (Pty) Ltd, with its french fry processing facility in Viljoens'kroom, South Africa

McCain acquires the production facilities and food service business of Anchor Food Products Inc., a leading US manufacturer of frozen appetizers, with sales of $503 million in 2000

2002   McCain acquires ethnic Chinese frozen food companies Goodman Fielder International (Taiwan) Lin Limited of Australia, and Wong Wing Foods of Montreal, Canada's leading manufacturer of frozen, authentic Chinese entrées, egg rolls, and dim sum

2003   McCain announces a $29-million expansion and upgrading of its Grand Falls pizza plant

2004   McCain begins construction of a $43.3 million french fry processing plant north of Ahmedabad, Gujarat Province, India

Notes

PREFACE

1   Frank McKenna, "Harrison McCain Eulogy," Florenceville, NB, 16 March
    2004, 7.

INTRODUCTION

1   See Michael Woloschuck, *Family Ties: The Real Story of the McCain Feud*
    (Toronto: Key Porter Books, 1995), 1.
2   Canada, Department of Finance, "What Is Equalization?," n.d. http://www.
    fin.gc.ca/fedprov/eqp-eng.asp.
3   See Donald J. Savoie, *Visiting Grandchildren: Economic Development in the
    Maritimes* (Toronto: University of Toronto Press, 2006).
4   Interview with John Bragg, October 2012.
5   See, among others, Savoie, *Visiting Grandchildren.*
6   Sam Walton, with John Huey, *Sam Walton: Made in America* (New York:
    Bantam Books, 1992), 1.
7   Quoted in Woloschuck, *Family Ties*, 25.
8   Frank McKenna, "Harrison McCain Eulogy," Florenceville, 16 March 2004,
    7.
9   See Daniel Stoffman, *From the Ground Up: The First Fifty Years of McCain
    Foods* (Toronto: McCain Foods, 2007), 25.
10 Ibid.
11 Gordon Pitts, *The Codfathers: Lessons from the Atlantic Business Elite*
    (Toronto: Key Porter Books, 2006); Paul Waldie, with Kate Jenison, *A House*

Divided: The Untold Story of the McCain Family (Toronto: Viking, 1996); and Woloschuck, *Family Ties*.

CHAPTER ONE

1 Daron Acemoglu and James A. Robinson, *Why Nations Fail: The Origins of Power, Prosperity and Poverty* (New York: Crown Publishers, 2012).

2 Brian W. Hutchison, *Descendants of John McCain from Stranorlar Parish, Co. Donegal, Ireland*, prepared for Wallace McCain, gen-find Research, Nanaimo, bc, 2005.

3 Edward M. Patterson, *The County Donegal Railways* (Devon: David and Charles, 1982), and County Donegal, Central Statistics Office, 2011, http://www.cso.ie/en/studentscorner/statisticalfactsaboutyourcounty/donegal/.

4 Hugh J. Gordon, "The McCain Family of Florenceville, New Brunswick, Canada," prepared for the McCain family, 12 December 1983, 5.

5 Ibid., 8.

6 James Hannay, *History of New Brunswick* (Saint John: John A. Bowes, 1909), 1:395.

7 Ibid., 1:396.

8 Ibid., 1:430.

9 Ibid., 1:7.

10 Dudley Mills, "The Duke of Wellington and the Peace Negotiations at Ghent in 1814," *Canadian Historical Review* 2, no. 1 (1921): 19–32.

11 Quoted in W.S. MacNutt, *New Brunswick: A History: 1784–1867* (Toronto: Macmillan of Canada, 1963), 269.

12 Ibid., 26.

13 Ibid., 270.

14 Jacques Poitras, *Imaginary Line: Life on an Unfinished Border* (Fredericton: Goose Lane, 2011), 75.

15 See Hutchison, *Descendants of John McCain*, 90.

16 Gordon, "McCain Family of Florenceville," 44.

17 New Brunswick, Department of Agriculture, Aquaculture and Fisheries, "For the King and County (1760–1860)," n.d., http://www.gnb.ca/0168/20/0168200003-e.asp.

18 Joseph McLeod, quoted in "History of New Brunswick – Early Church History," ElectricCanadian.com, n.d., http://www.electriccanadian.com/history/nb/history/appendix6.htm.

19   Gordon, "McCain Family of Florenceville," 90.

20   Ibid., 51.

21   Ibid.

22   New Brunswick, *Synoptic Report of the Proceedings of the Legislative Assembly of the Province of New Brunswick – For the Session of 1898* (Saint John, NB: Progress Print, Printers and Publishers, 1899), 162.

23   To gain a sense of the time, see Annie Kenney, *Memoires of a Militant* (London: Edward Arnold, 1924).

24   Paul Waldie, *A House Divided: The Untold Story of the McCain Family* (Toronto: Penguin, 1997), 20.

25   Gordon, "McCain Family of Florenceville," 91.

26   Waldie, *House Divided*, 20–1.

27   "Hartland Bridge Google Doodle Makes New Brunswick the Centre of Social Media," *National Post*, 4 July 2012.

28   Waldie, *House Divided*, 21.

29   Robert Craig Brown, "Carvell, Frank Broadstreet," *Dictionary of Canadian Biography Online*, vol. 15, http://www.biographi.ca/en/bio/carvell_frank_broadstreet_15E.html.

30   Hutchison, *Descendants of John McCain*, 91.

31   Ibid., 92.

32   Ibid., 126.

33   Barry M. Moody, "Acadia University," *The Canadian Encyclopedia*, n.d., http://www.thecanadianencyclopedia.com/articles/acadia-university.

34   Waldie, *House Divided*, 22.

35   Moody, "Acadia University."

36   See, among others, Omer Lavallée, *Narrow Gauge Railways of Canada* (Montreal: Railway Book, 1972).

37   Hutchison, *Descendants of John McCain*, 94.

38   For an excellent book on the New Brunswick–Maine border, see Jacques Poitras, *Imaginary Line: Life on an Unfinished Border* (Fredericton: Goose Lane, 2011).

CHAPTER TWO

1   See, for example, James Struthers, "Great Depression," *Canadian Encyclopedia*, n.d., http://www.thecanadianencyclopedia.com/articles/great-depression.

2 H.B. Neatby, *The Politics of Chaos: Canada in the Thirties* (Toronto: Macmillan of Canada, 1972).

3 S.A. Saunders, *The Economic History of the Maritime Provinces* (Fredericton: Acadiensis, 1984), 58.

4 New Brunswick, Provincial Archives, "Pioneers, Ploughs and Politics: New Brunswick Planned Settlements," n.d.

5 Hants A. White, *Potatoes without Gravy* (Jericho, NY: Exposition, 1972).

6 "1920–1945: The Countryside at Midcentury," Maine History Online, n.d., http://www.mainememory.net/sitebuilder/site/907/page/1318/display.

7 Victor Howard, "Unemployment Relief Camps," *Canadian Encyclopedia*, n.d., http://www.thecanadianencyclopedia.com/articles/unemployment- relief-camps.

8 Hugh J. Gordon, "The McCain Family of Florenceville, New Brunswick, Canada," prepared for the McCain family, 12 December 1983, 71; and Brian W. Hutchison, *Descendants of John McCain from Stranorlar Parish, Co. Donegal, Ireland*, prepared for Wallace McCain, gen-find Research, Nanaimo, BC, 2005, 126.

9 Hutchison, *Descendants of John McCain*, 127.

10 Paul Waldie, *A House Divided: The Untold Story of the McCain Family* (Toronto: Penguin, 1997), 24.

11 See Michael Woloschuk, *Family Ties: The Real Story of the McCain Feud* (Toronto: Key Porter Books, 1995), 11.

12 Quoted in ibid., 24.

13 Hutchison, *Descendants of John McCain*, 127.

14 Ibid.

15 "PM Delivers Remarks in Beaubassin, NB," 29 August 2012, Prime Minister's Office, speeches, 8.

16 Quoted from an interview Harrison McCain gave to James Downey, 19 February 2001.

17 Hutchison, *Descendants of John McCain*, 168.

18 See, among others, Gordon, "McCain Family of Florenceville," 73.

19 Interview with James Downey.

20 See, among others, Waldie, *House Divided*, 38-9.

21 Ibid., 32.

22 Quoted in ibid., 34.

23 Hutchison, *Descendants of John McCain*, 171.

24 See, among others, Donald J. Savoie, *Regional Economic Development: Canada's Search for Solutions* (Toronto: University of Toronto Press, 1986).

25 Robert Bothwell, Ian M. Drummond, and John English, *Canada since 1945: Power, Politics and Provincialism* (Toronto: University of Toronto Press, 1989)

26 Interview with James Downey, 5.

27 See, among others, Waldie, *House Divided*, 35.

28 Interview with James Downey, 6.

29 Waldie, *House Divided*, 35.

30 Interview with James Downey, 15.

31 Frank McKenna, "Harrison McCain Eulogy," Florenceville, New Brunswick, 16 March 2004, 8.

32 Interview with James Downey, 56.

33 Ibid.

34 Carmen Miller, "The 1940s: War and Rehabilitation," in *The Atlantic Provinces in Confederation*, ed. E.R. Forbes and D.A. Muise (Toronto: University of Toronto Press, 1993), 320.

35 See Legislative Assembly of New Brunswick, "John McNair," n.d., www.gnb.ca/legis/publications/tradition/premiers/mcnairj-e.asp.

36 Quoted in Waldie, *House Divided*, 41.

37 Consultation with Janet Scarfe, 3 December 2012.

38 Interview with James Downey, 57.

CHAPTER THREE

1 This story is told by James Downey in his "A Toast to Harrison McCain," Toronto, 17 January 2009, 2.

2 See, among others, Donald J. Savoie, *Visiting Grandchildren: Economic Development in the Maritimes* (Toronto: University of Toronto Press, 2006).

3 Quoted from an interview Harrison McCain gave to James Downey, 19 February 2001, 12.

4 Ibid., 12 and 13.

5 Ibid., 12.

6 Harrison McCain, quoted in Paul Waldie, *A House Divided: The Untold Story of the McCain Family* (Toronto: Penguin, 1997), 37.

7 See Dean Jobb, "Rich 100: Inside Irving," *Canadian Business*, 22 December 2009.

8 See "New Brunswick," *Globe and Mail*, 21 February 1987.

9   J.D. Irving, quoted in "Canada's Second-Richest Family Demystified," *Canadian Business Magazine*, 22 December 2002.

10 Quoted in Michael Woloschuk, *Family Ties: The Real Story of the McCain Feud* (Toronto: Key Porter Books, 1995), 36.

11 Donald J. Savoie, *Roots Matter: I'm from Bouctouche, Me* (Montreal and Kingston: McGill-Queen's University Press, 2009), 31.

12 Downey interview, 14.

13 Ibid., 17.

14 Quoted in Waldie, *House Divided*, 38.

15 Ibid., 37.

16 Downey interview, 18–19.

17 Ibid., 17.

18 Quoted in Daniel Stoffman, *From the Ground Up: The First Fifty Years of McCain Foods* (Florenceville: McCain Foods, 2007), 1.

19 Downey interview, 20.

20 Ibid., 17.

21 Waldie, *House Divided*, 44.

22 See, among others, "The Growth of the Potato Industry in Idaho," Food Reference.com, n.d., http://www.foodreference.com/html/a-idpot-grwth.html.

23 Woloschuk, *Family Ties*, 43.

24 Quoted in ibid., 50.

25 See, among many others, John F. Love, *McDonald's: Behind the Arches* (New York: Bantam Books, 1995).

26 Quoted in Woloschuk, *Family Ties*, 52.

27 Ibid., 49.

28 Quoted in Waldie, *House Divided*, 58.

29 Ibid., 59.

30 Stoffman, *From the Ground Up*.

CHAPTER FOUR

1   Daniel Stoffman, *From the Ground Up: The First Fifty Years of McCain Foods* (Toronto: McCain Foods, 2007), 9.

2   Quoted from an interview Harrison McCain gave to James Downey, 19 February 2001, 42.

3   Ibid.

4 · Legislative Assembly of New Brunswick, "Hugh John Flemming," n.d., http://www.gnb.ca/legis/publications/tradition/premiers/flemmingh-e.sp.

5 See, for example, Donald J. Savoie, *Visiting Grandchildren: Economic Development in the Maritimes* (Toronto: University of Toronto Press, 2006).

6 See, among many others, N.H. Lithwick, ed., *Regional Economic Policy: The Canadian Experience* (Toronto: McGraw-Hill Ryerson, 1978).

7 Quoted in Paul Waldie, *A House Divided: The Untold Story of the McCain Family* (Toronto: Penguin, 1997), 64.

8 Quoted in Stoffman, *From the Ground Up*, 8.

9 Ibid.

10 See, among others, Savoie, *Visiting Grandchildren*.

11 "New Food Plant Formally Opened," *Saint John (NB) Telegraph Journal*, 25 February 1957.

12 Quoted in Waldie, *House Divided*, 67.

13 "Carleton County Council Asked for Tax Concession, Building Plans under Way," *Fredericton (NB) Daily Gleaner*, 21 June 1956.

14 See, among others, Waldie, *House Divided*, 66.

15 He made that very point to me on several occasions.

16 "Obituaries – Olof P. Pierson," *Aroostook Republican and News*, 10 November 1993.

17 Ibid.

18 Quoted in Stoffman, *From the Ground Up*, 5.

19 The exchange can be found in Waldie, *House Divided*, 67.

20 Quoted in ibid., 68–9.

21 See, for example, Stoffman, *From the Ground Up*.

22 Quoted in ibid., 17.

23 Ibid., 14–15.

24 Ibid., 18.

25 Ibid., 19.

26 Stoffman, *From the Ground Up*, 28.

27 The reader may wish to consult Stoffman, *From the Ground Up*, for a complete listing of the key players.

28 The process has been described in a number of documents. See, for example, Waldie, *House Divided*, 73.

29 Quoted in Stoffman, *From the Ground Up*, 12.

30 Ibid., 29.

31 Ibid., 13.

32 Interview with James Downey, 49 and 69.

33 Quoted in Stoffman, *From the Ground Up*, 34.

34 See, among others, Donald J. Savoie, *What Happened to the Music Teacher: How Government Decides and Why* (Montreal and Kingston: McGill-Queen's University Press, 2013).

35 See Donald J. Savoie, *Court Government and the Collapse of Accountability in Canada and the United Kingdom* (Toronto: University of Toronto Press, 2008).

36 "New Food Plant Formally Opened."

37 New Brunswick, *Synoptic Report of the Proceedings of the Legislative Assembly, Fredericton*, 30 March 1954.

38 This story was told by long-time residents of Florenceville in a McCain Foods video produced to celebrate its fiftieth anniversary.

39 Quoted in Stoffman, *From the Ground Up*, 63.

40 Ibid., 34.

41 "The McCains of Florenceville," *Executive Magazine*, September 1967, 7.

CHAPTER FIVE

1 Quoted in "Wallace McCain: From Small Potatoes to Big-Time Success," *Globe and Mail*, 24 August 2012.

2 "Cedric E. Ritchie," Executive Profile, Bloomberg Businessweek, http://investing.businessweek.com/research/stocks/people/person.asp?personId=1993045&ticker=CNR:CN&previousCapId=4271575&previousTitle=University%20Of%20Windsor.

3 Quoted in Michael Woloschuk, *Family Ties: The Real Story of the McCain Feud* (Toronto: Key Porter Books, 1995), 61.

4 Quoted from an interview Harrison McCain gave to James Downey, 19 February 2001, 44.

5 Ibid., 50–1.

6 I had full access to Harrison McCain's personal and business files while carrying out research for this book.

7 Quoted in Daniel Stoffman, *From the Ground Up: The First Fifty Years of McCain Foods* (Florenceville: McCain Foods, 2007), 22.

8 Interview with James Downey, 44.

9 Ibid., 27.

10 Quoted in ibid., 45.

11 Ibid., 44–5.

12 I was present when the exchange took place at Harrison's house in Florenceville. I had the sense that it was not the first time they had the same conversation.

13 Frank McKenna, "Harrison McCain Eulogy," Florenceville, New Brunswick, 16 March 2004, 13.

14 Chris Morris, "Harrison McCain, 76: French Fry King," *Toronto Star*, 29 July 2004.

15 Quoted in Stoffman, *From the Ground Up*, 32.

16 Ibid.

17 Quoted in Paul Waldie, *A House Divided: The Untold Story of the McCain Family* (Toronto: Penguin, 1997), 97.

18 Quoted in "McCain Foods: Branching Out on a Spud-Spangled Strategy," conversation with Dean Walker in *Executive*, December 1983, 11.

19 "McCain's Equals Spud Power," *Atlantic Insight*, December 1979, 60.

20 Quoted in "A Star in the Business Sky," *Atlantic Business*, May–June 1982, 4.

21 "The McCain Phenomenon," *Atlantic Advocate*, November 1978, 24.

22 Quoted in "McCain Foods," 9.

23 Interview with James Downey, 41.

24 Quoted in "McCain Foods," 11.

25 "McCain Phenomenon," 22.

26 Ibid.

27 See Waldie, *House Divided*, 80.

28 See, among others, David Lewis, *Louder Voices: The Corporate Welfare Bums* (Toronto: James Lewis and Samuel Publishers, 1972).

29 "Adrienne Clarkson and the Fifth Estate," Yahoo! Voices, n.d., http://www.voices.yahoo.com/adrienne-clarkson-fifth-estate-9080367.html.

30 "McCain Foods and the Fifth Estate," *Winnipeg Free Press*, 16 December 1976.

31 See Donald J. Savoie, *Regional Economic Development: Canada's Search for Solutions* (Toronto: University of Toronto Press, 1992). See also Dan Usher, "Some Questions about the Regional Development Incentives Act," *Canadian Public Policy* 1, no. 4 (Autumn 1975): 557–75.

32 Ibid.

33 See, among others, ibid.

34 Canada, Department of Finance, *Economic Development for Canada in the 1980s* (Ottawa: Queen's Printer, 1981), 11.

35 Canada, Department of Regional Industrial Expansion (drie) "Speaking Notes: The Honourable Ed Lumley to the House of Commons on Industrial and Regional Development Program," 27 June 1983, 1 and 2.

36 See appendices B and C in Savoie, *Regional Economic Development.*

37 See, for example, David Smith, *Prairie Liberalism: The Liberal Party in Saskatchewan 1905–1971* (Toronto: University of Toronto Press, 1975).

38 I was given access to Donald Tansley's personal memoirs in 2008 from a friend who worked with Tansley in the Department of Fisheries and Oceans.

39 Day & Ross Transportation Group, "History," n.d.,

40 Woloschuck, *Family Ties*, 103–6.

41 Quoted in ibid., 106.

42 Quoted in Stoffman, *From the Ground Up*, 153–4.

43 Quoted in "Wallace McCain."

44 Interview with James Downey, 46.

CHAPTER SIX

1 Frank McKenna, "Harrison McCain Eulogy," Florenceville, New Brunswick, 16 March 2004, 6.

2 Ibid.

3 Quoted in Daniel Stoffman, *From the Ground Up: The First Fifty Years of McCain Foods* (Florenceville: McCain Foods, 2007), 41.

4 Quoted from an interview Harrison McCain gave to James Downey, 19 February 2001, 22-3.

5 Stoffman, *From the Ground Up*, 43.

6 Ibid., 43.

7 Interview with James Downey, 47.

8 Quoted in Michael Woloschuk, *Family Ties: The Real Story of the McCain Feud* (Toronto: Key Porter Books, 1995), 71.

9 Ibid., 74.

10 See, for example, Stoffman, *From the Ground Up*, 51.

11 Ibid., 65.

12 See, among others, ibid., 75.

13 Harrison McCain, "A Talk to the Harvard Business School Club of Toronto," 7, n.d., McCain personal papers.

14 McCain, quoted in Paul Waldie, *A House Divided: The Untold Story of the McCain Family* (Toronto: Penguin, 1997), 111.

15 Quoted in Stoffman, *From the Ground Up*, 83.

16 It currently ranks 34 out of 185 jurisdictions in the World Bank ranking. See "Economy Rankings," International Finance Corporation, n.d., http://doing-business.org/rankings.

17 Quoted in Stoffman, *From the Ground Up*, 55–6.

18 See, for example, ibid., 66.

19 See *York Press*, 5 January 2013; *Gazette* and *Herald*, 22 January 2013. See also "Charles McCarthy: Obituary," *Scarborough News*, 4 January 2013, http://www.thescarboroughnews.co.uk/news/local/tributes-paid-to-scarborough-s-mr-chips-84-1-5274482.

20 Quoted in Stoffman, *From the Ground Up*, 56.

21 Harrison McCain more than once mentioned George McClure in our conversations, always in a positive light.

22 Quoted in Stoffman, *From the Ground Up*, 76.

23 Ibid.

24 See, for example, *Women on the Labour Market* (Brussels: European Parliament: Directorate-General for Internal Policies, Policy Department C, 2008).

25 Catalyst, *Women in the Labour Force in France* (Zurich: Catalyst, 2011).

26 It will be recalled that McCain Foods bought the two plants in the Netherlands.

27 Alistair Cole, *François Mitterrand: A Study in Political Leadership* (London: Routledge, 1994).

28 See Donald J. Savoie, *Thatcher, Reagan, Mulroney: In Search of a New Bureaucracy* (Toronto: University of Toronto Press, 1994).

29 This account is drawn from Stoffman, *From the Ground Up*, 79–81.

30 Quoted in Woloschuk, *Family Ties*, 74.

31 Stoffman, *From the Ground Up*, 86.

32 Quoted in "McCain Foods: Branching Out on a Spud-Spangled Strategy," *Executive*, December 1983, 10.

33 Quoted in "Harrison McCain," *Financial Post* Magazine, 1990, special issue. The single issue was published when Harrison McCain became the inaugural recipient of the CEO of the Year award in Canada.

34 He also made this point in "Family Feud," *MacLean's*, 6 September 1993.

35 The article was published in the *Harvard Business Review*, July–August 1985, 8.

36 Thomas J. Peters and Robert H. Waterman, *In Search of Excellence: Lessons from America's Best Run Companies* (New York: Harper & Row Publishers, 1982).

37 McCain, "Talk to the Harvard Business School Club," 8.

38 Peters and Waterman, *In Search of Excellence.*

39 McCain, "Talk to the Harvard Business School Club," 4.

40 See "History," McCain, n.d., http://www.mccain.com/GoodBusiness/Pages/History.aspx.

CHAPTER SEVEN

1 Ernest Small, "Fiddleheads," http://www.thecanadianencyclopedia.com/articles/fiddleheads, n.d.

2 "McCain's Equals Spud Power," *Atlantic Insight*, December 1979, 9.

3 Quoted from an interview Harrison McCain gave to James Downey, 19 February 2001, 50–1.

4 Daniel Stoffman, *From the Ground Up: The First Fifty Years of McCain Foods* (Florenceville: McCain Foods Ltd, 2007), 32.

5 Quoted in ibid., 103.

6 The exchange is captured in Stoffman, *From the Ground Up*, 112–13.

7 See ibid., 104.

8 Quoted in ibid.

9 Ibid., 123.

10 Quoted in "McCain Foods: Branching Out on a Spud-Spangled Strategy," *Executive*, December 1983, 8.

11 Quoted in Stoffman, *From the Ground Up*, 121.

12 Harrison McCain, "McCain Foods Strategy," memo, January 1981, McCain personal papers.

13 McCain personal papers.

14 Ibid.

15 Stoffman, *From the Ground Up*, 114.

16 Ibid., chapter 6.

17 These figures were obtained from McCain Foods in late 2012.

18 Harrison McCain, "Speech on the Occasion of the 2001 Business Leader Award Dinner of the Richard Ivey School of Business," 11 October 2001, 9, McCain personal papers.

19 See, among others, Lynn R. Kahle, "The Nine Nations of North America and the Value Basis of Geographic Segmentation," *Journal of Marketing* 50, no. 2 (April 1986): 37–47.

20 For a detailed account of the negotiations, see Paul Waldie, "Shady Chicago – Part 1, The Sting," *New Brunswick Reader-Telegraph Journal*, 5 October 1996, 6–9.

21 Charles Enman, "The Lawsuit: Part II, How the McCain Brothers Got Squeezed for $5 million," *New Brunswick Reader-Telegraph Journal*, 5 October 1996, 9.

22 See, "3 Charged with Juice Conspiracy," *Chicago Tribune*, 26 July 1989; and Paul Waldie, *A House Divided: The Untold Story of the McCain Family* (Toronto: Penguin, 1997), 213.

23 Quoted in Stoffman, *From the Ground Up*, 171.

24 Ibid., 174.

25 David Stoffman writes that Harrison McCain resisted recommendations to acquire the large US frozen food firm in Lamb Weston and buy factories owned by Nestlé and Universal because he did "not think that McCain had the management strength" to take it on. See Stoffman, *From the Ground Up*, 172.

26 Florenceville, McCain Foods, "Growth of McCain Foods and the McCain Group," news release, January 1988, McCain personal papers.

27 Information drawn from Harrison McCain's personal papers, Florenceville.

28 This and other quotes and information in this chapter come from material found in Harrison McCain's personal files, Florenceville.

29 Quoted in Stoffman, *From the Ground Up, 148.*

30 Information drawn from Harrison McCain's personal papers, Florenceville.

31 "McCain-Cavendish French Fry Feud Festering: Result Is a Draw," *Bangor Daily News*, 30 January 1990.

32 Harrison McCain – note to file, conversation with Jim Martin at *McLean's*, n.d.

33 Quoted in "McCain-Cavendish French Fry Feud Festering."

34 Quoted in Waldie, *House Divided*, 232.

35 Harrison McCain, "Talk to the Harvard Business School Club of Toronto," 5–6, n.d., McCain personal papers.

36 "The Truth about Frozen French Fries," *Bangor Daily News*, 6 November 1993.

37   "McCain Foods," 6.

38   Quoted in ibid., 7.

39   See, for example, Ann Gibbon and Peter Hadekel, *Steinberg: The Breakup of a Family Empire* (Toronto: Macmillan of Canada, 1990).

40   Quoted in "Bad Blood," *Toronto Star*, 24 January 1988.

41   Manfred F.R. Kets de Vries, "The Dynamics of Family Controlled Firms: The Good and the Bad News," 1 January 1993, Access My Library, http://www.accessmylibrary.com/article-1G1-13929168/dynamics-family- controlled-firms.html.

CHAPTER EIGHT

1   See, for example, Ehud Kamar, Pinar Karaca-Mandic, and Eric L. Talley, *Going-Private Decisions and the Sarbanes-Oxley Act of 2002: A Cross-Country Analysis* (Santa Monica, CA: Rand Corporation, April 2006).

2   "Good Governance and Tough Times," and "Board Reforms Face Crucial Tests," *Globe and Mail*, 10 November 2008.

3   James Gillies in his preface to Caroll Hansell, *What Directors Need to Know: Corporate Governance* (Toronto: Davis Ward Phillips and Vineberg, 2003), iii.

4   Robert Zafft, "When Corporate Governance Is a Family Affair," *Observer* (Paris: OECD, 2001), 1.

5   The reader may wish to consult the Family Business Institute on this and other family business–related issues at www.family.business.com.

6   Manfred F.R. Kets de Vries and Randel S. Carlock, with Elizabeth Florent-Treacy, *Family Business on the Couch: A Psychological Perspective* (Chichester, UK: Wiley, 2007), 112.

7   See, among his other publications, John L. Ward, Amy Schuman, and Stacy Stutz, *Family Business as Paradox* (New York: Palgrave Macmillan, 2010).

8   Fred D. Tannenbaum is a manager partner in the Chicago-based firm Gould and Ratner. He made the comment in a talk "All in the Family: Corporate Governance Issues Facing Family-Owned Business," n.d., http://www. gouldratner.com/Assets/News/FDT%20All%20in%20the%20 Family-Corporate%20Governance.pdf.

9   Manfred F.R. Kets de Vries, "The Dynamics of Family Controlled Firms: The Good and the Bad News," *Organizational Dynamics* 21, no. 3 (Winter 1993): 316 and 320.

10 See, among many others, Reginald Litz, "The Family Business: Toward Definitional Clarity," *Family Business Review* 8, no. 2 (June 1985): 71–81.

11 See, among others, M.A. Gallo and Alvaro Vilaseca, "A Financial Perspective on Structure, Conduct and Performance in the Family Firm: An Empirical Study," *Family Business Review* 11, no. 1 (March 1998): 35–47.

12 Ronald C. Stevenson, *In the Matter of an Arbitration: G. Wallace McCain et al., and McCain Foods Group Inc. et al.* (Fredericton, 20 April 1994), 8 and 9.

13 Quoted in Michael Woloschuk, *Family Ties: The Real Story of the McCain Feud* (Toronto: Key Porter Books, 1995), 151.

14 Ibid., 152.

15 Quoted in Stevenson, *In the Matter of an Arbitration*, 15.

16 See ibid.

17 This information was reproduced from Stevenson, *In the Matter of an Arbitration*, 19–20.

18 The reader may wish to consult ibid., 21–5. I also found a number of Harrison's memos in his personal files as well as copies of Wallace's responses.

19 Based on Harrison McCain's personal papers, Florenceville.

20 Stevenson, *In the Matter of an Arbitration*, 30.

21 The exchange is captured in Paul Waldie, *A House Divided: The Untold Story of the McCain Family* (Toronto: Penguin, 1997), 244.

22 Drawn from documents found in Harrison McCain's personal papers, Florenceville.

23 Stevenson, *In the Matter of an Arbitration*, 40–9.

24 Ibid.

CHAPTER NINE

1 See, for example, Paul Waldie, *A House Divided: The Untold Story of the McCain Family* (Toronto: Viking, 1996).

2 Reuben Cohen, *A Time to Tell* (Toronto: Key Porter Books, 1998), 208.

3 Ibid., 289.

4 Ibid., 306.

5 Frank McKenna, "Harrison McCain Eulogy," Florenceville, NB, 16 March 2004, 7.

6 "Canadian Family's Feud," *New York Times*, 30 October 1994.

7   Waldie, *House Divided*; and Michael Woloschuk, *Family Ties: The Real Story of the McCain Feud* (Toronto: Key Porter, 1995).

8   Carl Morris, interview.

9   Ibid.

10 As outlined in "In the Matter of an Arbitration between G. Wallace F. McCain and GWF Holdings Inc. and McCain Foods Group Inc. et al.," *Arbitrator's Award and Reasons*, Date of Award (New Brunswick: Fredericton, 20 April 1994), 5–6.

11 Ibid., 38.

12 Ronald C. Stevenson, *In the Matter of an Arbitration: G. Wallace McCain et al., and McCain Foods Group Inc. et al.* (Fredericton: New Brunswick, 20 April 1994), 21.

13 I saw a number of exchanges and other material in going through Harrison McCain's personal and business files in Florenceville. Justice Stevenson also had access to that material. See Stevenson, *In the Matter of an Arbitration*.

14 Terry Bird, interview.

15 "Family Feud," *Maclean's*, 6 September 1993.

16 Drawn from Harrison McCain's personal papers, Florenceville.

17 See Stevenson, *In the Matter of an Arbitration*, 58.

18 Ibid., 61.

19 Ibid., 63.

20 Ibid., 73.

21 Ibid., 74.

22 Woloschuk, *Family Ties*, 176.

23 "What's Yours Is Mine," *Forbes*, 2 August 1993, 68–9; and "No Small Potatoes," *Financial Post*, 14 August 1993.

24 Information drawn from Harrison McCain's personal papers, Florenceville.

25 See, among others, Waldie, *House Divided*; and Woloschuk, *Family Ties*.

26 Stevenson, *In the Matter of an Arbitration*, 70.

27 Quoted in ibid., 94.

28 Ibid., 106.

29 Ibid., 108.

30 Ibid., 110.

31 Harrison McCain's personal papers.

32 Ibid.

33 Justice Creaghan, G. Wallace F. McCain et al. and McCain Foods et al., Moncton, New Brunswick Court of Queen's Bench, Moncton, judgment filed 23 September 1994.

34   Drawn from Harrison McCain's documents, Florenceville.

35   "Family Feud," *Maclean's*.

CHAPTER TEN

1   Quoted from an interview Harrison McCain gave to James Downey, 19 February 2001, 50.

2   See, among others, "Revised Speech by Harrison McCain," 2001 Business Leaders Annual Dinner of the Richard Ivey School of Businesses, 11 October 2001, 6.

3   Ibid., 8.

4   Frank McKenna, "Harrison McCain Eulogy," Florenceville, New Brunswick, 16 March 2004, 11.

5   See "McCain Foods Completes Ore-Ida Food Service Acquisition," PR News-wire, 30 June 1997.

6   "Harrison McCain on the Family Feud, Frozen Food and the Future," *Financial Post*, 13 December 1998.

7   Daniel Stoffman, *From the Ground Up: The First Fifty Years of McCain Foods* (Florenceville: McCain Foods, 2007), 177–8.

8   Ibid., 178.

9   Ibid., 179.

10 Ibid., 177.

11 "McCain Going Cold on Juice Business," *Financial Post*, 13 November 1998.

12 See, among others, World Health Organization, "20 Questions on Genetically Modified Foods," n.d., http://www.who.int/foodsafety/publications/biotech/20questions/en.

13 Drawn from documents in Harrison McCain's papers, Florenceville.

14 See, for example, Paul Waldie, *A House Divided: The Untold Story of the McCain Family* (Toronto: Penguin, 1997).

15 Quoted in McKenna, "Harrison McCain Eulogy," 6.

16 Stoffman, *From the Ground Up*, 145.

17 Ibid.

18 Quoted in Michael Woloschuk, *Family Ties: The Real Story of the McCain Feud* (Toronto: Key Porter Books, 1995), 263.

19 Drawn from Harrison McCain's personal papers, Florenceville.

20 Quoted in McKenna, "Harrison McCain Eulogy," 14.

21 See Gordon Pitts, *The Godfather: Lesson from the Atlantic Business Elite* (Toronto: Key Porter Books, 1995), 30.

22 David Adams Richards, *Lord Beaverbrook* (Toronto: Penguin Books, 2008), 40.

23 "Revised Speech by Harrison McCain," 12–14.

24 See, for example, Stoffman, *From the Ground Up.*

CHAPTER ELEVEN

1 Quoted in "Harrison McCain," *Financial Post Magazine*, 1990, special issue, 15.

2 Based on a discussion with Camille Thériault who was at the convention in support of his father, 20 September 2012.

3 Ernest R. Forbes, "New Brunswick," *Canadian Encyclopedia Historica*, n.d., http://www.thecanadianencyclopedia.com/articles/new-brunswick.

4 See Donald J. Savoie, *I'm from Bouctouche Me* (Montreal and Kingston: McGill-Queen's University Press, 2009), 112.

5 Quoted in ibid., 78.

6 Quoted from an interview Harrison McCain gave to James Downey, 19 February 2001, 34.

7 The letter is dated 16 April 2003 in response to her request for information on Pierre Trudeau.

8 See Savoie, *I'm from Bouctouche, Me*, 75.

9 Interview with James Downey, 28–30.

10 Ibid., 30.

11 McCain to John Turner, McCain papers.

12 See, for example, Donald J. Savoie, *Pulling against Gravity: Economic Development in New Brunswick during the McKenna Years* (Montreal: Institute for Research of Public Policy, 2001).

13 Interview with James Downey, 35.

14 Camille Thériault, interview.

15 Dave Kearney, interview.

16 Ibid., 31–2.

17 Ibid., 33.

18 Ibid., 36.

19 Bud Bird, *A Family History* (Fredericton: privately printed, 2003), chap. 8.

20 Ibid.

21 Frank McKenna, "Harrison McCain Eulogy," Florenceville, New Brunswick, 16 March 2004, 7.

22 Drawn from Harrison McCain papers, Florenceville.

23 Ibid.

24 Ibid.

25 See, among many others, Daniel Trefler, *The Long and Short of the Canada-US Free Trade Agreement* (London: Toyota Centre, London School of Economics and Political Science, 2006).

26 See, among others, Downey, interview, 35.

27 Drawn from the papers of Harrison McCain, Florenceville.

28 Harrison McCain, McGill convocation speech, 7 June 1991, 4 and 5.

29 Michael Woloschuk, *Family Ties: The Real Story of the McCain Feud* (Toronto: Key Porter Books, 1995), 97–8.

30 "Harrison McCain," *Financial Post Magazine*, 1990, special issue, 15.

31 "National Gallery of Canada Saddened by Death of Harrison McCain," National Gallery of Canada, 19 March 2004, http://www.gallery.ca/en/about/564.php.

32 David O'Brien, interview.

33 "Neighbors, Aides Remember Mayor Koch's Indomitable Spirit," CBS *New York,* 2 Febr55uary 2013, http://newyork.cbslocal.com/2013/02/02/neighbors-aides-remember-mayor-kochs-indomitable-spirit/.

34 John M. Saulnier, "Farewell to Harrison McCain, a Food Industry Giant," *Quick Frozen Foods International*, April 2004, 114.

CHAPTER TWELVE

1 Frank McKenna, "Harrison McCain Eulogy," Florenceville, New Brunswick, 16 March 2004, 8.

2 *Spud*, newsletter of the New Brunswick potato industry, June 2004.

3 Reuben Cohen, *A Time to Tell: The Public Life of a Private Man* (Toronto: Key Porter Books, 1998).

4 McCain personal papers.

5 Ibid.

6 Ibid.

7 Ibid.

8 Ibid.

9 He said this to Frank McKenna. See McKenna, "Harrison McCain Eulogy," 16.

10 I also tell this story in my *I'm from Bouctouche, Me* (Montreal and Kingston: McGill-Queen's University Press, 2009), 201.

11   James Downey makes this point in "A Toast to Harrison McCain," Toronto, 17 January 1998, 3.

12   Ibid., 1 and 2.

13   Quoted from an interview Harrison McCain gave to James Downey, 19 February 2001, 8 and 9.

14   Ibid., 37.

15   See, for example, "The Grotesque Campeau failure," *New York Times*, 17 January 1990.

16   Dick Currie, "Tribute to Harrison McCain, CEO of the Year Dinner," 25 November 2004, Toronto, 2.

17   George McClure, interview.

18   The exchange is captured in Dean Walker, "McCain Foods: Branching Out on a Spud-Spangled Strategy," *Executive*, December 1983.

19   Ibid.

20   "McCain's Equals Spud Power," *Atlantic Advocate*, December 1979, 19.

21   Ibid., 18.

22   Ibid.

23   Walter Stewart, *Hard to Swallow: Why Food Prices Keep Rising and What Can Be Done about It* (Toronto: Macmillan of Canada, 1979).

24   "McCain's equals spud power," 18.

25   Downey interview, 42.

CHAPTER THIRTEEN

1   Quoted from an interview Harrison McCain gave to James Downey, 19 February 2001, 60.

2   Carl Morris, interview.

3   Ibid.

4   Ibid.

5   Ibid.

6   Frank McKenna, "Harrison McCain Eulogy," Florenceville, 16 March 2004, 8.

7   Jan Aart Scholts, "Global Capitalism and the States," *International Affairs* 33, no. 3 (July 1995): 439.

8   Ibid.

9   Donald J. Savoie, *Visiting Grandchildren: Economic Development in the Maritimes* (Toronto: University of Toronto Press, 2006).

10 See Gordon Pitts, *The Godfather: Lesson from the Atlantic Business Elite* (Toronto: Key Porter Books, 1995), 37.

11 Ibid., 7.

12 Ibid.; and Reuben Cohen, *A Time to Tell: The Public Life of a Private Man* (Toronto: Key Porter Books, 1998).

13 Donald H. Akenson, *Conor: A Biography of Conor Cruise O'Brien* (Montreal and Kingston: McGill-Queen's University Press, 1994),1:5.

14 See publications from Citizenship and Immigration Canada.

15 See Canada, Citizenship and Immigration Canada, *2012 Annual Report to Parliament on Immigration* (Ottawa: Citizenship and Immigration Canada, 2012), s. 2, 12.

16 Canada, Citizenship and Immigration Canada, *Facts and Figures 2010: Immigration Overview Permanent and Temporary Residents* (Ottawa: Citizenship and Immigration Canada, 2010), section by territory and urban area.

17 Quoted in "McCain Foods: Branching Out on a Spud-Spangled Strategy," *Executive*, December 1983, 37.

18 See "More Than One-Fifth of Canadians Are Foreign-Born: National Household Survey," *Globe and Mail*, 8 May 2013.

19 Canada, Citizenship and Immigration Canada, *The Interprovincial Mobility of Immigrants in Canada* (Ottawa: Citizenship and Immigration Canada, n.d.). See section on province of nomination versus province of residence in the 2006 tax year.

20 "Schumpeter-Fixing the Capitalist Machine," *Economist*, 29 September 2012, 22.

21 *Conclusions of the Meeting of the Territorial Development Policy Committee at ministerial level* (Paris: OECD, March 2009).

22 Mario Polèse and Richard Shearmur make this point in their *The Periphery in the Knowledge Economy: The Spatial Dynamics of the Canadian Economy and the Future of Non-Metropolitan Regions in Québec and the Atlantic Provinces* (Montreal: INR, 2002), xxvii.

23 Richard Florida, *The Rise of the Creative Class and How It's Transforming Work, Leisure and Everyday Life* (New York: Basic Book, 2002).

24 Interview with Gillian McCain. She serves as president of the board of directors of the Poetry Project in New York City and is co-author of *Please Kill Me: The Uncensored Oral History of Punk*.

25 See Savoie, *Visiting Grandchildren*, 29. See also, among many others, the work of David Alexander, Philip A. Buckner, and Ernest Forbes.

26 John Ibbitson, *Loyal No More: Ontario's Struggle for a Separate Destiny* (Toronto: Harper Collins, 2001), 5.

27 See Donald J. Savoie, *Whatever Happened to the Music Teacher?: How Government Decides and Why* (Montreal and Kingston: McGill-Queen's University Press, 2013).

28 Based on a conversation with Ghislain Pelletier, vice-president corporate agriculture, McCain Foods, 30 January 2013.

29 See, among others, "Tories Doing Away with Research in More Cuts at Agriculture and Agri-Food Say Unions," *Hill Times*, 13 May 2013.

30 See Savoie, *Visiting Grandchildren.*

31 A copy of the letter was given to me by Wade MacLauchlan, former president of the University of Prince Edward Island, April 2013.

32 See, among others, Garth Hopkins, *Clairtone: The Rise and Fall of a Business Empire* (Toronto: McClelland Stewart, 1978).

33 Quoted in Savoie, *Visiting Grandchildren*, 43.

34 See, among others, "Does Harper Still Believe in Atlantic Canada's 'Culture of Defeat'?," 15 June 2007, http://www.canadafreepress.com/2007/higgins061507.htm. See also Savoie, *Visiting Grandchildren*, 269.

35 Stephen G. Tomblin, *Ottawa and the Outer Provinces* (Toronto: Lorimer, 1995), 16.

36 "Liberal MP McGuinty Apologizes for Comments: Resigns as Energy Critic," *Globe and Mail*, 21 November 2012.

37 Harry Bruce, *Down Home* (Toronto: Key Porter Books, 2002).

38 Jeffrey Simpson, "The Truth about Atlantic Canada's Economy," *Globe and Mail*, 20 June 2001.

39 R.A. Young, "Teaching and Research on Maritime Politics: Old Stereotypes and New Directions," in *Teaching Maritime Studies*, ed. P.A. Buckner (Fredericton: Acadiensis, 1986), 153.

40 Edith Robb, "It's Now Time to Change Our Image," *Moncton Times and Transcript*, 10 July 2004.

41 See, among others, Claire Morris, "The New Brunswick Experience," remarks before the Ontario Management Forum, June 1995, 11–12.

42 "Venture Capital Fund Good News for the Atlantic Economy," *Chronicle Herald*, 14 October 2012.

43 Quoted in Donald J. Savoie, *Power: Where Is It?* (Montreal and Kingston: McGill-Queen's University Press, 2010), 58.

44 Ibid.

45   Ibid.

46   Donald J. Savoie, "Notes: Canadian Business Hall of Fame Dinner," 1 April
     1993, 2.

47   Savoie, *Visiting Grandchildren*, 243–4.

48   Both quoted in "We Are Too Rural for Our Own Good: Pollster," *Telegraph
     Journal*, 5 February 2013.

49   I owe this insight to a discussion I had with former Nova Scotia premier
     Gerald Regan, 5 February 2013.

Index